Tom Wright is Research Professor of New Testament and Early Christianity at the University of St Andrews, and was previously Bishop of Durham. Widely regarded as one of the world's foremost New Testament theologians, he has lectured and broadcast in many countries. In addition to producing a fresh translation of the New Testament (*The New Testament for Everyone*, SPCK, 2011) drawn from his popular For Everyone commentaries, he is the author of over fifty books, including (as N. T. Wright) the monumental works in the series Christian Origins and the Question of God.

SIMPLY JESUS

Who he was, what he did, why it matters

TOM WRIGHT

Published in the United States of America in 2011 by
HarperCollins Publishers, 10 East 53rd Street, New York, NY 10022

First published in Great Britain in 2011

Society for Promoting Christian Knowledge
36 Causton Street
London SW1P 4ST
www.spckpublishing.co.uk

British Library Cataloguing-in-Publication Data
A catalogue record for this book is available from the British Library

ISBN 978-0-281-08672-6
eBook ISBN 978-0-281-06728-2

Typeset by Graphicraft Limited, Hong Kong
Manufacture managed by Jellyfish
First printed in Great Britain by CPI Group
Subsequently digitally printed in Great Britain

Produced on paper from sustainable forests

To the beloved memory of Nicholas Irwin Wright
26 February 1920–16 March 2011

Contents

Preface

Jesus of Nazareth poses a question and a challenge two thousand years after his lifetime. The question is fairly simple: who exactly was he? This includes the questions, What did he think he was up to? What did he do and say, why was he killed, and did he rise from the dead? The challenge is likewise fairly simple: since he called people to follow him, and since people have been trying to do that ever since, what might 'following him' entail? How can we know if we are on the right track?

I have spent much of my life puzzling over these questions and trying, from various angles, to address and answer them. This has been exhilarating as well as challenging. Having grown up in a Christian household, and having experienced the growth and development of my own personal faith from my early years through to adulthood, I have been aware of a vocation which our present culture usually splits into two but which I persist in seeing as a single whole. I have been called to be a historian and theologian, a teacher and writer specializing in the history and thought of early Christianity, and also a pastor within the church. Sometimes I have been able to combine these two elements, the academic and the pastoral; sometimes the jobs to which I have been led have forced me to specialize in one rather than the other, leaving an imbalance which I have then tried to correct. The relevance of this autobiographical remark for the present topic should, I think, be clear: writing about Jesus has never been, for me, a matter simply of 'neutral' historical study (actually, there is no such thing, whatever the topic, but we'll leave that aside for the moment); the Jesus whom I study historically is the Jesus I worship as part of the threefold unity of the one God. But, likewise, writing about Jesus has never been a matter simply of pastoral and homiletic intent; the Jesus whom I preach is the Jesus who lived and died as a real human being in first-century Palestine. Modern Western culture has done its best to keep these two figures, the Jesus of history and the Jesus of faith, from ever meeting. I have done my best to resist this trend, despite the howls of protest from both sides.

This book is entitled *Simply Jesus*, in conscious succession to an earlier book of mine, *Simply Christian*. However, there is simplicity and simplicity. Often, when I give a public lecture and then invite questions from the audience, someone will stand up and say, 'I have a very simple question.' Then out comes something like, 'Who exactly is God?' or 'What was there before creation?' or 'If God is good, why is there evil?' As I always say to such people, the question may be simple, but the answer may well not be. In fact, if we try to give a 'simple' answer, we may well oversimplify matters and end up just being quizzical. (When someone asked Augustine what God was doing before creation, he quoted, albeit with disapproval, the suggestion that God was making hell for people who ask silly questions.) Simplicity is a great virtue, but oversimplification can actually be a vice, a sign of laziness.

This is, of course, a familiar problem. Suppose I am standing outside my college in St Andrews and a car pulls up. 'A simple question,' says the driver. 'How do I get to Glasgow from here?' Again, the question is simple, the answer less so. If I simply say, 'Keep heading west and a bit south, and you can't miss it,' I am telling the truth, more or less. The roads are reasonably well signed. But the roads are not straight, and without more help one might easily go wrong. It might be useful to point out that there is a large river in the way, a mile wide at its narrowest point until a long way inland, and that the bridge over the river is sometimes closed because of high winds, but that the alternative route involves going through several small towns and villages and skirting around one or two ranges of hills. The driver doesn't want to know all that, or not at the moment. But unless I draw attention to some of it, I may be oversimplifying, and the driver may resent my 'simple' advice for being too simple by half when, stuck in a village somewhere, he reflects that a little complexity might actually have helped.

I feel a bit like that with the present book. I set out to write a 'simple' book about Jesus. But Jesus was not simple in his own time, and he is not simple now. One might have thought that it would be comparatively easy to take my earlier books, particularly *Jesus and the Victory of God* and *The Challenge of Jesus*,[1] and turn them into something quite 'simple'. But I was surprised, in sketching out this book and then writing it, to discover how many new twists and turns I am now aware of that I did not deal with in those earlier works.

It isn't just that scholarship has moved on, though of course it has; this book, though, is not the place to explore those debates. It is, just as much, that I have spent most of the last decade working as a bishop in the Church of England, and, though in some popular imaginings bishops don't have very much to do with Jesus, I found myself thinking, talking and preaching about Jesus pretty much all the time. In particular, I was of course vitally interested in the way in which Jesus and the struggle to follow him might make a difference in real lives and real communities, from the old mining villages of County Durham, where I lived and worked from 2003 to 2010, right down to the corridors of power in Westminster.

For most of that time I didn't stop to ask how all that ministry, and the life of prayer and sacrament that sustained it, might be changing my view of Jesus. Now, however, when the car pulls up and someone says, 'A simple question: tell me about Jesus,' I find myself wanting to explain about the river, the bridge, the high winds, the small towns and the hills. I could just say, 'Just start reading the gospels and try to follow Jesus,' and that might do the trick, like telling the traveller just to head west and south and hope for the best. But I decided to answer the simple question by putting together, layer upon layer, in as simple a fashion as I could, what I thought might help someone who really wanted to find the way to Jesus, to Jesus as he really was, and so to find the way *through* Jesus both to God himself and to a life in which 'following Jesus' would make sense.

The book then falls, more or less, into three parts. Part 1 consists of the first five chapters, in which I try to explain what the key questions are, why they matter, and why we today find them difficult to answer.

Then, in the central part of the book, Part 2 (Chapters 6—14), I try, as simply as I can, to say what I think Jesus' public career was all about, what he was trying to accomplish, and how he went about it. At this point, to be honest, the material is so rich and dense that I have found myself, like a gardening expert given half an hour to guide a visitor around the Chelsea Flower Show, both spoiled for choice as to what to talk about and anxious about maintaining some shape and direction to the conducted tour. I have found it necessary, here and there, to indulge in the cinematic technique of 'flashbacks', and indeed 'flash-forwards', taking readers away from Jesus for a moment to remark on other leaders or would-be leaders in Jewish movements of the period. (I didn't want to put those up front, or readers might have become tired, and might have despaired of ever arriving at Jesus himself. By placing them where I have, I trust they illuminate Jesus rather than distract attention from him.)

In this section I ask readers to try various thought experiments. This is absolutely necessary, because first-century Jews thought very differently from the way we do now – and, indeed, from the ways in which other first-century people such as the Greeks and the Romans thought. We have to make a real effort to see things from a first-century Jewish point of view, if we are to understand what Jesus was all about.

All this brings us, in the end, to Jesus' death, resurrection and ascension and the meaning of those events. Throughout the whole book, as will quickly become apparent, I have done my best to explore the meaning of the phrase Jesus used as the great slogan for his whole project, the 'kingdom of God'. Jesus himself spent quite a bit of time explaining what he meant by this phrase, and I have tried to track those explanations and get to the heart of his meaning.

Part 3 of the book consists of one long final chapter, which could be entitled, 'So what?' In other words, what does it all mean for us now? I sketch four ways in which people today have tried to understand the contemporary relevance of Jesus' inauguration of God's kingdom, and allow them to enter into discussion with one another. From this there emerges a sense, which is central to the New Testament itself, that Jesus' way of running the world here and now is, however surprisingly, through his followers. The heart of their life is Spirit-led worship, through which they are constituted and energized as 'the body of Christ'. The agenda that follows from this is set by those memorable sayings we call the Beatitudes, which offer a vantage point from which to explore the ways in which the project of God's kingdom, which Jesus announced and which he believed would be accomplished through his death, can become a reality not only *in* the lives of his followers, but *through* the lives of his followers. This final chapter is only a signpost to the much larger proposals that might be advanced at this point, but it is clearly important, granted the subject-matter of the book as a whole, that something at least should be said along these lines. I have been encouraged by the many ways in which

Christians from very different traditions have been exploring these issues both in theory and in practice in recent years, and I hope that this book will give a firmer biblical and theological grounding, and perhaps shaping, to these explorations and efforts.

I mentioned first-century Jews just now, and how they thought. I am of course aware that there were many different varieties of Judaism in the ancient world, as there are in our own day, and that all gener-alizations about Jews, or for that matter Greeks or Romans, are bound to ignore whole libraries full of complex detail. I have written about some of that elsewhere too (particularly in *The New Testament and the People of God*[2]). But some things have to be made simple if we are going to get anywhere.

I am grateful, as ever, to my two publishers, HarperOne in San Francisco and SPCK in London, and to their respective editorial teams. My thanks, too, to Jamie Davies, my research assistant, for many discussions of this project, and for compiling the indexes.

This is the first book I have written since the death of my beloved father, at the age of ninety-one. Having read little or no theology or biblical scholarship until his mid sixties, when I started writing, he then read everything I wrote within days of its publication and frequently telephoned me to tell me what he thought about it. I cherish some of his comments. 'I've looked up "eschatology" three times in the dictionary,' he once complained, 'and I keep forgetting what it means.' When my big book on the resurrection came out, he read it, all 700 pages, in three days, commenting that he had really started to enjoy it after about page 600. Presumably, with the end in sight, he was starting to *experience* hope as well as reading about it. Particularly with my popular writings, I now realize that he was always part of the 'target audience' of which I was subconsciously aware. Writing a book like this feels different now that he's not there to read it. In any case, though I hope he learned a few things from me, this book – particularly its concluding chapter – hints at some of the many things I learned from him. As I grieve his passing, I dedicate this book to his memory with gratitude, love and, yes, hope.

Tom Wright
St Mary's College
St Andrews

Part 1

1

A very odd sort of king

'As Jesus was going along, people kept spreading their cloaks on the road. When he came to the descent of the Mount of Olives, the whole crowd of disciples began to celebrate and praise God at the tops of their voices' (Luke 19.36–37). The crowd went wild as he got nearer. This was the moment they'd been waiting for. All the old songs came flooding back, and they were singing, chanting, cheering and laughing. At last their dreams were going to come true.

But in the middle of it all their leader wasn't singing. 'When he came near and saw the city, he wept over it' (v. 41). Yes, their dreams were indeed coming true. But not in the way they had imagined.

He was not the king they expected. He wasn't like the monarchs of old who sat on their jewelled and ivory thrones, dispensing their justice and wisdom. Nor was he the great warrior-king some had wanted. He didn't raise an army and ride into battle at its head. He was riding on a donkey. And he was weeping, weeping for the dream that had to die, weeping for the sword that would pierce his supporters to the soul. Weeping for the kingdom that wasn't coming as well as for the kingdom that was.

Jesus' arrival in Jerusalem a few days before his death is one of the best-known scenes in the gospels. But what was it all about? What did Jesus think he was doing?

I have a clear, sharp memory of the moment when that question first impinged on my consciousness. It was the autumn of 1971. It was a month or so after our wedding, and I had just begun my training for ordination. New worlds were opening in front of me. But I hadn't expected this one. A friend lent me the album *Jesus Christ Superstar.*

I had known about Jesus all my life. Indeed, I venture to say that I had known Jesus all my life; better still, perhaps, to say that he had known me. He was a presence, a surrounding love, whispering gently in scripture, singing at the top of his voice in the beauty of creation, majestic in the mountains and the sea. I had done my best to follow him, to get to know him, to find out what he wanted me to do. He wasn't an undemanding friend; he was always a disturbing, challenging presence, warning against false trails and grieving when I went that way anyway. But he was also a sigh-of-relief healing presence; like Bunyan's hero, I knew what it was to see burdens roll away. I had been many times around the cycle we find in the gospels in the character of Peter: firm public declarations of undying loyalty, followed by miserable failure, followed by astonishing, generous, forgiving love.

But as my bride and I moved into our basement apartment, I listened to *Superstar*. Andrew Lloyd Webber was then still a brash young pup, not a Peer of the Realm, and Tim Rice was still writing lyrics with real force and depth. Some were worried about *Superstar*. Wasn't it cynical? Didn't it raise all kinds of doubts? I didn't hear it that way. I heard the questions: 'Who are you? What have you sacrificed? . . . Do you think you're what they say you are?' These were the proper next questions, the other side of the story I had learned (or at least *an*other side of the story).

It was as though all the energy of the popular culture of the 1960s had suddenly swung around, away from its preoccupation with sex, drugs and rock 'n' roll, and was looking again at the Jesus it had almost forgotten. There was a sense of, 'Oh, you're still there, are you? Where do you fit? What was it all about anyway?' Western culture bounced back at Jesus the question with which he had teased his own followers. Instead of 'Who do you say that I am?' *we* were asking *him*, 'Who do *you* say that *you* are?'

Rice and Lloyd Webber didn't give an answer. That wasn't their aim. I often point out to students that they come to a university not to learn the answers, but to discover the right questions. The same was true of *Superstar*. And the question it asked was, I am convinced, right and proper. It's not the only question about Jesus, not the only question we should ask *of* Jesus, but it's utterly appropriate in its own way. And necessary. Unless you ask this question ('Are you who they say you are?'), your 'Jesus' risks disappearing like a hot-air balloon off into the mists of fantasy. This problem remains enormously important.

It is the question of who Jesus actually was. What he did, what he said, what he meant. It is, by implication, the question that any grown-up Christian faith must address. Is our sense of Jesus as a presence, disturbing but also healing, confronting but also comforting, simply a figment of our imagination? Was Freud right to see it as just a projection of our inner desires? Was Marx right to say that it was just a way of keeping the hungry masses quiet? Was Nietzsche right to say that Jesus taught a wimpish religion that has sapped the energy of humankind ever since? And – since those three gentlemen are now a venerable part of the cultural landscape in their own right – are today's shrill atheists right to say that God himself is a delusion, that Christianity is based on a multiple mistake, that it's all out of date, bad for your health, massively disproved, socially disastrous and ridiculously incoherent?

Faced with these questions, whether from Rice and Lloyd Webber, Richard Dawkins or anybody else, Christians have a choice. They can go on talking about 'Jesus', worshipping him in formal liturgy or informal meetings, praying to him, and finding out what happens in their own lives and communities when they do so – and failing to address the question that has been in the back of everyone else's mind for the last century at least. Or they can accept the question (even if, like many questions, it needs redefining, the closer you get to it) and set about answering it.

I was not yet ready, in the autumn of 1971, to do the latter. But within a few years I had realized that I could no longer put it off. By then, in the late 1970s, I was ordained, preaching regularly, leading Confirmation classes, organizing worship. I was finishing my doctorate and teaching undergraduates. My wife and I had two children and more on the way. We were facing the challenges of 'real life' on several levels. Why should I avoid the challenge of the real Jesus? Every time I opened the gospels and thought about my next sermon, I was faced with questions. Did he *really* say that? Did he really *do* that? What did it mean? There were plenty of voices around to say he hadn't said it, he didn't really do it, and that the only 'meaning' is that the church is a big confidence trick. If I was going to preach and, for that matter, if I was going to counsel people to trust Jesus and get to know him for themselves,

I couldn't do it with integrity unless I had faced the hard questions for myself.

It's been a long journey. No doubt there is much more to discover. But this book will tell you, as simply as possible, what I've found out so far.

The challenge to the churches

With Jesus, it's easy to be complicated and hard to be simple. Part of the difficulty is that Jesus was and is much, much more than people imagine. Not just people in general, but practising Christians, the churches themselves. Faced with the gospels – the four early books that give us most of our information about him – most modern Christians are in the same position I am in when I sit down in front of my computer. My computer will, I am reliably informed, do a large number of complex tasks. I only use it, however, for three things: writing, email, and occasional Internet searches. If my computer were a person, it would feel frustrated and grossly undervalued, its full potential nowhere near realized. We are, I believe, in that position today when we read the stories of Jesus in the gospels. We in the churches use these stories for various obvious things: little moralizing sermons on how to behave in the coming week, aids to prayer and meditation, extra padding for a theological picture largely constructed from elsewhere. The gospels, like my computer, have every right to feel frustrated. Their full potential remains unrealized.

Worse, *Jesus himself* has every right to feel frustrated. Many Christians, hearing of someone doing 'historical research' on Jesus, begin to worry that what will emerge is a smaller, less significant Jesus than they had hoped to find. Plenty of books offer just that: a cut-down-to-size Jesus, Jesus as a great moral teacher or religious leader, a great man but nothing more. Christians now routinely recognize this reductionism and resist it. But I have increasingly come to believe that we should be worried for quite the opposite reason. Jesus – the Jesus we might discover if we really looked! – is larger, more disturbing, more urgent than we – than the church! – had ever imagined. We have successfully managed to hide behind other questions (admittedly important ones) and to avoid the huge, world-shaking challenge of

Jesus' central claim and achievement. It is we, the churches, who have been the real reductionists. We have reduced the kingdom of God to private piety, the victory of the cross to comfort for the conscience, and Easter itself to a happy, escapist ending after a sad, dark tale. Piety, conscience and ultimate happiness are important, but not nearly as important as Jesus himself.

You see, the reason Jesus wasn't the sort of king people had wanted in his own day is – to anticipate our conclusion – that he *was* the true king, but they had become used to the ordinary, shabby, second-rate sort. They were looking for a builder to construct the home they thought they wanted, but he was the architect, coming with a new plan that would give them everything they needed, but within a quite new framework. They were looking for a singer to sing the song they had been humming for a long time, but he was the composer, bringing them a new song to which the old songs they knew would form, at best, the background music. He was the king, all right, but he had come to redefine kingship itself around his own work, his own mission, his own fate.

It is time, I believe, to recognize not only who Jesus was in his own day, despite his contemporaries' failure to recognize him, but also who he is, and will be, for our own. 'He came to what was his own,' wrote one of his greatest early followers, 'and his own people did not accept him' (John 1.11). That puzzle continues.

Perhaps, indeed, it has been the same in our own day. Perhaps even 'his own people' – this time not the Jewish people of the first century, but the would-be Christian people of the Western world – have not been ready to recognize Jesus himself. We want a 'religious' leader, not a king! We want someone to save our souls, not rule our world! Or, if we want a king, someone to take charge of our world, what we want is someone to implement the policies we already embrace, just as Jesus' contemporaries did. But if Christians don't get Jesus right, what chance is there that other people will bother much with him?

This book is written in the belief that the question of Jesus – who he really was, what he really did, what it means, and why it matters – remains hugely important in every area, not only in personal life, but also in political life, not only in 'religion' or 'spirituality', but also in such spheres of human endeavour as worldview, culture, justice, beauty, ecology, friendship, scholarship and sex. You may be relieved, or perhaps disappointed, to know that we won't have space to address all of these. What we will try to do is to look, simply and clearly, at Jesus himself, in the hope that a fresh glimpse of him will enable us to gain a new perspective on everything else as well. There will be time enough to explore other things in other places.

Getting inside the gospels

Jesus of Nazareth was a figure of history. That's where we have to start. He was born somewhere around 4 BC (the people who invented our present system of dating got it nearly right, but not quite) and grew up in the town of Nazareth in northern Palestine. His mother was related to the priestly families, and Jesus had a cousin, John, who in the ordinary course of events would have worked as a priest. His mother's husband, Joseph, was from the ancient royal family, the family of King David, of the tribe of Judah, though by this time there was no particular social status attached to such family membership. We know very little of Jesus' early life; one of the gospels tells a story of him as a precocious twelve-year-old, already able to ask key questions and debate with adults. His later life indicates that, like many Jewish boys, he was from an early age taught to read Israel's ancient scriptures, and that by adulthood he knew them inside out and had drawn his own conclusions as to what they meant. The strong probability is that he worked with Joseph in the family business, which was the building trade.

So far as we know, he never travelled outside the Middle East. Likewise, he never married; despite the speculations of occasional fantasy literature, there is not the slightest historical trace of any such relationship, still less of any children. (Jesus' blood relatives were well known in the early church; if he himself had had a family, we would certainly have heard about it. And we don't.) From complete obscurity Jesus suddenly came to public attention in the late 20s of the first century, when he was around thirty years old. Virtually everything we know about him as a figure of history is crammed into a short space of time; it's not easy to tell if it lasted one, two or three years, but pretty certainly it wasn't any longer. He was then picked up by the authorities in Jerusalem and, after some kind of trial or trials, was executed on the charge of being a would-be rebel leader, a 'king of the Jews'. Like many thousands of young Jews in that period, he died by crucifixion, a horrible method of killing designed to torture the victim as long as possible. It happened at Passover-time, most likely in AD 30 or possibly 33.

We are therefore in a curious position when we try to place Jesus in his proper historical context. We know a very great deal about the short, final period of his life and hardly anything about the earlier period. Jesus himself wrote nothing, so far as we know. The sources we have for his public career – the four gospels in the New Testament – are dense, complex and multilayered. They are works of art (of a sort) in their own right. But it is quite impossible to explain their very existence, let alone their detailed content, unless Jesus was himself not only a figure of real, solid history, but also pretty much the sort of person they make him out to be. If he wasn't that – if cunning people made him up out of thin air to validate their own new movement, as some have ridiculously suggested – he's not worth bothering with. But if he was a figure of history, we can try to discover what he did and what it meant in his own day. We can try to get, not 'behind' the gospels, as some sneeringly suggest is the purpose of historical research, but *inside* them, to discover the Jesus they've been telling us about all along, but whom we had managed to screen out. That will occupy the bulk of the book.

But Christians have always believed, as well, that Jesus is alive in the present and that he will play a crucial role in the eventual future towards which we are heading. He is the same, declared another wise early Christian writer, 'yesterday, today and for ever' (Hebrews 13.8). This book is mostly about the 'yesterday', not least because that's the part many today simply don't know. But towards the end of the book I shall deal a little with the 'tomorrow' part (what will Jesus be in God's ultimate future?) and suggest ways in which this combination of 'yesterday' and 'tomorrow' might condition us to think and behave differently in relation to Jesus 'today'.

2

The three puzzles

Jesus of Nazareth, then, stands out in the middle of history. Tens of millions call him 'Lord' and do their best to follow him. Countless others, including some who try to ignore him, find that he pops up all over the place – a line in a song, an image in a film, a cross on a distant skyline. Most of the world has adopted a dating system based, supposedly, on his birth (it's a few years off, but near enough). Jesus is unavoidable.

But Jesus is also deeply mysterious. This isn't just because, like any figure of ancient history, we don't know as much about him as we might like. (In fact, we know more about him than we do about most other people from the ancient world; but even some who wrote about him at the time admitted that they were only scratching the surface.) Jesus is mysterious because what we *do* know – what our evidence encourages us to see as the core of who he was and what he did – is so unlike what we know about anybody else that we are forced to ask, as people evidently did at the time: who, then, *is* this? Who does he think he is, and who is he in fact? Again, people who listened to him at the time said things like, 'We've never heard anyone talking like this,' and they didn't just mean his tone of voice or his skilful public speaking. Jesus puzzled people then, and he puzzles us still.

There are three reasons for this. The first reason for our being puzzled is that, for most of us, Jesus' world is a strange, foreign country. I don't mean just the Middle East, a major international trouble spot then as now. I mean that people in his day and in his country thought differently. They looked at the world differently. They told different stories to explain who they were and what they were up to. We do not habitually think, look and tell stories in the way they did. We have to get inside that world if the sense Jesus made then is going to make sense to us now.

An example may help. In today's Western world it's common for young adults to ask their parents for financial help to get them started in life. If well-to-do parents refused such a request, we might think them mean. But when Jesus told a story about a younger son asking his father for his inheritance while the father was still alive, his hearers would have been shocked. They would have seen the son's action as putting a curse on the father, saying, in effect, 'I wish you were dead.' That gives the whole story a different flavour. You can't assume that things worked in those days the way they work now.

But if the first reason for the puzzle is that Jesus' *world* is strange to us, the second is that Jesus' *God* is strange to us. That idea may itself seem odd. Isn't God simply God? Isn't it just a matter of whether you believe in God or not? No. The word 'God' and its various equivalents in other languages, ancient and modern, may *mean* 'the supreme or ultimate reality' or 'a being or object believed to have more than natural attributes and powers and to require human worship'. Those are, actually, the two basic definitions offered by *Merriam-Webster's Collegiate Dictionary*. But a brief study of the world's great religions, including those of the ancient Egyptians, Greeks, Romans, Indians and Chinese, or for that matter a glance at the different religious movements in the Western world over the last few centuries, will show that there are many different views of what this 'supreme or ultimate reality' is like. It isn't enough to ask whether someone believes or does not believe in 'God'. The key question is which God we're talking about. Part of the reason why Jesus puzzled the people of his day was that he was talking about 'God' most of the time, but what he was saying both did and did not make sense in relation to the 'God' his hearers had been thinking of.

We need, then, to get inside Jesus' world. And, as we do so, we need to try to catch a glimpse of what he meant when he spoke of God. These are two of the key puzzles. Once we grapple with these two puzzles, though, we begin to discover something much of our world, including much of today's church, has ignored or forgotten altogether. This is the hidden puzzle behind the other two. Throughout his short public career Jesus spoke and acted *as if he was in charge.*

Jesus did things people didn't think you were allowed to do, and he explained them by saying he had the right to do them. He wasn't, after all, merely a teacher, though of course he was that too – in fact, one of the greatest teachers the world has ever known. He spoke and acted as more than a teacher. He behaved as if he had the right, and even the duty, to take over, to sort things out, to make his country and perhaps even the wider world a different place. He behaved suspiciously like someone trying to start a political party or a revolutionary movement. He called together a tight and symbolically charged group of associates (in his world, the number twelve meant only one thing: the new Israel, the new people of God). And it wasn't very long before his closest followers told him that they thought he really *was* in charge, or ought to be. He was the king they'd all been waiting for. If we look for a parallel in today's world, we won't find it so much in the rise of a new 'religious' teacher or leader as in the emergence of a charismatic, dynamic politician whose friends are encouraging him to run for president – and who gives every appearance of having what it takes to sort everything out when he gets there.

You might have thought, and people certainly did at the time, that Jesus' untimely death dashed all those hopes once and for all. But not long after his death his associates started to claim that he *was* now in charge, for real. And they started to act as if it was true. This isn't about 'religion' in the sense the Western world has imagined for over two hundred years. This is about everything: life, art, the universe, justice, death, money. It's about politics, philosophy, culture and being human. It's about a God who is so much bigger than the 'God' of ordinary modern 'religion' that it's hardly possible to think of the two in the same breath. The really striking, and really puzzling, thing about Jesus – then and now – is that he seems not only to have been talking about this much bigger God, but actually launching the transformative new project this God had planned all along. And his followers really believed it had happened.

Talking about someone new being in charge was dangerous talk in Jesus' day, and it's dangerous talk still. Someone behaving as if they possess some kind of authority is an obvious threat to established rulers and other power brokers. Perhaps that's why, particularly in the last two or three hundred years, this side of Jesus hasn't been explored too much. Our culture has become used to thinking of Jesus as a 'religious' figure rather than a 'political' one. We have seen those two categories as watertight compartments, to be kept strictly separate. But it wasn't like that for Jesus and others of his time. What would happen if we took the risk of going back into his world, into his vision of God, and asking, 'Suppose it really is true?' What would it look like, in other words, if Jesus not only was in charge then, but is in charge today as well?

A ridiculous idea, you might say. It's blindingly obvious that Jesus isn't in charge in our world. Murder, misery and mayhem still continue, as they always have. Even Jesus' own so-called followers contribute their fair share. (As I write this, a 'Christian' mob is vowing to take violent revenge on adherents of another religion who have bombed a packed church.) What could we possibly mean by saying, 'Jesus is in charge'?

Well, we'll come to that later. But before we can even get going, we have to face a problem that is peculiarly our own. Behind the three historical puzzles (Jesus' world, Jesus' God and Jesus' behaviour – acting as if he was in charge) are additional difficulties that, like the elements of a perfect storm, have come together to pose severe challenges for anyone trying to address the questions about Jesus, let alone to do so simply.

3

The perfect storm

It was late October 1991. The crew of the fishing boat *Andrea Gail*, out of Gloucester, Massachusetts, had taken the vessel five hundred miles out into the Atlantic. A cold front moving along the Canadian border sent a strong disturbance through New England, while at the same time a large high-pressure system was building over the maritime provinces of south-eastern Canada. This intensified the incoming low-pressure system, producing what locals called the 'Halloween Nor'easter'. As Robert Case, a meteorologist, put it, 'These circumstances alone could have created a strong storm, but then, like throwing gasoline on a fire, a dying Hurricane Grace delivered immeasurable tropical energy to create the perfect storm.'[1] The hurricane, sweeping in from the Atlantic, completed the picture. The forces of nature converged on the helpless *Andrea Gail* from the west, the north and the south-east. Ferocious winds and huge waves reduced the boat to matchwood. Only light debris was ever found. There had, of course, been earlier 'perfect storms', but this was the one made famous by the book and film of that title.

Those of us who study and write about Jesus find ourselves at the mercy of our own perfect storm. The very mention of Jesus raises all kinds of winds and cyclones today. Listen to the build-up of the western wind. 'How do we know those things really happened? Isn't it the sort of legend people always tell about remarkable characters? Hasn't modern science and history shown we can't believe that kind of tale? And anyway, weren't the books about Jesus written a long time later, by people who wanted to make him out to be someone extra special, so that they could boost their own religious beliefs or even establish some kind of power for themselves? Isn't it time we got rid of these old superstitions once and for all?'

But as that storm whistles in from the west, watch the skies darken to the north, as other voices clamour for our attention. 'Of course

Jesus did it! The Bible is the word of God, and we have to believe it! Anyway, he was the son of God, so he could do that kind of thing. Miracles were his stock-in-trade. We have to stand up for the truth of the gospels against the blasts of modern scepticism. We can't let the atheists and the nay-sayers have it all their own way. It's time to roll back the climate of suspicion and once again learn to trust – to trust the canon of scripture, to trust the great traditions of the church, to trust the God of miracles, to trust Jesus himself. Even to ask the historical question shows that you've sold out to the rationalists before you go any farther.'

It's not comfortable being out on an open boat when these two winds strike from their different directions. Believe me – it's where I've lived for the last forty years. The winds are howling around you, you can hardly hear yourself think, and you suspect that neither side can hear too well either. It's a dialogue of the deaf.

If the westerly wind here stands for the rationalistic scepticism of the last two hundred years and the high-pressure system to the north stands for the 'conservative' Christian reaction to that sneering modernist denial, what is the tropical hurricane? We'll come to that presently. For the moment, let's examine these first two storm systems a bit more closely.

The distortions of scepticism and conservatism

The two violent winds of scepticism and conservatism have picked up extra energy from massive social, political and cultural storms that have raged across the Western world over the last two or three hundred years and that seem, as we speak, to be coming to something of a climax. In the United States, for example, the general picture seems to be that a lot of people taking the 'sceptical' position vote Democrat, and a lot of people taking the 'trusting' position vote Republican. I could introduce you to several people who buck those trends, but the picture is nonetheless worryingly accurate. Can it really be the case that people's judgment about who to vote for and what policies are best for a country and for the world can be mapped so easily onto questions of whether or not to believe a strange set of stories from the first century?

Unlikely though it seems, I think that is exactly what has happened. In a complicated, confused and dangerous world, anything will serve as a guardrail for people blundering along in the dark. We oversimplify complex problems. We bundle up very different social and political issues into two packages, and with a sigh of relief – now at least we know who we are, where we stand! – we declare ourselves to be in favour of *this* package and against *that* one. And we make life uncomfortable for anyone who wants to sit loose, to see things differently.

Jesus, as always, gets caught in the middle – along with a good number of his followers. To continue the US example, many people in America today were brought up in strict Christian homes and churches of one sort or another. There was a set package. Jesus, the Bible (if you were Protestant), the Mass (if you were Catholic), family, strict morals, the Rapture (for some Protestants), purgatory (for some Catholics), and ultimately a straight choice between heaven and hell: anyone familiar with life in modern America knows that all of this describes the world many remember only too well. And many of those who do remember it remember it with a shudder. That's the small, narrow world from which (phew!) the healthy scepticism of the modern world has rescued them. So, for many Americans today, and others elsewhere too, Jesus is part of the tight little world, closed and closed-minded, from which they have thankfully escaped. If you want to know why the 'new atheists' like Richard Dawkins, Christopher Hitchens and Sam Harris sell so many books, the answer is that they're offering the modernist version of the good old-fashioned theological term 'assurance'. They are assuring anxious ex-believers that the nightmare of small-minded and stultifying 'religion' is gone for ever.

Of course, things are a bit different in the UK, where few people today have had that kind of strict upbringing. But scepticism still thrives. Those same atheistic books denouncing the church, Christianity and religion in general sell by the cartload. Two generations after most people stopped sending their children to Sunday school, it seems that people still want to strike out at the religion they haven't got. Do they suspect that God, or someone, is still out there and might be dangerous? In any case, such rumours need to be stifled. The general public wants them to be stifled. We have our dreams of being free, grown-up humans, and we don't want to bend the knee to anyone, especially that fussy old God or that strange character Jesus! Actually, the sceptics, who take grim comfort from the apparent decline of many mainstream churches, don't often focus on Jesus himself. They have far softer targets to aim at (badly behaved clergy, for a start). But if they do mention Jesus, they tend to dismiss him with a wave of the hand. Just a first-century fanatic whose wild-eyed followers turned him into a god. Or, damning him with faint praise, just a mild-mannered first-century moralist, one of many great teachers down through the ages. Those are the internal dynamics of the westerly wind, the howling gale of contemporary scepticism.

Meanwhile, however, millions around the world, and tens of thousands in Britain and the United States too, tell a different story. They claim to have discovered Jesus as a living, challenging, healing presence. Stories abound of changed lives, of physical and emotional healing. New churches have sprung up, full of eager and excited people, often young people. Addicts are cured. Dysfunctional families are reunited. Real help is given to the sick, the poor, the prisoners. Failing schools are turned around. New energy is found for creative social and cultural projects. For such people, the whole thing is real enough. It's hard to argue with a radically changed life or, indeed, with still being alive when the doctors had given you up for dead. That's why there is such energy behind the northern high-pressure system, the powerful force of a newly energized, but often very 'conservative', Christian faith.

Many sceptics simply ignore these current Christian phenomena. Many of these newer, high-octane Jesus-followers simply return the compliment. That's unhealthy – on both sides. We need to think things through. Jesus himself was open to all comers. He told his followers to love God with their minds as well as every other part of themselves. There is nothing to lose and everything to gain by proper enquiry.

For what it's worth, my long-lasting impression is that the 'Jesus' who gets caught in the crossfire of these cultural wars may be considerably less than the Jesus we actually find in the pages of the early Christian writings – and in real, first-century history itself. After all, just as it's quite possible for sceptics to be mistaken, so it's quite possible, as church history shows in plenty, for devout Jesus-followers to be mistaken as well. It is vital to look again at Jesus himself.

Two Jesus myths

There are, then, two myths that swirl around our heads, around the churches, around the TV studios, and around the editorial offices of news magazines. Let's name them even more clearly and, to some extent, shame them, so we can be clear about the present confusions before we turn to the equally confusing world of the first century. We'll take them in the reverse order this time. First, the high-pressure system of conservative Christianity.

Here we find the classic Western Christian myth about Jesus, which is still believed by millions around the world. In this myth, a super-natural being called 'God' has a supernatural 'son' whom he sends, virgin-born, into our world, despite the fact that it's not his natural habitat, so that he can rescue people out of this world by dying in their place. As a sign of his otherwise secret divine identity, this 'son' does all kinds of extraordinary and otherwise impossible 'miracles', crowning them all by rising from the dead and returning to 'heaven', where he waits to welcome his faithful followers after their deaths. In the Catholic version of this classic Western myth, Jesus calls his close friend Peter to found the church; anyone who wants to be with Jesus, here or hereafter, must join Peter's movement. In the Protestant version, Jesus commissions his followers to write the New Testament, which reveals the absolute truth about Jesus and, once more, how to get to heaven.

(Already I hear that wind getting up. 'What d'you mean it's a myth? Don't you believe that? Are you one of those dangerous liberals after all? Aren't you a bishop?' OK, OK, I hear you. Please wait. Patience is a Christian virtue.)

The second myth, prevalent in the sceptical 'westerly wind' of our perfect storm, is the new classic modernist myth, which is widely believed in secular society and in several mainstream churches too. In this new myth of Christian origins, Jesus was just an ordinary man, a good first-century Jew, conceived and born in the ordinary way. He was a remarkable preacher and teacher, but he probably didn't do all those 'miracles'. Some people seem to have felt better after meeting him, but that was about it. He certainly didn't think he would die for the sins of the world. He was simply trying to teach people to live differently, to love one another, to be kind to old ladies, small children and (that blessed postmodern category) the 'marginalized'. He was talking about God, not about himself. The idea of being a super-natural 'son of God' never occurred to him; he'd have been horrified to hear such a thing and even more to have had a 'church' founded in his memory.

He certainly didn't rise from the dead; yes, his followers, feeling that his work would continue, used careless language that seemed to imply that that's what had happened, but of course it didn't. Then these followers began to tell stories about him that snowballed into legends, which then sprouted fresh interpretations. The 'gospels' we now have in the Bible are the product of that free-floating – and perhaps self-serving – inventive process. They tell us a lot about the new aims and agendas of the early 'Christians' and about how they settled down and adapted the original message of Jesus to different circumstances. But if we want to find out about Jesus himself, we have to work our way back through the fog of subsequent hero wor-ship and, above all, through the process by which he was 'divinized'. We might even need to call on some of the 'other gospels', the ones that boring old 'orthodox' Christianity left out of its 'canon'.

(At this point I hear the other wind rattling the window panes. 'And you don't believe that? Don't you realize that the gospels are full of later invention and interpretation? Are you one of those right-wing fundamentalist fanatics who think that all of that stuff just happened the way it says in the gospels? Which stone have you been living under for the last two hundred years?' All right, all right, I hear you too. If you're representing the world of sweet reasonableness, then calm down and take the argument one step at a time.)

When I say that these two stories are 'myths', I mean it in the following way. A 'myth' in this strict sense is a story that purports to be in some sense 'historical' and that encapsulates and reinforces the strongly held beliefs of the community that tells it. Serious 'myths' are regularly expressed not only in narrative, but also in symbol and action. Much of the life of the broadly 'conservative' Western church acts out the first myth. Much of the life of 'liberal' Christianity, on the one hand, and of the wider secular world, on the other, acts out the second. Both are very, very powerful stories. They have shaped the lives of millions, and they still do. But they are both, in this sense, myths. Neither of them will stand up to full-on, hard-edged, no-nonsense historical scrutiny. Or, for that matter, theological scrutiny.

The underlying problem with both these myths is that they pose the question in the wrong place. First, 'Did it all happen or didn't it?' This is the plain, blunt question of a typical eighteenth-century Westerner. No frills, no metaphors, no interpretation, just 'facts'. Did it happen or not? The 'conservative' or 'orthodox' brigade, driven onto the back foot (to use a cricketing metaphor) marshals its forces to say, 'Yes, it really did happen.' And there the matter ends. Those in the 'liberal' or 'sceptical' brigade shrug their shoulders: 'No, it didn't really happen. Or not much of it, anyway.' Again, that's the end of it. Facts or no facts. But what about meaning?

The second related question – I was asked it just yesterday by a journalist – is: so was Jesus the son of God, or wasn't he? And for most people the phrase 'son of God' carries with it all the connotations of that first myth, in which the supernatural being swoops down to reveal secret truth, do extraordinary 'miracles' to prove his 'divinity', die a redemptive death, and get back to heaven at once, enabling others to get there too. And if I say – as I'm going to – that I don't think that story is the right way to talk about Jesus, some will say, 'So you don't think he's the son of God, then?' and condemn me as a hopeless liberal. Whereas if I say – as I'm going to – that I *do* think Jesus was and is the 'son of God', albeit within a very different sort of story, others will condemn me as a hopeless conservative.

The problem of historical complexity

And now at last we are ready to take up the third element in the perfect storm we face today when we talk about Jesus. Out in the Atlantic, but heading for shore fast, is a hurricane. It was coming anyway, but when it meets these two winds we should expect a storm of what people today, perhaps confusingly, call 'apocalyptic' proportions.

The third element is the sheer historical complexity of speaking about Jesus. The world of first-century Palestinian Judaism – his world – was complex and dense in itself. Anyone who has tried to understand today's Middle Eastern problems can be assured that life was every bit as complicated in the first century as it is now. We have a thousand sources on which to draw for constructing a picture of today's problems, everything from newspaper reports to Facebook and Twitter postings. But for historians of the first century – and if we want to talk about Jesus himself, as opposed to making up fantasies about him, we are all bound to become to some extent historians of the first century – we are faced with a strange challenge.

Take an example. John F. Kennedy is perhaps one of the best-known figures of the mid twentieth century. His presidency was of course cut short by his sudden and violent death, a death that had, and perhaps still has, iconic significance for many Americans and others around the world. Those of us alive at the time all still remember where we were when we heard the news. Now suppose we had four books containing very detailed accounts of what Kennedy did and said during his three-year presidency, with only a brief glance at what went before. Suppose it was quite clear that these were put together by people who believed that what Kennedy had done and said had lasting importance for their own day. But suppose as well that, instead of the overwhelming multitude of sources we actually possess for the decades before his day, we simply had a history book written in the early years of the twenty-first century (i.e. forty years after his death) plus a scattering of other material – a few letters, tracts, coins, souvenir artefacts, that kind of thing – to help us reconstruct the world within which what Kennedy did and said made the sense it did at the time, and particularly to get some idea of why some thought him a hero and others thought he had to be killed. One can imagine all the theories – the reconstructions of the cold war mentality, the social and cultural tensions of 1960s America, the state of the main political parties at the time, the dynastic ambitions of Kennedy's father, and so on. There would be plenty of wiggle room for interpretation.

That is more or less our challenge with the historical evidence for Jesus. We have the four 'gospels', written later by people who believed passionately that what Jesus had done and said, coupled with his death and what happened afterwards, was of massive ongoing significance. The gospels are highly detailed; one of the problems of writing the present book has been trying to decide what to leave out. They are clearly written from particular (pro-Jesus) points of view. But, unlike today's historian studying JFK in his actual context, we have simply a history book written forty or fifty years later (by Josephus, an aristocratic Jew who went over to the Roman side in the war of AD 66–70) and a scattering of other material, bits and pieces, tracts, coins, letters and so forth. Out of these very disparate sources we have to reconstruct the setting in which what Jesus did and said made the sense it did, so much sense that some thought he was God's Messiah and others thought he had to be killed at once. If we don't make the effort to do this reconstruction, we will, without a shadow of doubt, assume that what Jesus did and said makes the sense it might have made in some other context – perhaps our own. That has happened again and again. I believe that this kind of easy-going anachronism is almost as corrosive to genuine Christian faith as scepticism itself.

This tropical storm – the challenge of writing history about Jesus – would be threatening enough even without the cultural pressures of the westerly wind (modernist scepticism) and the high-pressure system to the north (would-be 'Christian' conservatism). Or, if you like, angry voices from the left, angry voices from the right, and a major historical puzzle sweeping in on us with full force. If, trying to make things simple, we fail to recognize this multilayered complexity, we will simply repeat the age-old mistake of imagining Jesus in our own image or at least placing him, by implication, in our own culture. And part of the whole point of the Christian message is that what happened back then, what happened to Jesus, what happened *through* him, was a one-time, never-to-be-repeated piece of history.

Hence the perfect storm of present-day discussion. I have on my desk as I write two brand-new books about Jesus, one written by the pope himself and another by a well-known English sceptic. Both are learned, sophisticated, engaging. They cannot both be true. Behind me are twenty shelves of books about Jesus and the gospels written over the last two hundred years. They cannot all be true either. What are we to do?

Faced with this massive storm brewing, some earnestly advise us to stay in the harbour. It's too dangerous out there just now; let's just tell the story the way we learned it, let's rely on the great tradition of the church, let's be faithful to our scriptures. This amounts, of course, to a sophisticated version of the northern high-pressure system: take shelter from the westerly wind, pretend the hurricane isn't happening, and just let the northerly wind blow wherever it wants. To do anything else, such voices say, is to capitulate to the forces of scepticism and cynicism, to collude with post-Enlightenment reductionist notions of 'history'.

Not so. The westerly wind of modernist scepticism and the easterly hurricane of historical puzzle are not the same thing. There were historians before the Enlightenment; please God, there will be historians after postmodernity. History studies what actually happened (and when, and where, and how) and particularly *why* people did what they did. These are good questions. We should be grateful to the whole post-Enlightenment movement we loosely call 'modernism' for reminding us that they matter, even as we should firmly decline the same movement's unwarranted restriction of the kinds of answers it is prepared to accept.

Part of our difficulty here – this has been another serious problem I've faced in writing this book – is that the world of first-century Palestinian Judaism was complex and (to us) often highly confusing. Imagine, again, trying to explain the America of the early 1960s to a visitor from Mars with short, dense books of Kennedy memorabilia as your main sources. In any particular historical context, certain things made sense, certain ideas and actions went together in a way that felt entirely natural at the time, but that we may well have to reconstruct with considerable difficulty. Sometimes, doing first-century history, people use this difficulty as a way of saying that Jesus and his followers couldn't have thought like this or like that: if *we* find a certain idea difficult or puzzling, how could they (poor, pre-Enlightenment souls!) possibly have got their minds round it?

Sometimes people argue the other way round. We, today, are eager to ask certain questions (for instance, 'Do heaven and hell exist, and how can I get to the first and avoid the second?'); and so we assume, too readily, that people in Jesus' day were eager to ask those questions as well, meaning pretty much the same by them as we do now. But if we are to do real history, we have to allow people in other times and other places to be radically different from us – even though, in order to do history at all, we have to exercise disciplined imagination and try as best we can to relate to those very different people. It's a challenge. But it's one I believe we can meet.

What matters, I have become convinced, is that we need to understand how *worldviews* work. If you have been born and bred within a culture that tells certain stories, observes certain customs and festivals, practises particular domestic habits, and sings particular songs, and if these things all go together and reinforce one another, a single phrase or action may well carry multiple layers of meaning. Imagine our visiting Martian landing this time in the middle of a game of cricket. Those of us who have played it appreciate the subtleties, the nuances, the finely balanced match, the implications of how the ball is bowled, of who it is that's coming in to bat next. You or I would take all of that in at a glance, but it might take us an hour or more to explain it, in all its detail, to our alien guest. That doesn't mean it's horribly theoretical or abstract. It only means that most people, most of the time, live more complex lives than we often realize.

That complexity is likely to increase when you go to a place like first-century Jerusalem at Passover-time, with pilgrims singing those Psalms again and families getting ready to tell one another the story they already know, the story of God and Moses and Pharaoh and the Red Sea and the hope of freedom at last, while the Roman soldiers are looking down from their watchtowers and while an excited procession comes over the Mount of Olives, led by a man on a donkey, and starts to sing about the kingdom that is going to appear at any minute . . .

So how can we go about the task of trying to understand Jesus himself? There is a whole other book to be written about the kind of evidence we have for Jesus and how we can use it responsibly. What are the gospels? What about those 'other gospels'? What sources did these books use, and how can we evaluate them historically? What non-Christian sources are there for Jesus? (Answer: a reference in the Jewish historian Josephus, a reference in the Roman historian Tacitus, and one possible allusion in a more scurrilous Roman writer, Suetonius.) How were the stories of Jesus shaped by the needs of his first followers as they went out into the wider world? What were the motives and intentions of the writers themselves? What can we know about the communities within which they themselves lived, prayed, thought and wrote?

All of these questions have been the subject of intensive study over the last two hundred years. But the present book isn't the place to address any of them. I have written about them myself in various other places and hope to do so more in the future. But actually all such questions are themselves not 'neutral'. There is no place where we can gain a 'fixed point' from which to begin. The way you treat the sources will reflect the way you already understand Jesus, just as the way you understand Jesus will reflect the way you understand the sources. This isn't a vicious circle. The same would be true in the study of Napoleon, or John F. Kennedy, or indeed Margaret Thatcher. It just means that we have to go forward carefully, round and round the loop, checking that we're talking sense about both the subject and the sources. The present book represents one part of one journey around one element in that loop.

In fact, I increasingly suspect that a good deal of the 'methods' developed within professional biblical scholarship over the last two hundred years have been, themselves, the product of a worldview that may not have been truly open to discovering the real Jesus. The worldview of post-Enlightenment Europe and America was determined, often enough, to see Jesus as a religious teacher and leader offering a personal spirituality and ethic and a heavenly hope. It had no intention of seeing him as someone who was claiming to be in charge of the world; some might say that the 'methods' of supposedly 'historical scholarship' were designed, whether accidentally or not, to screen out that possibility altogether. This doesn't mean that those 'methods' – the study of the sources, the forms of the early Jesus stories, the motives of the gospel writers – have nothing to say. On the contrary, they have a great deal to say. But there comes a time when it may be appropriate to stand back, having heard it all, and to have another shot at saying, 'Actually, I think *this* was what was going on.' This, I think, is one of those times.

So if we are going to approach Jesus himself in a fresh way and ask the right questions instead of the wrong ones, we need to get our minds and imaginations into Jesus' own day by examining another 'perfect storm', the one into which Jesus himself was walking. What were the winds that gathered speed just then, rushing in upon him from various directions? What did it mean for him to be caught in the eye of this storm? As he rode into Jerusalem that fateful spring day, what did he think he was doing?

4

The making of a first-century storm

A really good metaphor deserves more than one outing – as Jesus himself seems to have found, using and reusing ideas and scenes in his kaleidoscopic display of parables. Let's have another go at the perfect storm, then, but now set in the first century. This time, the forces converging on a spot off the Massachusetts coast stand not for today's particular cultural pressures, but for the pressures that were building up in Jesus' own day. And the place where they are converging is Jerusalem.

We smile at those medieval maps that placed Jerusalem at the centre of the earth, with everything else radiating out from that point. How quaint, we think. But maybe there's a truth there, buried under the rubble of successive social, cultural, political and religious earthquakes. Maybe that's the point. Maybe the reason Jerusalem was seen as the centre of the world was because that's where all the pressure was concentrated. That's where the fault lines all came together, where the tectonic plates ground relentlessly into one another, as indeed they still do. And it is to Jerusalem that we have to go to understand Jesus of Nazareth. That's where the real perfect storm took place. That's where all the dark forces converged, one spring day in, most likely, the year we call AD 30 (or, less likely, 33).

How can we tell the story of Jesus in a simple way, when so many elemental forces came rushing together at that point in space and time? So much history, so many bad memories, such high expectations and aspirations, such a tangled web of faith and fear and hatred and hope. And so many memorable characters crowding onto the stage, catching our eye and firing our imagination: Mary Magdalene, Peter, Pontius Pilate, Judas . . . the list goes on. And then we catch a glimpse – or was it just our imagination? – of Jesus himself, towering over them but without ever appearing aloof. Who was he? What was he about? What was he trying to do? Why should we care, two thousand years later?

These were, of course, the questions his closest friends wanted to ask as they woke him up in the middle of an actual storm on the Sea of Galilee. It's still a dangerous place today. There are signs in the car parks on the western side of the sea warning that high winds can sweep giant waves right over parked vehicles. But Jesus wasn't fazed. According to the story, he got up and told the storm to be quiet (Matthew 8.23–27; Mark 4.35–41; Luke 8.22–25). And it obeyed him. I think his friends told that story not only because it was striking and dramatic in itself, but because they saw in it something of the larger story they were struggling to tell: the story of a man in the eye of the storm, the storm of history and culture, of politics and piety, a man who seemed to be asleep in the middle of it all, but who then stood up and told the wind and the waves to stop.

Come back, then, to the Massachusetts coast in October 1991. The wind from the west, the storm from the north, and the hurricane from the south-east – they are all converging on a single point. This is not the place to be, not the time to be out on the open sea. Now think of the Middle East in the first century. There was a gale, there was a storm, and there was a hurricane. And Jesus was caught in the middle of it all.

The Roman storm

The gale blowing steadily from the far west was the new social, political and (not least) military reality of the day. The new superpower. The name on everyone's lips, the reality on everyone's minds. Rome.

Rome had been steadily increasing in power and prominence as a world force over the previous two or three hundred years. But until thirty years before the birth of Jesus of Nazareth, Rome had been a republic. An intricate system of checks and balances ensured that nobody could hold absolute power, and those who did have power didn't have it very long. Rome had had tyrants many centuries before and was proud to have rid itself of them.

But with Julius Caesar all that changed. 'Caesar' was simply his family name, but Julius made it a royal title from that day on (the words 'Kaiser' and 'Tsar' are variations on 'Caesar'). A great military hero out on the frontiers, he did the unthinkable: he brought his army back to Rome itself and established his own power and prestige there. It seems that he even allowed people to think he was divine.

The traditionalists were furious, and they assassinated him. But this threw Rome into a long and bloody civil war from which one winner emerged, Caesar's adopted son, Octavian. He took the title 'Augustus', which means 'majestic' or 'worthy of honour'. This, along with 'Caesar', became the name or title of his successors as well. He declared that his adoptive father, Julius, had indeed become divine; this meant that he, Augustus Octavian Caesar, was now officially 'son of god', 'son of the divine Julius'. If you'd asked anybody in the Roman Empire, from Germany to Egypt, from Spain to Syria, who the 'son of god' might be, the obvious answer, the politically correct answer, would have been 'Octavian'.

In a world where mainstream religion was emphatically a branch of the state, Augustus took the senior priestly roles. He became *pontifex maximus* ('chief priest' in Latin) and passed that role too to his successors. Meanwhile, Augustus's court poets and historians did a great job with their propaganda. They told the thousand-year story of Rome as a long and winding narrative that had reached its great climax at last; the golden age had begun with the birth of the new child through whom peace and prosperity would spread to the whole world. The whole world is now being renewed, sang Virgil in a passage[1] that some later Christians saw as a pagan prophecy of the Messiah. (The fathers of the American Constitution borrowed a key phrase from this poem, *novus ordo seclorum*, 'a new order of the ages', not only for the Great Seal of the United States, but also for the dollar bill. They were thereby making the striking claim that history turned its vital corner not with Augustus Caesar, nor even with Jesus of Nazareth, but with the birth and Constitution of the United States.)

Virgil's poem goes on to promise that from now on, in this new age, under the divine kingship of Apollo himself, the earth will produce all that one could require. Earth, sea and heaven will rejoice at the child now to be born. Nobody knows which child Virgil was referring to, but the point is clear: the new age, for which we have waited for a millennium, is now here at last through the peaceful and joyful rule of Augustus Caesar. The message was carved in stone, on monuments and in inscriptions, around the known world: 'Good news! We have an Emperor! Justice, Peace, Security and Prosperity are ours for ever! The son of God has become King of the World!'

Augustus ruled the Roman world, an increasingly massive empire, from 31 BC to AD 14. After his death, he too was divinized, and his successor, Tiberius, took the same titles. I have on my desk, as I write this, a coin from the reign of Tiberius. On the front, encircling Tiberius's portrait, is the abbreviated title: AUGUSTUS TI CAESAR DIVI AUG F, short for AUGUSTUS TIBERIUS CAESAR DIVI AUGUSTI FILIUS, 'Augustus Tiberius Caesar, son of the Divine Augustus'. On the reverse is a picture of Tiberius dressed as a priest, with the title Pontifex Maximus. It was a coin like this one that they showed to Jesus of Nazareth, a day or two after he had ridden into Jerusalem, when they asked him whether or not they should pay tribute to Caesar. 'son of God'? 'Chief Priest'? He was in the eye of the storm.

That tells us almost all we need to know about the first element of our first-century 'perfect storm'. But why was Rome particularly interested in the Middle East?

For reasons surprisingly similar to those of today's Western powers. Rome needed the Middle East for urgent supplies of necessary raw materials. Today it's oil; then it was grain. Rome itself was grossly overpopulated and underemployed. There were far too many people to be fed on local produce alone. Grain shipments from Egypt were vital. In the first century, as in the twenty-first, sea traffic was a tempting target for pirates and other hostile action. To avoid that, it was vital to keep the whole area stable. The job of a Roman governor in a place like Jerusalem was to keep the peace, to administer justice, to collect the taxes, and particularly to suppress unrest. After all, as the propaganda insisted, the rule of Caesar, the Roman 'son of god', was the 'good news' that had brought blessings and benefits to the whole world. Surely, once the locals saw what blessings Rome was so generously offering, they would happily come into line? Could it really be that difficult to win over their hearts and minds to the great ideals of the empire to the west?

That was the westerly gale, the first element in the perfect storm at whose centre Jesus of Nazareth found himself. We now turn to the high-pressure system.

The Jewish storm

The second great element in Jesus' perfect storm, the overheated high-pressure system, more turbulent and complex than the first element, is the story of Israel. As far back as we can trace their ancient scriptures, the Jewish people had believed that their story was going somewhere, that it had a goal in mind. Despite many setbacks and disappointments, their God would make sure they reached the goal at last. This is the story within which many Jews of Jesus' day believed, passionately, that they themselves were living. They were not just telling it as an ancient memory. They were, themselves, actors within its ongoing drama.

It is, I think, hard for people today to imagine what it's like to live within a long story in this way. The closest we come, perhaps, is the widespread assumption that ever since the rise of the modern Western world we are acting out a story of 'progress'. This is the so-called Whig view of history writ large: history is the story of movements of progressive freedom, and we must go forward and make the next one happen, and the next one after that. Despite all the tyrannies of the last century, people today still believe this myth of progress, as evidenced by the numerous proposals you read or hear that begin, 'Now that we live in this day and age . . .' or 'Now that we live in the twenty-first century . . .' Those phrases signal the presence of some kind of 'progressive' agenda. People who think like that are actors in a play whose script they already know. They believe themselves called to take the drama forward towards a supposed libertarian utopia. On the day I am revising this chapter, the day after the wedding of Prince William and Catherine Middleton in Westminster Abbey, there is a grumpy letter in *The Times*, complaining that this event and the public reaction to it have 'turned the clock back a hundred years'. That only makes sense if you assume that the 'clock' had been inexorably moving towards republicanism – a myth that many have found consoling down through the years, but that many more around the world seem determined to resist.

Take that rather vague, though still powerful, notion of 'progress' and multiply it many times over. We have lived with the 'progressive' dream for two or three centuries, but the Jews had been living in their great story for, they believed, well over a thousand years. Their story, like a great costume drama going on over many generations, stretched back to Abraham, Moses, David and other heroes of the distant past. But it was all going to come to its great climax, they believed, any moment now. It was a single story, and they were at its leading edge.

So far as we know, this story was unique in the ancient world. Even the Romans had not thought of themselves in this way, with the sense of a great story now at last reaching its climax, until Augustus and his court poets used the idea in their propaganda. (This is interesting in itself. It's clear from earlier Jewish texts that the Jews didn't get the idea from Livy or Virgil. But it's equally obvious that the Roman poets didn't borrow it from the Jews either. Faced with these two parallel movements, we can see already why they crashed into each other, as you would expect in a perfect storm.) As far back as we can trace their ancient scriptures – what Christians call the Old Testament – the Jewish people and their ancestors had believed, or had been told by their prophets to believe, that their story was going somewhere, that it had a goal in mind. Despite many setbacks and disappointments, their God would make sure they reached the goal at last.

After all, they were taught that their God was the one true God of all the world. He wasn't simply one more god among many. It was therefore impossible that his will for the world would ultimately be thwarted. And, since the present state of affairs was clearly less than ideal, he would do whatever it took to sort things out. His people would, in the meantime, find themselves caught up in the story of how that would happen. Thus, whereas the Romans had what we might call a *retrospective eschatology*, in which people looked *back* from a 'golden age' that had already arrived and saw the whole story of how they had arrived at that point, the Jews cherished and celebrated a *prospective eschatology*, looking *forward* from within a decidedly ungolden age and longing and praying fervently for the freedom, justice and peace that, they were convinced, were theirs by right. God would do it! It was going to happen at last!

The stories the Jews told (and when I say 'told', I mean not only told one another, read out aloud in their meeting-houses, studied privately, and turned into prayer, but also celebrated in national festivals, which involved most of the population and brought vast pilgrim crowds from all over the world) were not simply stories of small beginnings, sad times at present, and glorious days to come. They were more specific, more complex, dense with detail and heavy with hope. Their theme came to its fullest flowering in the great story of the Exodus, when, roughly fifteen hundred years before the time of Jesus, Moses had led the Israelites out of slavery in Egypt, across the Red Sea (which miraculously parted to let them through), and through the desert to the promised land. The Jews lived on the hope that it would happen again. The tyrants would do their worst, and God would deliver the people. Understand the Exodus, and you understand a good deal about Judaism. And about Jesus. Jesus chose Passover, the great national festival celebrating the Exodus, to make his crucial move.

We will look in more detail at the Exodus story a little later. It was celebrated annually at Passover and in other festivals too. But the Exodus, in turn, looked back farther, to the divine call to the original patriarchs, Abraham, Isaac and Jacob. Their story in turn looked back farther still, to the mysterious but powerful story of creation itself, when Israel's God had brought his beautiful, ordered and living creation out of the primal waters of chaos. *The God who brought order out of chaos and who brought his enslaved people out of Egypt would do it again.* Creation and covenant: God made the world, God called Israel to be his people, and God would remake his world in order to rescue his people Israel. Every time the Jewish people told the story (and they told it often), that was what they were thinking and hoping and praying for. It was this hope, this story that generated the second great storm wind, the powerful high-pressure system, into whose path Jesus of Nazareth decided to walk. And, eventually, to ride a donkey.

Long before that point, two more elements had entered the story of Israel and continued thereafter to dominate the horizon. When I lived in Jerusalem for three months in 1989, I frequently walked through the ultra-Orthodox Jewish quarter, Mea Shearim. Among the fascinating and evocative sights and sounds of that community I observed many posters. Some of them were warning visitors to dress modestly: no bare flesh here, please! But many of them were harping on a darker, more powerful double theme. Many of the families in Mea Shearim had escaped from Eastern Europe around the time of the Holocaust. The horror of that period had shaped their imagination. It was because of what Hitler did that one must now observe the ancestral law. It was because of what Hitler did that God would now do a new thing. And it was because of what Hitler did that this Jewish community was praying and waiting and longing for – the Messiah. 'Hitler and the Messiah!' 'Hitler and the Messiah!' The great wicked ruler and the coming great deliverer! That was the message I saw then.

And that, with the first name changed to suit different circumstances (Caesar? Herod?), is the message you would have heard in Jesus' day. These two themes – the great evil empire and the coming royal deliverer – look back partly to the Exodus itself, when Moses delivered Israel from Pharaoh's Egypt. But they increased in power with the long story of Israel's monarchy and the spectacular national disasters that had befallen the people during that period. These themes are, if you like, the particular dust storms that the great high-pressure system of Israel's history picked up along the way, gathering momentum with every passing decade. Memories of King David and his famous victories over the surrounding pagan nations were kept alive, as prophets promised a coming day when a king from David's family would bring justice, peace and prosperity to the whole world. (Had the Roman poet Virgil been reading Isaiah 11? Probably not, but the coincidence of themes is striking.) Memories of King Solomon building the Temple in Jerusalem were kept alive by those who defended, cleansed, restored or beautified the Temple, a process that was still going on in Jesus' day under the patronage of the Herod family. The coming king would defeat the wicked, oppressive nations and would build, or rebuild, God's Temple! Hitler and the Messiah! Down with the one! Bring on the other!

For 'Hitler', then, also read 'Babylon'. Other disasters had come crashing down on the Israelites. But easily the worst was when the

Babylonians captured Jerusalem in the early sixth century BC, decimated the royal family, smashed the Temple to bits, and carried away its treasures, dragging off most of the population into an exile from which few would ever return. It was like Egypt all over again: enslavement in a foreign land. 'By the rivers of Babylon,' wrote one of their poets, 'there we sat down and there we wept' (Psalm 137.1). And it was memories of Jerusalem, of 'Zion', that made the tears bitter. They had lived at the fault line in world history and geography, and the earthquake had swallowed them up alive.

And now here comes the extraordinary bit, the part of the story many miss out, the twist in the tale responsible for the fact that, by the time the high-pressure system of Jewish history reached the first century, it was already dangerously close to storm force. Though many Jews had, remarkably enough, been brought back from Babylon and by the end of the sixth century had even rebuilt the Temple, there remained a strong sense that this was not yet the real 'new Exodus' for which they longed. Babylon itself had fallen, overthrown by a rival empire (Persia); but the phenomenon of which Egypt a thousand years before had been one classic example, and Babylon the most recent, was continuing. New wicked empires had arisen, and Israel was still enslaved to them. And there grew up a sense that a new Exodus, a real 'return from exile', was still to be awaited, had not yet happened. It would come when the last great world empire had done its worst. Indeed, it would result in the overthrow of that dark power.

This is the long story, the great narrative of hope, the prospective eschatology, within which many Jews of Jesus' day were living, had been living for a long time, and would continue to live. In Jesus' day it was obvious which world power had taken on the role of Egypt and Babylon. This is where our high-pressure system meets our gale. The long story of Israel must finally confront the long story of Rome. This is no time to be out on the sea in an open boat. Or riding into Jerusalem on a donkey.

The clash of these two stories produced several movements within a couple of hundred years on either side of the time of Jesus. We shall look at these in a later chapter. For the moment we move on to the third element in the perfect storm of the first century.

5

The hurricane

The gale of Rome and the high-pressure system of Jewish hopes. It takes one more wind to make the perfect storm. And, as in the original Massachusetts disaster, this one was of a different order altogether.

To understand this great cyclone, this tropical hurricane, you have to understand, as I said before, something about the ancient Jewish vision of God. This always was the highly unpredictable element within the Jewish story itself. God remained free and sovereign. Again and again in the past, the way Israel had told its own story was different from the way God was planning things. The people, no doubt, hoped that the way they were telling their own story would fit in comfortably enough with the way God was seeing things, but again and again the prophets had to say that this was not so. Often God's way of telling the story cut clean against the national narrative. *And Jesus believed that this was happening again in his own time.*

God had promised to come back, to return to his people in power and glory, to establish his kingdom on earth as in heaven. The Jewish people always hoped that this would simply underwrite their national aspirations; he was, after all, their God. They wanted a divine hurricane simply to reinforce their already overheated high-pressure system. But the prophets, up to and including John the Baptist, had always warned that God's coming in power and in person would be entirely on his own terms, with his own purpose – and that his own people would be as much under judgment as anyone, if their aspirations didn't coincide with God's.

Jesus not only believed that this was another of those moments where the true, prophetic vision of the divine hurricane would clash with the current national mood. He believed, it seems – the stories he told at the time bear this out quite strikingly – that as he came to Jerusalem *he was embodying, incarnating, the return of Israel's God to his people* in power and glory.

But it was a different kind of power, a different kind of glory. This is another point that *Jesus Christ Superstar* got exactly right. Jesus is approaching Jerusalem, and Simon the Zealot urges him to mount a proper revolution. Jesus, he says, will then get the power and the glory for ever. But then Jesus sings, hauntingly, the lines that make clear that there is a radical difference between the national aspiration, as voiced by the Zealots, and the divine purpose. Neither Simon nor the crowds nor the other disciples nor Jerusalem itself have any idea what power is. They don't understand what glory is. They simply haven't a clue. So he continues with the warning, which, in all our sources, he went on to enact in a dramatic symbol. Jerusalem itself was going to be thrown down, stone by stone. The harsh wind of western empire would blast away the Temple itself, the central symbol of national identity and the building that made Jerusalem what it was, because Jerusalem and its leaders had not recognized the moment when God was visiting them, was coming back to them in person (Luke 20.44).

The wind of God

Here, then, is the third element in the first-century perfect storm: the strange, unpredictable and highly dangerous divine element. The wind of God. This is God's moment, declares Jesus, and you were looking the other way. Your dreams of national liberation, leading you into head-on confrontation with Rome, were not God's dreams. God called Israel, so that through Israel he might redeem the world; but Israel itself needs redeeming as well. Hence God comes to Israel riding on a donkey, in fulfilment of Zechariah's prophecy of the coming peaceful kingdom, announcing judgment on the system and the city that have turned their vocation in upon themselves and going off to take the weight of the world's evil and hostility onto himself, so that by dying under them he might exhaust their power.

All his public career Jesus had been embodying the rescuing, redeeming love of Israel's God, and Israel's own capital city and leaders couldn't see it. The divine hurricane sweeps in from the ocean, and to accomplish its purpose it must meet, head-on, the cruel westerly wind of pagan empire and the high-octane high-pressure system of national aspiration. Jesus seizes the moment, the Passover moment, the Exodus moment, not least because these too speak of the sovereign freedom and presence of God as much over his rebellious and incomprehending people as over the tyranny of Egypt. And as we watch the events of Jesus' final days unfold, we cannot simply look on and register them as an odd quirk of history. The claim being made in the stories of Jesus is that this was the perfect storm. This was where the hurricane of divine love met the cold might of empire and the overheated aspiration of Israel. Only when we reflect on that combination do we begin to understand the meaning of Jesus' death. Only then might we begin to understand how it is that the true son of God, the true High Priest, has indeed become king of the world.

This is, of course, to run too far ahead of ourselves. If we are to approach that density of understanding, we must first grasp just how powerful, within the ancient scriptures, this theme of God's sovereign, independent action really was.

Sometimes, indeed, Israel's God was envisaged, as in our present running metaphor, in terms of the violent forces of nature, rampaging through the heavens and coming to the rescue of his people:

> The earth reeled and rocked;
>> the foundations also of the mountains trembled
>> and quaked, because he was angry.
> Smoke went up from his nostrils,
>> and devouring fire from his mouth;
>> glowing coals flamed forth from him.
> He bowed the heavens, and came down;
>> thick darkness was under his feet.
> He rode on a cherub, and flew;
>> he came swiftly upon the wings of the wind.
> He made darkness his covering around him,
>> his canopy thick clouds dark with water.
> Out of the brightness before him
>> there broke through his clouds
>> hailstones and coals of fire.
> YHWH also thundered in the heavens,
>> and the Most High uttered his voice.
> And he sent out his arrows, and scattered them;
>> he flashed forth lightnings, and routed them.

Then the channels of the sea were seen,
  and the foundations of the world were laid bare
at your rebuke, O yhwh,
  at the blast of the breath of your nostrils.
                                    (Psalm 18.7–15)

That sounds pretty much like a hurricane to me. And perhaps something more. Whatever else the ancient Israelites believed about their God, he was not a tame God. He was not the cool, detached God of ancient Epicureanism or modern Deism. But nor was he simply the personification of those forces of nature. He uses them, riding on the wind. At other times he tells the winds to be quiet. He remains sovereign over the elements. He is, after all, their creator.

This is a different sort of wind altogether. In a sense, it's strange even to put it alongside the other two. But the reason for doing so is that the first-century Jews told stories not only about their national history, but about their God. They celebrated his power, singing Psalms like the one I've just quoted. They held together, with fierce devotion, their robust beliefs that their God was the one and only God, their anguish with the pain of the world, and the agony of their own people at the heart of that world. Jerusalem, as ever, stood at the point where the tectonic plates of the world crashed together. It was, it seemed, the appropriate place of prayer for a world in pain.

Who should be king?

But it was also, in Jesus' day, a deeply puzzling place in its own right. This is where the story of God, the great hurricane that would sweep in from the third angle of the triangle, came into its own. Jesus' contemporaries believed, because their ancient prophets had told them so, that their God had promised to live in their midst, in the Jerusalem Temple, which was the lineal descendant of Solomon's Temple, which was itself the successor to the wilderness tabernacle constructed by Moses. But – again, as the prophets had said – Israel's God had abandoned the Temple at the time of the exile to Babylon. Ezekiel saw it happen (chs 10—11).

Ever afterwards, the same prophets had promised that he would one day return. He would come back to Mount Zion, to the holy city, to the Temple, to Jerusalem. 'The Lord whom you seek will suddenly come to his temple' (Malachi 3.1). 'The glory of YHWH will be revealed, and all people shall see it together' (Isaiah 40.5). 'Your sentinels lift up their voices, together they sing for joy; for in plain sight they see the return of YHWH to Zion' (52.8). On and on go the promises, resonating through the minds and hearts and prayers of Israelites, of the Jewish people, of the Jerusalemites, of the pilgrims. Of Jesus of Nazareth.

The point is this. At exactly the time when Jesus was growing up, there was a movement – call it a political movement, a religious movement, or (as Josephus calls it) a 'philosophy' – that said that *it was time for God alone to be king.* The people were waiting for the cyclone. They were praying for it. Did they know what it would mean?

They knew what it wouldn't mean. They were fed up with their own 'kings' – the Hasmonean dynasty of the last hundred years, such as it was, and then Herod and his second-rate sons. They saw no prospect of any human leader arising from such quarters to do what had to be done, to fight the battle, to overthrow the pagans, to cleanse and restore the Temple, to establish the long-awaited rule of justice and peace. In between the long years of hope and the even longer years of crushing sorrow, this movement emerged saying that God, only God, could and would be king. God would come back and would rule his people. The Jewish historian Josephus tells us about some of the forms of this movement; there were undoubtedly many more. And even when the hope didn't turn into action, it smouldered on in private dreams and prayers. Theocracy! Yes, that's what they wanted – as long as it was the right God doing the ruling. As Bob Dylan once said, ' "I am the Lord thy God" is a fine saying, as long as it's the right person who's saying it.'

This idea of theocracy wasn't as extraordinary as it might sound to modern ears (though, as we shall see, the debate about such matters has recently come back into public prominence). The ancient scriptures were full of the theme. In fact, the Bible relates how, when the people first asked for a king, the divine response was that it was inappropriate: God himself was their king, so they didn't need a human king as well (1 Samuel 8.7; 12.12). At that time, a compromise was reached: after the failure of Saul, the first king, God chose David, 'a man after his own heart'. Somehow, right from the start, there was a sense in which God was king – through David.

That, presumably, is part of what it means to say that, when Samuel anointed David with oil to proclaim him king, 'the spirit of YHWH came mightily on David from that day forward' (1 Samuel 16.13). That didn't mean that David had a smooth, easy path to power. Far from it. He was on the run, hunted by Saul, moving from place to place, resorting to tricks and deceit to stay out of trouble.

But, at last, Saul died in battle against the Philistines. He had failed in the main royal task of defeating the national enemy. David, who had earlier killed the Philistine hero Goliath and had thereby marked himself out as potential royalty, came into the kingdom for which he had been anointed several years before. This story is heavy with resonances for the story of Jesus of Nazareth. Indeed, Jesus himself refers to it as part of the explanation for his own strange itinerant public career, under the eagle eyes of critical opponents (Mark 2.23–28).

David, of course, made big mistakes, as did his successors. The story of his reign shows the cracks starting to appear that would ruin the kingdom of his successors bit by bit, starting with the splitting off of the northern kingdom and ending with the devastation of Jerusalem itself and the shameful and horrific exile. But in the beginning, right after David's establishment as king, the scriptures report a promise made to him by God. David had decided he wanted to build a house for his God, a great Temple, so that the God who had lived among his people in the tabernacle would now live with them permanently. This permanent dwelling would be the focal point of the city, which would thereby be established for ever as the capital city of God's people: Jerusalem. The city at the centre of the earth.

A fine ambition, you might think. But then Nathan, David's court prophet, comes to him with a message and a promise. David is not, actually, to build the house for God. His son will do it. But, more important, God will make David a 'house' – a house, that is, not made with stone and timber, but a 'house' in the sense of a family:

When your days are fulfilled and you lie down with your ancestors,
I will raise up your offspring after you, who shall come forth from
your body, and I will establish his kingdom. He shall build a house
for my name, and I will establish the throne of his kingdom for ever.
I will be a father to him, and he shall be a son to me.

(2 Samuel 7.12–14)

That promise was remembered and pondered again and again
in the days to come, right up to the time of Jesus. Nobody, it seems,
was absolutely sure what it would mean in practice. But many saw
the royal house of Israel as the means by which the living God would
establish his own kingdom, his own rule or reign. There is a sense
in which it isn't an either/or choice, *either* God *or* David. Somehow
it seems to be both. This is the point at which we can understand
only too well how it was that the Israelite people of old, and the Jewish
people of Jesus' day, could very easily forget that *their* national dream
and *God's* purposes for them might actually be two quite different
things. The prophets existed to remind them of the fact; but prophets
were easy to ignore or forget. Or kill.

God as king

As it was, the more the story of Israel went on, the more the ancient
poets and prophets spoke explicitly about God himself being king,
taking charge, coming to sort everything out. They sang memorable
songs about what it would be like when God did this. These poems,
we should remind ourselves, continued to be sung in the Jerusalem
Temple right through to the time of its destruction in AD 70, as they
continue to be sung in synagogues and private homes, wherever Jews
say their prayers, to this day. What follows is a small selection of many
similar passages:[1]

YHWH is king for ever and ever;
   the nations shall perish from his land.
O YHWH, you will hear the desire of the meek;
   you will strengthen their heart, you will incline your ear
to do justice for the orphan and the oppressed,
   so that those from earth may strike terror no more.

(Psalm 10.16–18)

The hurricane

Clap your hands, all you peoples;
  shout to God with loud songs of joy.
For YHWH, the Most High, is awesome,
  a great king over all the earth.
He subdued peoples under us,
  and nations under our feet.
He chose our heritage for us,
    the pride of Jacob whom he loves.

God has gone up with a shout,
  YHWH with the sound of a trumpet.
Sing praises to God, sing praises;
  sing praises to our King, sing praises.
For God is the king of all the earth;
  sing praises with a psalm.

God is king over the nations;
  God sits on his holy throne.
The princes of the peoples gather
  as the people of the God of Abraham.
For the shields of the earth belong to God;
  he is highly exalted.
                              (Psalm 47.1–9)

For YHWH is a great God,
  and a great King above all gods.
In his hand are the depths of the earth;
  the heights of the mountains are his also.
The sea is his, for he made it,
  and the dry land, which his hands have formed.

O come, let us worship and bow down,
  let us kneel before YHWH, our Maker!
For he is our God,
  and we are the people of his pasture,
  and the sheep of his hand.
                              (Psalm 95.3–7)

Say among the nations, 'YHWH is king!
  The world is firmly established; it shall never be moved.
  He will judge the peoples with equity.'

Let the heavens be glad, and let the earth rejoice;
  let the sea roar, and all that fills it;
  let the field exult, and everything in it.
Then shall all the trees of the forest sing for joy
  before YHWH; for he is coming,
  for he is coming to judge the earth.
He will judge the world with righteousness,
  and the peoples with his truth.

(Psalm 96.10–13)

I will extol you, my God and King,
  and bless your name for ever and ever . . .
All your works shall give thanks to you, O YHWH,
  and all your faithful shall bless you.
They shall speak of the glory of your kingdom,
  and tell of your power,
to make known to all people your mighty deeds,
  and the glorious splendour of your kingdom.
Your kingdom is an everlasting kingdom,
  and your dominion endures throughout all generations.

(Psalm 145.1, 10–13)

We notice a constant triple theme in these songs. First, Israel's God is celebrated as king especially in Jerusalem, in his home in the Temple. Second, when Israel's God is enthroned as 'king', the nations are brought under his rule. Israel rejoices, but all the other nations will be included as well – sometimes, it seems, so that they may be punished for all their wickedness, particularly their oppression of Israel, but sometimes too so that they may be brought in to share the life of God's people and join in with Israel's praise of the one God. Indeed, the whole of creation will join in the celebration. Third, when God is king, the result is proper justice, real equity, the removal of all corruption and oppression.

One can see all too easily how these songs would give rise, among a people weary of corrupt and self-serving rulers, to the longing for YHWH himself to come and take charge. He and he alone would give the people what they needed and wanted. He would take control and sort everything out. The singing of these songs week in and week out, while watching the dreary procession of corrupt officials and regimes come and go, would provide a natural seedbed for the hope for Israel's God to be king – and nobody else.

This longing would only be increased by the prophetic passages that spoke in the same way:[2]

> How beautiful upon the mountains
>> are the feet of the messenger who announces peace,
> who brings good news,
>> who announces salvation,
>> who says to Zion, 'Your God reigns' [i.e. 'Your God is king'].
> Listen! Your sentinels lift up their voices,
>> together they sing for joy;
> for in plain sight they see
>> the return of YHWH to Zion.
> Break forth together into singing,
>> you ruins of Jerusalem;
> for YHWH has comforted his people,
>> he has redeemed Jerusalem.
> YHWH has bared his holy arm
>> before the eyes of all the nations;
> and all the ends of the earth shall see
>> the salvation of our God.
>
> (Isaiah 52.7–10)

Sometimes, of course, this theme resulted in a note of severe warning:

> Cursed be the cheat who has a male in the flock and vows to give it, and yet sacrifices to the Lord what is blemished; for I am a great King, says YHWH of hosts, and my name is reverenced among the nations.
>
> (Malachi 1.14)[3]

So far I have only quoted passages in which the word 'king' or 'kingdom' or a near equivalent actually occurs. But it isn't hard to extend the range. Consider, for example, passages in which Israel's God is spoken of as the true 'shepherd' of his people – remembering that, in a rural economy where looking after livestock was one of the most common occupations, 'shepherd' was a frequent image for 'king'. We think again of the Psalms:

YHWH is my shepherd; I shall not want.
　　He makes me lie down in green pastures;
he leads me beside still waters;
　　　he restores my soul.

(23.1–3)

Give ear, O Shepherd of Israel,
　　you who lead Joseph like a flock!
You who are enthroned upon the cherubim, shine forth . . .
Stir up your might,
　　and come to save us!

(80.1–2)

And also of the prophets:

> See, the Lord YHWH comes with might,
> 　　and his arm rules for him;
> his reward is with him,
> 　　and his recompense before him.
> He will feed his flock like a shepherd;
> 　　he will gather the lambs in his arms,
> and carry them in his bosom,
> 　　and gently lead the mother sheep.
> (Isaiah 40.10–11)

Hear the word of YHWH, O nations,
　　and declare it in the coastlands far away;
say, 'He who scattered Israel will gather him,
　　and will keep him as a shepherd a flock.'
For YHWH has ransomed Jacob,
　　and has redeemed him from hands too strong for him.
They shall come and sing aloud on the height of Zion,
　　and they shall be radiant over the goodness of YHWH.
(Jeremiah 31.10–12)

And then, in particular, an extraordinary passage in which YHWH, the true shepherd of Israel, is contrasted with the human rulers who have failed in their task of looking after the 'sheep', Israel:

Mortal, prophesy against the shepherds of Israel: prophesy, and say to them – to the shepherds: Thus says the Lord YHWH: Ah, you shepherds of Israel who have been feeding yourselves! Should not shepherds feed the sheep? You eat the fat, you clothe yourselves with the wool, you slaughter

46

the fatlings; but you do not feed the sheep. You have not strengthened the weak, you have not healed the sick, you have not bound up the injured, you have not brought back the strayed, you have not sought the lost, but with force and harshness you have ruled them. So they were scattered, because there was no shepherd; and scattered, they became food for all the wild animals. My sheep were scattered, they wandered over all the mountains and on every high hill; my sheep were scattered over all the face of the earth, with no one to search or seek for them . . .

For thus says the Lord YHWH: I myself will search for my sheep, and will seek them out. As shepherds seek out their flocks when they are among their scattered sheep, so I will seek out my sheep. I will rescue them from all the places to which they have been scattered on a day of clouds and thick darkness . . . I will feed them with good pasture, and the mountain heights of Israel shall be their pasture; there they shall lie down in good grazing land, and they shall feed on rich pasture on the mountains of Israel. I myself will be the shepherd of my sheep, and I will make them lie down, says the Lord YHWH. I will seek the lost, and I will bring back the strayed, and I will bind up the injured, and I will strengthen the weak, but the fat and the strong I will destroy. I will feed them with justice.   (Ezekiel 34.2–6, 11–12, 14–16)

This could hardly be clearer. The human 'shepherds' have been a dismal failure; only YHWH himself will now do. He and he alone will give the 'sheep' – the people of Israel – what they need and what the other shepherds have so obviously not given them. There is a radical break between the way Israel's rulers have been telling and living the national story and the way God wants to tell it. But then comes the shock, sending us all the way back to 2 Samuel to revisit the strange long-term relationship between the kingship of God and the kingship of David:

I will set up over them one shepherd, my servant David, and he shall feed them: he shall feed them and be their shepherd. And I, YHWH, will be their God, and my servant David shall be prince among them; I, YHWH, have spoken.   (Ezekiel 34.23–24)

The result is that Israel will be YHWH's sheep indeed:

They shall know that I, YHWH their God, am with them, and that they, the house of Israel, are my people, says the Lord YHWH. You are my sheep, the sheep of my pasture, and I am your God, says the Lord YHWH.
                    (Ezekiel 34.30–31)

Ezekiel 34 is all about Israel's God becoming king, to do for his people what other kings and rulers have failed to do. That is clear. But it is also clear that the prophet reserves a role for the eventual king (or 'prince') from the line of David. How these two relate he does not say. Somehow, when God is king, 'David' (i.e. the coming king from David's family) will be king. These will not cancel one another out. When we read, among the stories of Jesus, hints and promises about a shepherd who cares for the sheep, these are the resonances we should be picking up.

A similar result emerges from a Psalm that was well known and widely quoted and adapted at the time. It functioned, for Jews of the period and then for the early Christians, as a model of how YHWH would set up his kingdom over the turbulent nations – by establishing the true Davidic king:

> Why do the nations conspire,
>   and the peoples plot in vain?
> The kings of the earth set themselves,
>   and the rulers take counsel together,
>   against YHWH and his anointed . . .
>
> He who sits in the heavens laughs;
>   YHWH has them in derision.
> Then he will speak to them in his wrath,
>   and terrify them in his fury, saying,
> 'I have set my king on Zion, my holy hill.'
>
> I will tell of the decree of YHWH:
> He said to me, 'You are my son;
>   today I have begotten you.
> Ask of me, and I will make the nations your heritage,
>   and the ends of the earth your possession.
> You shall break them with a rod of iron,
>   and dash them in pieces like a potter's vessel.'
>   (Psalm 2.1–2, 4–9)

Here we have it. YHWH is in charge and will establish his own rule over the rest of the world from his throne in Zion. But he will do this through his 'anointed', through the one he calls 'my son'.

I have deliberately set out these passages at some length to show just how strong, just how deep-rooted in scripture, is the idea of YHWH himself coming to rule and reign as Israel's king. Several of the themes one can observe in the sorry sequence of would-be kings from the Maccabees to bar-Kochba (see Chapter 9) emerge in a clear light: victory over the nations, the rescue of Israel from oppression, Jerusalem and the Temple as the proper dwelling place for God's glory, and so on. But it is YHWH himself who will bring this about – or, in that final twist in Ezekiel 34, echoed in Psalm 2, YHWH himself *acting in and through the Davidic king.*

The idea of YHWH alone as king, as expressed by the extreme revolutionaries in the first century, thus raises a big question. What will this mean in practice, in reality? What will it look like? How does all this line up, if it does, with the national expectation and hope? Will it underwrite it, will it overthrow it, or will it perhaps do both of those at the same time? Paying attention to the prophets would indicate that something like this third possibility was likely; but what would it actually mean?

In particular, the question was raised: would YHWH actually appear, visibly and in person, to take charge? If so, what could people expect to see? How would it happen? Or, if not, would he act through chosen representatives – perhaps specially inspired prophets? (There was no shortage of people in the first century claiming prophetic inspiration, speaking urgent words from YHWH to his suffering and anxious people, sometimes promising them immediate and spectacular supernatural deliverance.) And if YHWH did choose to act in that way – acting in one sense all by himself, but in another through particular representatives – how would those people be equipped for the task?

This, again, is where the ancient idea of 'anointing' comes into play. An individual is solemnly smeared with holy oil as a sign, and perhaps a means, of a special 'equipping', or 'enabling', from YHWH himself to perform the necessary tasks. Such persons are no longer acting on their own authority or initiative, but on God's. A dangerous claim, and one can imagine people being instantly cynical: 'Claiming to speak for YHWH? What, another one? We've heard that before. You're probably just a fraud like all the others.'

There was, after all, no obvious model for what it might look like, how it might happen, that YHWH would do what all those Psalms and prophets said and come in person to take charge, ruling the world, rescuing Israel, establishing his presence in the Temple, judging the nations, and causing the trees and the animals to shout for joy. The ancient scriptures are quite unhelpful on the matter. When YHWH visits Abraham, Abraham sees three men and entertains them at a meal. When YHWH meets Moses, what Moses sees is a burning bush. When, later, YHWH guides Moses and the Israelites through the desert, what they see is a pillar of cloud by day and a pillar of fire by night. When YHWH reveals his glory to the prophet Isaiah, all Isaiah tells us (in his terror) is that YHWH was high and lifted up, surrounded by angels, with the hem of his robe filling the Temple. Was that, we wonder, what was meant when, in the same book, we are told that the sentinels would shout for joy as in plain sight they saw YHWH returning to Zion? Was that what was meant when it said, 'The glory of YHWH will be revealed, and all people shall see it together' (Isaiah 40.5)? When Ezekiel saw the glory of YHWH, all he offered by way of a description was a strange account of YHWH's chariot-throne, with its whirling wheels darting this way and that. Which of these models, if any, ought one to expect? Or would it be something different?

The notion of YHWH himself as Israel's true king thus became closely bound up with the idea of his powerful *return*. At the time of the exile, it was widely believed that Israel's God had abandoned the Temple and the city of Jerusalem, leaving them to their fate. (How else, people reasoned, could they have fallen?) Ezekiel saw the glory depart because of the people's wickedness (chs 10—11). But then, towards the end of his majestic book, he was given another vision of YHWH's glory returning to the newly rebuilt Temple (43.1–5). For Isaiah and Ezekiel, then, not only would Israel return to its land, but YHWH would return to the Temple. That is at the heart of the vision of King YHWH in Isaiah 52. And that, we may suppose, is what devout Jews hoped and prayed for as they sang all those Psalms about YHWH becoming king, taking charge at last, rescuing his people and bringing justice to the world.

But it hadn't happened yet – or not as far as the prophets after the exile were concerned. Yes, they had returned from Babylon to Judaea. Yes, they had rebuilt the Temple. But YHWH had not returned to fill the house once more with his glory. The last two prophets in the canon both promise that he *will* indeed come, but this makes it all the clearer that *he has not yet done so*:

> Thus says YHWH: I will return to Zion, and will dwell in the midst of Jerusalem; Jerusalem shall be called the faithful city, and the mountain of YHWH of hosts shall be called the holy mountain . . . Thus says YHWH of hosts: I will save my people from the east country and from the west country; and I will bring them to live in Jerusalem. They shall be my people and I will be their God, in faithfulness and in righteousness.
>
> (Zechariah 8.3, 7–8)

> See, I am sending my messenger to prepare the way before me, and the Lord whom you seek will suddenly come to his temple. The messenger of the covenant in whom you delight – indeed, he is coming, says YHWH of hosts. But who can endure the day of his coming, and who can stand when he appears? For he is like a refiner's fire and like fullers' soap; he will sit as a refiner and purifier of silver, and he will purify the descendants of Levi and refine them like gold and silver, until they present offerings to YHWH in righteousness . . . Then I will draw near to you for judgement . . .
>
> (Malachi 3.1–3, 5)

All this brings into sharp focus the theme I have described as the third great storm, the hurricane from the south-east – and the final type of 'king' that people in Jesus' day were eager to see. The people who were longing for God alone to be their king were clinging to the hope set out in scripture: the hope that, after all these years, Israel's God would return to be with his people, to rescue them, to restore them, to condemn their oppressors, to take charge, to do justice, to sort things out, to rule over them like a good king should, but unlike any actual human king they had ever known. And, bearing in mind not only Ezekiel 34, but also a remarkable passage in Zechariah, it appears that the divine king might after all come in the form of a human king:

> Rejoice greatly, O daughter Zion!
>   Shout aloud, O daughter Jerusalem!
> Lo, your king comes to you;
>   triumphant and victorious is he,
> humble and riding on a donkey,
>   on a colt, the foal of a donkey.

He will cut off the chariot from Ephraim
  and the warhorse from Jerusalem;
and the battle-bow shall be cut off;
  and he shall command peace to the nations;
his dominion shall be from sea to sea,
  and from the River to the ends of the earth.
As for you also, because of the blood of my covenant with you,
  I will set your prisoners free from the waterless pit.

(9.9–11)

We notice the echoes of promises made to David in Psalm 2 and elsewhere: when the true king of Israel arrives, he will be king not only of Israel, but of the whole world. That is part of the point, as we have seen again and again with the promises about God's victory over the nations (or, just possibly, God's welcoming of them into a kind of extended holy people). When God acts as Israel believes he will, it will be not only to rescue his people, but to establish his sovereign rule over the whole world. God will finally be in charge from one sea to the other, from the River to the ends of the earth. And what will it look like? Like a humble figure, riding into Jerusalem on a donkey.

The coming anointed one

Nobody in the two hundred years before Jesus and nobody in the hundred years of continuing struggle after his time seems to have put all this together and suggested that Israel's God might come *in the form and person of the Davidic king*. Or, if they did, we have no record of it. The closest we come might be bar-Kochba, proclaiming himself in AD 132 to be a great light from heaven, the promised and long-awaited 'star'. We will look at his movement later on.

But of course the prime example of a movement that held together the themes of God's kingdom, on the one hand, and a messianic kingdom, on the other, was indeed that of Jesus himself. Within a few years of his death, the first followers of Jesus of Nazareth were speaking and writing about him, and indeed singing about him, not just as a great teacher and healer, not just as a great spiritual leader and holy man, but as a strange combination: *both* the Davidic king *and* the returning God. He was, they said, the anointed one, the one who had been empowered and equipped by God's Spirit to do all kinds of things, which somehow meant that he was God's anointed, the Messiah, the coming king. He was the one who had been exalted after his suffering and now occupied the throne beside the throne of God himself.

But they also believed that Jesus had thereby fulfilled the dreams of those who wanted God, and God alone, to be king. Jesus, they believed, had lived and worked within the same overall story as other would-be kings of the time. But he had transformed the story around himself. In Jesus, they believed, God himself had indeed become king. Jesus had come to take charge, and he was now on the throne of the whole world. The dream of a coming king – of God himself as the coming king, ruling the world in justice and peace – had come true at last. Once we get inside the world of Jesus' day and begin to understand what he might have meant by the word 'God', we begin to understand too the breathtaking claim that Jesus was, himself, now in charge. He was the one who had 'an everlasting dominion' (Daniel 7.14), a kingship that would never be destroyed.

This claim can never be, in our sense or indeed in the ancient sense, merely 'religious'. It involves everything, from power and politics to culture and family. It catches up the 'religious' meanings, including personal spirituality and transformation, and the philosophical ones, including ethics and worldview. But it places them all within a larger vision that can be stated quite simply: God is now in charge, and he is in charge in and through Jesus. That is the vision that explains what Jesus did and said, what happened to Jesus, and what his followers subsequently did and said. And what happened to them too.

But here is the puzzle – the ultimate puzzle of Jesus. This puzzle boils down to two questions.

First, why would anyone say this of Jesus, who had not done the things people expected a victorious king to do? Why, indeed, did Jesus end up being crucified with the words 'King of the Jews' above his head? And why would anyone, three minutes, three days, or three hundred years after that moment, ever dream of taking it seriously?

Second, what on earth might it mean today to speak of Jesus being 'king' or being 'in charge', in view of the fact that so many things in the world give no hint of such a thing?

Those are the questions that will now occupy us in the rest of this book.

In Part 2, we shall look at Jesus' public career, watching him stake the claim that God's kingdom was being launched then and there and hearing him explain it to his puzzled hearers. We shall then see where it led him and learn how he understood his own forthcoming death as the means by which, in a strange and dark mystery, God's kingdom would be established for ever. That will open a new way for us to consider, in Part 3, what it might mean in today's and tomorrow's world to speak of Jesus as being truly in charge – and, equally important, not just to speak of it, but to help make it happen.

But, as we draw these introductory chapters to a close, we return to the image of the perfect storm. We have felt the force of the westerly gale: the relentless power of Rome, its emperor, its armies, its steely-eyed ambition to rule the world. We have sensed the build-up of hope and national aspiration within the high-pressure system that emerged from the age-old stories of Israel, producing a complex but coherent narrative in which many of Jesus' contemporaries believed themselves still to be living, in which indeed they were eager for the denouement, the fulfilment, the great final day. These two by themselves would have been enough, and were enough in many other instances, to produce a terrible storm with devastating results.

But, from the moment Jesus of Nazareth launched his public career, he seems to have been determined to invoke the third part of the great storm as well. He spoke continually about the hurricane of which the Psalmists had sung and the prophets had preached. He spoke about God himself becoming king. And he went about doing things that, he said, demonstrated what that meant and would mean. He took upon himself (this is one of the most secure starting points for a historical investigation of Jesus) the role of a prophet, in other words, of a man sent from God to reaffirm God's intention of over-throwing the might of pagan empire, but also to warn Israel that its present way of going about things was dangerously ill-conceived and leading to disaster. And with that, the sea is lashed into a frenzy; the wind makes the waves dance like wild things; and Jesus himself strides out into the middle of it all, into the very eye of the storm, announcing that the time is fulfilled, that God's kingdom is now at hand. He commands his hearers to give up their other dreams and to trust his instead. This, at its simplest, is what Jesus was all about.

Part 2

6

God's in charge now

The reason there were crowds with Jesus that day as he rode into Jerusalem is that there were always crowds around Jesus, from the beginning. He attracted them. The first thing most people knew about Jesus was that when he arrived in the village there was a party. A celebration – whoops of delight, people dancing, women ululating. The prophet's in town, and it's good news all around!

You didn't have to look far to discover the reason for the celebration either. People were being healed – healed of any and every disease you can think of. Ancient medicine wasn't quite as unsophisticated as we moderns sometimes imagine, but it wasn't that effective either. In any given community there would be many suffering from long-term problems, from the broken bone that hadn't healed properly to the persistent, year-in-and-year-out haemorrhage. And with almost every bodily problem came some sort of social problem: the farm worker who couldn't plough any more, the 'unclean' woman who couldn't share food with her family. So wherever Jesus went, he healed people. 'He went on through the whole of Galilee,' says Matthew, 'teaching in their synagogues and proclaiming the good news of the kingdom, healing every disease and every illness among the people' (4.23). There is every reason to suppose that this is exactly what most people saw going on as Jesus of Nazareth launched his strange, short public career.

Already we are back again in the eye of our own, modern historical storm. Sceptics have always scoffed at these stories. We know, they say, that 'miracles' don't happen. People are attracted to a charismatic leader, and so they make up stories to boost his reputation. In any case, what sort of a 'god' is it who 'intervenes' in this way? But then others say, no, 'miracles' are what you'd expect if there's a 'supernatural' God and if Jesus is his son. And then a third element asks: what do we actually know about these things within first-century history anyway?

It's a shame to stop the story when it's hardly begun, but let's freeze the frame for a moment and address these well-known questions. If we don't, seeds of doubt may be planted. There's no time for extensive answers; four quick ones will do for the moment.

First, Jesus attracted large crowds. A thousand little features of the stories put this beyond doubt. When we ask why, the gospels all say it was because he was healing people. The link between healing and crowds is made in all the sources.

Second, we find reports at various points of opponents accusing Jesus of being in league with the devil – with the 'Shame Lord' (Beelzebul) or something similar. Scholars have often suggested that many Jesus stories were invented by his followers later on. But those who loved and worshipped Jesus wouldn't have invented tales of his being involved in dark arts. People don't accuse you of being in league with the devil unless you are doing pretty remarkable things.

Third, as we shall see, the explanation Jesus gave for what was going on was that something new was happening – something powerful, dramatic, different. If all he'd been doing was encouraging people to feel better about themselves and not actually transforming their real lives, there would have been no sign of anything new. There would have been nothing to explain. His explanations only make sense if the thing they are explaining is sufficiently startling to raise questions.

Fourth, it may be time to be sceptical about scepticism itself. In Jesus' own day, there were plenty of people who didn't want to believe his message, because it would have challenged their own power or influence. It would have upset their own agenda. For the last two hundred years that's been the mood in Western society too. By all means, people think, let Jesus be a soul doctor, making people feel better inside. Let him be a rescuer, snatching people away from this world to 'heaven'. But don't let him tell us about a God who actually does things in the world. We might have to take that God seriously, just when we're discovering how to run the world our own way. Scepticism is no more 'neutral' or 'objective' than faith. It has thrived in the post-Enlightenment world, which didn't want God (or, in many cases, anyone else either) to be king. Saying this doesn't, of course, prove anything in itself. It just suggests that we keep an open mind and recognize that scepticism too comes with its own agenda. We should be prepared to follow where the story leads and see if these initially surprising bits of it make sense with the rest.

To the voices that trumpet their support for a 'supernatural' God doing 'miracles' through his divine 'Son', I would just say, for the moment, 'Be careful with your worldview. You're in danger of reaffirming the very split-level cosmos that Jesus came to reunite.'

Heralds of the king

So where does the story lead? It leads straight to the announcement that Jesus was making: 'God's in charge now – and this is what it looks like!'

I was trying to explain all this to someone earlier this morning and back came the reply, 'But I thought God was supposed to be in charge already, all the time?' Ah. Now we're talking. Yes, of course, in one sense the average first-century Jew did believe that Israel's God was already in charge. But she or he also knew, with every bone and breath, that there were all sorts of ways in which God was *not* in charge – otherwise why was the world such a mess? Why were God's people, the Jews, in such trouble? Why were ruthless, coarse, blaspheming foreigners running the show? Why were the Jewish leaders themselves such a corrupt lot? And why – in the middle of it all – is my child so sick? Why is my mother crippled? Why did the soldiers kill my son, my cousin, my husband? Surely, if God was really in charge, then all of this, from as far as the eye could see to as near as one's own family, should be put right. Jesus was going about sorting out the near-at-hand stuff. But he was talking, the whole time, about God being in charge on a larger scale as well. The close-up actions pointed to that greater reality. They were the signs that it was starting to come true.

When I say that Jesus was talking about God being king, I mean that he was *announcing* it. Think how football clubs and their support-ers get very excited when a new star player arrives. The announcement is made: we have a new star! At last, we're going to score some goals! He'll make all the difference. But they get even more excited when, after months or years of indifferent management, a new manager is appointed, especially if he comes with a reputation for turning things around and getting a club back on a winning streak. We've got a new boss! Everything's going to change now! This is an *announcement* about something that's *happened* because of which everything will be different. It isn't a piece of advice about how to live or a clue about how to give up watching football altogether now that the team have been playing so badly. It's a proclamation. Once the new manager has been announced, the players had better do what he says. Then, and only then, things will work out properly.

The same thing is true under a great empire. When Caesar's herald comes into town and declares 'We have a new emperor,' it isn't an invitation to debate the principle of imperial rule. It isn't the offer of a new feeling inside. It's a new fact, and you'd better readjust your life around it.

Of course, for a football club what then often happens is that within weeks, or even days, disappointment begins to set in. The team doesn't magically start winning all the trophies. And so another cycle begins. Maybe one day we'll get someone who can really sort it out, can really turn it around ...

Countries go through this cycle too. I remember the excitement and delight when Tony Blair won the general election in 1997. The country gave a sigh of relief, because the old government had run into trouble and run out of ideas, and now they were run out of town. Now at last we have a new vision! A new leader! Everything's going to be all right! But, with the sad wisdom of hindsight, many people are embarrassed at how enthusiastic they were on that occasion. The 'New Labour' party turned out to be like all the rest, getting some things right and a lot of things wrong.

I have watched other countries go through similar ups and downs. I remember the joy of many when Barack Obama was elected president of the United States in 2008, and I watched that joy turn to frustration when things didn't magically improve overnight. (I have also watched the horror of many at that same election, and I have watched that horror turn into paranoia.) We treat our political leaders as heroes and demigods; they carry our dreams, our fantasies of how things should be. When we find out that they are only human after all, we turn on them, blaming them for the intractable problems that they, like their predecessors, haven't been able to solve. So why did people think that Jesus might be any different?

It wasn't as though they hadn't had disappointments before. The long story of Israel had had its high points, but if you add up everything that had happened over the previous thousand years, the sequence of disappointments is so long, so repetitive and so dispiriting that you might forgive them for giving up hope altogether.

Some did. Most didn't. And the reasons why they didn't give up hope tell us a great deal about what they thought would happen if and when their God finally took charge. At this point we must take off the spectacles through which we normally see the world, not least the modern Western world, and put on a different set. If we are to understand Jesus, we have to learn to see the world as his contemporaries saw it. We have already begun to do this in the opening chapters. Now, tricky though this is for a historian (because our sources are thin and patchy), we must take this process a step further.

What went wrong?

To put it very simply, the Jews of Jesus' day believed that their God had made the world and that he had remained in charge of it. They didn't understand, any more than we do, why a world made by a good God would somehow go wrong, but clearly that had happened. The signs were all there: broken bodies, broken lives, broken systems, broken countries. The whole thing needed fixing, needed mending, needed to be put right. And the Jewish people believed that they, the family of Abraham, were part of the answer, part of the mending operation, part of the putting-right plan.

So if, as the Jewish people believed, they were the key element in God's global rescue-operation, it was doubly frustrating, doubly puzzling and doubly challenging that the Jews' own national life had itself been in such a mess for so long. By the time Jesus went about Galilee telling people that God was now in charge, it was close to six hundred years since Jerusalem had been destroyed by the Babylonians, the greatest superpower of the time. And though many Jews had come back from

Chronological outline of Jewish History

Babylonian period: 597–539 BC

597	Jerusalem taken by Nebuchadnezzar II
587	Jerusalem destroyed, people exiled to Babylon
539	Fall of Babylon

Persian/Greek period: 538–320 BC

538	Return of (some) exiles; rebuilding of Temple begun (completed 516)
450s/440s	Ezra and Nehemiah in Jerusalem
336	Alexander the Great comes to power
332	Alexander conquers Palestine
323	Alexander dies; empire divided

Egyptian period: 320–200 BC

Ptolemies of Egypt rule Palestine; local government by high priests

Syrian period: 200–63 BC

200	Antiochus III defeats Egyptians
175	Antiochus IV Epiphanes enthroned
171	Menelaus (high priest) favours Antiochus; Jews revolt
167	Antiochus desecrates Temple, builds altar to Zeus Olympus
166	Judas Maccabaeus ('Judah the Hammer') leads revolutionary group
164	Judas cleanses Temple
160	Death of Judas
160–63	Quasi-independent rule of Maccabean (Hasmonean) dynasty

Roman period: 63 BC onwards

63	Pompey (Roman general) takes Jerusalem
44	Death of Julius Caesar; Roman civil wars
37	Herod established as 'King of Judaea'
31	Octavian (Augustus) wins civil war, transforms Roman republic into an empire
7–4 BC (?)	Birth of Jesus of Nazareth
4 BC	Death of Herod; his kingdom is divided: Antipas rules Galilee, Archelaus Judaea. Civil unrest and 'messianic' movements
AD 6	Archelaus deposed after protests; Judaea ruled by 'prefects'
AD 14	Death of Augustus; accession of Tiberius
26–36	Pontius Pilate 'prefect' of Judaea
30 (33?)	Crucifixion of Jesus of Nazareth

exile in Babylon and had even rebuilt the Temple in Jerusalem, they knew things weren't right yet. One pagan nation after another took charge, ruling the Middle East in its own way. (See the chronological outline on page 64.)

In particular, the Jewish people believed that the Temple in Jerusalem was where their God was supposed to live. The Temple was the place on earth where 'heaven' and 'earth' actually met. They saw 'heaven' as God's space and 'earth' as our space, the created order as we know it, and they believed that the Temple was the one spot on earth where the two overlapped. But the Temple seemed empty. God hadn't come back.

So where did the hope come from? How on earth do you sustain hope over more than half a millennium, while you're watching one regime after another come and go, some promising better things, but all letting you down in the end? How can you go on believing, from generation to generation, that one day God will come and take charge?

Reliving the Exodus

Answer: you tell the story, you sing the songs, and you keep celebrating God's victory, even though it keeps on not happening. As we have seen, the story – the Story above all stories for the Jewish people – was the story of the Exodus, the time when God heard the cries of his people in their slavery in Egypt and came to rescue them, bringing them through the Red Sea at Passover-time, leading them through the desert and home to their promised land. Since Jesus himself seems to have deliberately chosen the Exodus story, the Passover story, as the setting for the carefully staged climax to his own public career, it's important that we think for a moment about the seven great features of this story, which all first-century Jews would have known in their bones. All this – we are still learning to take off our modern Western spectacles and put on first-century Jewish ones! – is essential if we are to understand what Jesus thought he was doing. If we don't get this straight, we shall simply squash Jesus into the little boxes of our own imaginations rather than seeing him as he was. Here are the seven themes of the Exodus:

- wicked tyrant
- chosen leader
- victory of God
- rescue by sacrifice
- new vocation and way of life
- presence of God
- promised/inherited land.

First, the Exodus story was all about a wicked tyrant – Pharaoh, the king of Egypt – who had enslaved God's people. Pharaoh is, as it were, the most visible symptom of the problem the people were facing.

Second, God chose a leader. Moses was called, along with his brother Aaron and sister Miriam, to tell the people that God was now at last coming to their rescue. Moses then, at God's behest, led the people out of slavery to freedom.

Third, God won a great victory over Pharaoh and his people. This took the form of divine judgment, beginning with a sequence of plagues and reaching its decisive climax when the Red Sea, which had parted to let the Israelites through, rushed back and drowned the Egyptian army. This divine victory was celebrated in a great song whose closing line gives us the direct link to what Jesus was saying: 'YHWH will reign for ever and ever' (Exodus 15.18). This is what it means to say that Israel's God has taken charge. He is reigning. He has won the victory over the wicked tyrant. He is the king.

Fourth, the rescue of God's people was achieved in such a way as to make it clear to them that this was an act of special favour and mercy. 'Passover' is called that because, on the last night in Egypt, the angel of death, bringing judgment on all the firstborn of Egypt, 'passed over' the Israelite houses where a lamb had been sacrificed and its blood daubed on the doorposts. The shared family meal of that night has been repeated ever since, constituting the people as the rescued, freed family of God. And it was during the preparations for Passover when Jesus rode into Jerusalem on the donkey.

Fifth, the Israelites arrived at Mount Sinai, where the 'marriage covenant' between them and their God was sealed. God, for his part, gave them his law, the way of life through which they were to show the world what its maker had had in mind.

Sixth, God himself went with the Israelites on their journey, in a pillar of cloud by day and fire by night. The book of Exodus closes with the making of the tabernacle, where God would come to live in the midst of his people. Half a millennium after Moses's day, David and Solomon would plan and build a permanent version of this tabernacle, the Temple in Jerusalem. It was to the Temple that Jesus of Nazareth came that day, to perform a strange, dramatic symbolic gesture and to debate with the teachers of the law, as the winds began to blow more fiercely and the perfect storm of history reached its height.

Seventh, all this happened in fulfilment of ancient promises. God had promised to Abraham, Isaac and Jacob that their family would have the land of Palestine as their inheritance. Now at last those promises were coming true. Hope had been deferred for a long time. Now it was being realized.

All this is what I meant when I said earlier that the festival Jesus chose as his moment to act was 'dense with detail and heavy with hope'. For us, the picture has to be assembled step by step; for them it was like a living room in their own home, full of pictures and ornaments they knew extremely well, and none of them without significance. And the significance, for everyone who shared in the festival, was hope. What God had done before God would do again.

Of course, as the biblical story itself abundantly shows, things were never that simple. The people at the time of the Exodus were fearful. Moses himself tried to get out of his dangerous new role. The people grumbled and sometimes clamoured to go back to Egypt. When the holy law arrived from Mount Sinai, its first task was to condemn the people – including Aaron! – for making an idol, a golden calf, instead of worshipping the one God, whose only appropriate 'image' is a living, breathing human being. The covenant was broken before it had even really begun, and God very nearly withdrew his promise to travel in person with the Israelites. Whatever the ancient promises meant, and whatever this new fulfilment might involve, it certainly didn't make the people pure, holy and faithful overnight.

But this was the story that sustained the Israelites for the next thousand years and more, up to the time of Jesus – and, of course, sustains the Jewish people to this day. This was the story Jesus knew from boyhood. This was the story – the tyrant, the leader, the victory, the sacrifice, the vocation, the presence of God, the promised inheritance – within which it made sense to talk about God taking charge. This was the story about God becoming king.

This was the story Jesus' hearers would have remembered when they heard him talking about God taking charge at last. Since we have reason to believe that Jesus was one of the greatest communicators of all time, we must assume that this was the story he wanted them to think of. He must have known what he was doing, what pictures he was awakening in people's minds. When he was talking about God taking charge, he was talking about a new Exodus.

7

The campaign starts here

Keep these spectacles on, then, as we come back to Jesus and to what he was saying about God – about Israel's God. Jesus was going about declaring, after the manner of someone issuing a public proclamation, that Israel's God was at last becoming king. 'The time is fulfilled!' he said. 'God's kingdom is arriving! Turn back, and believe the good news!' (Mark 1.15). 'If it's by God's finger that I cast out demons,' he declared, 'then God's kingdom has come upon you' (Luke 11.20).

Think for a moment of how a 'proclamation' like this works. Those of us who live in modern democracies are used to the idea of a new government taking office, with a new president or prime minister. We are used to hearing about this on the radio or TV. When this happens, almost all of us simply accept that this is how things now are. We believe in democracy. Even if we didn't vote for the eventual winner, we shrug our shoulders and recognize that the majority disagreed with us this time round. Whatever happens, it's unlikely to mean that all the old laws and all the old customs will be swept away, or that the new leader will invent a whole lot of new ones and expect us all to come into line. Some policies will shift this way or that, to be sure. But a new leader, a new government, won't transform our lives from top to bottom.

But imagine what it would be like if you'd lived for years and years under the vicious and repressive rule of a foreign tyrant. You have no system in place to change things. No elections are held, or if they are, they're rigged from start to finish. And imagine that this takes place in a world without radio, TV or printed media. The only way you hear about things is by rumour (often very effective, and sometimes remarkably accurate) or by some kind of public proclamation – perhaps as it finally filters down to your town, far away from the centre of power.

Proclamations would be used, too, to announce that the ruler was changing but that the system was carrying on. The old emperor dies, but the power brokers around him will take care that, before the bad news of his death is released, the good news of his successor is firmly in place. Then the heralds are sent off to provinces, cities and towns across the whole empire, with a message that carries weight, authority and a sense that this isn't a new idea you might like to think about, but a new fact that you'd better get used to. 'Good news – we have a new emperor!' So when Jesus was in his late teens, and the old emperor Augustus finally died after his four decades as master of the Western world, we can imagine Jesus, perhaps in the newly rebuilt city of Sepphoris, not far from Nazareth, being in the market square when the herald came in to read the proclamation. 'Good news – Tiberius Caesar is emperor!'

The herald might well be accompanied by a squad of soldiers, especially in potential trouble spots. Everybody knew then, as people who live under tyrannies today know equally well, that a change of ruler is a moment of vulnerability, a moment when a revolution could erupt. The reason Sepphoris had had to be rebuilt, perhaps with help from local carpenters such as Joseph and possibly even Jesus himself, was that it had been the centre of a major anti-Roman revolt after the death of Herod the Great, and the Romans had smashed it to the ground. The proclamation of a new emperor, then, carried weight. It wasn't a take-it-or-leave-it affair. It meant that Tiberius was now in charge – and that his local agents, with his backing, had to be obeyed. Or else.

Celebration, healing and forgiveness

So what about Jesus' own kingdom-announcement? His going around Galilee saying, like one of Caesar's heralds, that *God himself* was now becoming king would be a poke in the eye for two people at least. In the north of the country, where Jesus was launching his campaign, there was Herod Antipas, one of the many sons of Herod the Great. Herod Antipas wasn't particularly powerful, but, though the Romans hadn't allowed him to keep his father's title of 'king of the Jews', he was the nearest equivalent at the time. Indeed, it was he who had been rebuilding Sepphoris as his capital. In the south, there were the chief priests, with the (annually appointed) high priest at their head – a pseudo-aristocracy, kept in place, as was Herod Antipas himself, by Roman backing. The Romans liked to run their huge empire through local power brokers on whom they could rely to collect the taxes and keep the population under control. If either Herod or the high priest heard that someone was going around announcing that God was becoming king, they would smell trouble at once.

So when Jesus went around saying that God was now in charge, he wasn't walking (as it were) into virgin territory. He wasn't making his announcement in a vacuum. Imagine what it would be like, in Britain or the United States today, if, without an election or any other official mechanism for changing the government, someone were to go on national radio and television and announce that there was now a new prime minister or president. 'From today onwards,' says the announcer, 'we have a new ruler! We're under new government! It's all going to be different!' That's not only exciting talk. It's fighting talk. It's treason! It's sedition! By what right is this man saying this? How does he think he'll get away with it? What exactly does he mean, anyway? An announcement like this isn't simply a proclamation. *It's the start of a campaign.* When a regime is already in power and is simply transferring that power to the next person in line, you just announce that it's happening. But if you make that announcement while someone else appears to be in charge, you are saying, in effect, 'The campaign starts here.'

So what *did* Jesus mean? What sort of a campaign could this have been? Those were the questions, we can be sure, in his hearers' minds. Frustratingly, for us and for them, Jesus' answer to 'What exactly does he mean?' seems to have been partly, 'Wait and see.' But in the meantime he was still demonstrating what it meant, up close and personal. His healings and celebrations were part of the meaning of God becoming king. This is what it looked like.

But what had the curing of dozens, perhaps thousands, of people to do with the hopes and aspirations we studied earlier, the dream of a new Exodus, a victorious battle against the old tyrant, the rebuilding of the Temple, the creation of justice and peace?

Maybe that last one is the place to start. Justice and peace are about putting things right in the world. But, from whatever angle you look at Jesus, he was concerned not just with outward structures, but with realities that would involve the entire person, the entire community. No point putting the world right if the people are still broken. So broken people will be healed: paralytics, epileptics, demoniacs, people with horrible skin diseases, a servant on the point of death, an old woman with a high fever, blind men, deaf and mute men, a little girl who's technically already dead, an old woman with a persistent haemorrhage. And so on, and so on. Matthew lets the list build up until we almost take it for granted: yes, here's a person who's sick; Jesus will cure her.

But it wasn't just healings. It was also parties – celebrations. Jesus, to be sure, often spent long times alone in prayer. But he was also deeply at home where there was a party, a kingdom party, a celebration of the fact that God was at last taking charge. And, as is well enough known but not always fully understood, he seems to have specialized in celebrating God's kingdom with all the wrong people. Tax-collectors (always disliked; doubly so when they were working for Herod or the Romans or both) were a breed apart, and Jesus went out of his way to meet them, to eat and party with them, to call one of them to be part of his inner team. Matthew, telling the story of his own call (9.9–13), puts it as one in a long list of *healing stories*. Presumably this is because that's how he himself had experienced it. Prostitutes seem to have been another speciality. Jesus is said to have welcomed them too, and in the remarkable story of the Prodigal Son, which we shall look at more closely in a minute, the charge levelled against the prodigal by the older brother is that he has spent all the father's money on whores (Luke 15.30). That reflects the charge levelled against Jesus that precipitated the story in the first place ('This fellow welcomes sinners! . . . He even eats with them!', v. 2).

That chapter, in fact (Luke 15), is a sustained exposition of *the reason why there's a party taking place to begin with*. Something is happening, Jesus declares, that is bringing heaven and earth together. The angels are celebrating in heaven, so surely we should be celebrating here on earth as well. And the reason the angels are celebrating is that notorious sinners are seeing the error of their ways and turning away from them, even though the righteous and respectable, who can't bear to think there's anything wrong with *them*, are looking down their noses at such behaviour.

The point, as with the healings, is not that Jesus was simply mounting a one-man rescue operation for lost and battered souls – though that's what it must often have looked like. Jesus, aware as ever of the long stories of God's people and the ways in which those stories were expected to come true, knew as well as any trained teacher of the law that one of the great things Israel had to do so that God would launch his great renewal movement, his new Exodus, was 'to turn', to repent, to turn back from the evil ways of the heart, and to turn instead to God in penitence and faith. That's what Moses himself had said in Deuteronomy 30. Jeremiah and Ezekiel had made the same point. This was how it would have to be: when the Israelites had hit rock bottom, then they would turn back to God with all their heart and soul, and God would turn back to them, restoring them and making them his people indeed.

'So,' says Jesus, 'it's time to celebrate! It's happening! Not, perhaps, in the way you thought it would, not yet on a national scale, but it's happening all right. "How glad they will be in heaven over one sinner who repents" (Luke 15.7). "This brother of yours was dead and is alive again! He was lost, and now he's found!" (15.32). Resurrection, the ultimate hope of new life for Israel, is happening under your noses, and you can't see it. But for those of us who can – well, we're having a party, the same party that the angels are having in heaven, and you're not going to stop us.' This, it seems, is part at least of what it means that God's kingdom is coming 'on earth as in heaven'. The heavenly celebrations at the signs of renewal, the first flickers of a dawn that will soon flood the whole sky, are to be matched by the motley mob around Jesus here and there, in Matthew's house (Matthew 9.9–13) and Zacchaeus's house (Luke 19.1–10), in this tavern and that, with Mary Magdalene and her friends and anyone else who cares to join in. This is what it looks like when God's in charge. This is how the campaign gets under way.

This introduces us to another theme that is closely connected with the themes of healing and celebrating. Jesus spoke frequently of people being *forgiven*. Forgiveness, indeed, is a sort of healing. It removes a burden that can crush and cripple you. It allows you to stand up straight without pretending. It spreads out into whole communities. Think of Desmond Tutu, chairing that harrowing Commission for Truth and Reconciliation in South Africa. 'No Future Without Forgiveness' was the slogan, which became the title of Tutu's book. Forgiveness has a claim to be the most powerful thing in the world. It transforms like nothing else. It ranges from the top of the scale, 'forgiveness' of massive financial debt, all the way down deep to release from the quiet, secret horror of personal guilt and shame, which can, quite literally, paralyse you.

That was the case in one of the first and best-known stories (Mark 2.1–12). 'Child,' says Jesus to a man lying prone on a stretcher, unable to move, 'your sins are forgiven.' All very well to say that, you might think. A bit like walking into town and declaring that we have a new emperor. 'What d'you mean? How will this work? And isn't that pushing your luck? Isn't "forgiveness" what you normally get in the Temple, under the authority of the chief priests?' Yes, that's exactly how it normally works. But something else is going on here. A new dimension of the God-in-charge proclamation is being unveiled. 'You want to know', Jesus declares to the assembled company, 'that the son of man has authority on earth to forgive sins?' He turns to the paralysed man: 'I tell you,' he says, 'Get up, take your stretcher, and go home.' The man obeys. And the crowd in the house, which wouldn't part to let the sick man in, now parts, like the Red Sea, to let the healed man out.

Forgiveness and healing! The two go so closely together, personally and socially. Whole societies can be crippled by ancient grudges that turn into feuds and then into forms of civil war. Families can be torn apart by a single incident or one person's behaviour that is never faced and so never forgiven. Equally, societies and families as well as individuals can be reconciled, can find new hope and new love, through forgiveness. Jesus was tapping into something extremely deep in human life.

But, like the physical healings, forgiveness didn't stop with this kind of reconciliation. To understand this we must come forward from the Exodus to the other great defining moment in Israel's history: the exile. We've already mentioned the time when the people were taken away to Babylon. Well, the prophets of the time were quite clear why this had happened: it was because of the people's wickedness. Like their distant ancestors dancing around a golden calf in the desert, they had forgotten their true God. They had worshipped idols. So, instead of being a light to the nations, Israel had become a byword for a godforsaken nation. People looked at the Israelites and sneered at them and their God, the God who had apparently left them defence-less. Exile was seen, throughout the ancient scriptures, as the punish-ment for Israel's sin. In a culture where honour and shame were everything, the exile brought deep, deadly shame upon Israel. And, in the eyes of the watching world, on Israel's God.

But if that is so, then forgiveness must mean that exile is now over. 'Comfort, O comfort my people,' sang one of the greatest prophets. 'Speak tenderly to Jerusalem, and cry to her that she has served her term, that her penalty is paid, that she has received from YHWH's hand double for all her sins' (Isaiah 40.1–2). And, as the prophecy that follows makes clear, this word of forgiveness is part of the overall message that Israel's God is in fact king. He will be known as king through his victory over the tyrannical pagan kingdom of Babylon and his bringing of his people back home to their land. This was to be the new Exodus: tyrant, rescue, vocation, God's presence, inheritance. Just as physical healing is the up-close-and-personal version of what it looks like when God takes charge, to fix and mend the whole world, so individual forgiveness is the up-close-and-personal version of what it looks like when God does what he promised and restores his exiled people. As we saw, most Jews of Jesus' day saw the Babylonian exile as only the start of a much longer period of history in which God's people remained unredeemed, unrescued and unforgiven. When Jesus was announcing forgiveness, both on the one-to-one personal scale and more widely, this was the story people would have had in their heads. And this was the story we must assume Jesus intended them to have in their heads.

The first announcement

This is how we should understand both the big announcements and the intimate words of consolation. The most formal of the announcements comes, in Luke's gospel (4.16–30), at the start of Jesus' public career. Jesus goes back to his hometown of Nazareth and on the sabbath day goes to the synagogue – a place of worship, but also the communal 'gathering place' (that's what the word means), the place where people come together to discuss, to think things through, to study the law and to reflect on what it means. Jesus stands up to read from the prophet Isaiah and chooses another of the great passages about the coming new age, the release from slavery, the new Exodus, and restoration after the exile, which formed the hope that sustained so much Jewish life of his day. This is the passage often referred to as Jesus' 'Nazareth Manifesto':

> He came to Nazareth, where he had been brought up. On the sabbath, as was his regular practice, he went into the synagogue and stood up to read. They gave him the scroll of the prophet Isaiah. He unrolled the scroll and found the place where it was written:
>
> > The spirit of the Lord is upon me
> > because he has anointed me
> > to tell the poor the good news.
> > He has sent me to announce release to the prisoners
> > and sight to the blind,
> > To set the wounded victims free,
> > To announce the year of God's special favour.
>
> He rolled up the scroll, gave it to the attendant, and sat down. All eyes in the synagogue were fixed on him.
> 'Today,' he began, 'this scripture is fulfilled in your own hearing.'
>
> (Luke 4.16–21)

This is the message of forgiveness, all right, but it's not just forgiveness for individuals who are physically or emotionally crippled as a result of their guilt, real or imagined. It's a kind of corporate forgiveness, tapping into the ancient Jewish hope of the 'jubilee', the year when all debts would be forgiven, when slaves would be set free (Leviticus 25). The jubilee is the sabbath of sabbaths. If, every seven years, there is to be a sabbatical year, in which the land lies fallow and people rest, the jubilee is the sabbatical of sabbaticals, seven times seven years, producing a great celebration of release, forgiveness and rescue from all that has crippled human life. That's what Jesus was announcing.

> You shall count off seven weeks of years, seven times seven years, so that the period of seven weeks of years gives forty-nine years. Then you shall have the trumpet sounded loud; on the tenth day of the seventh month – on the day of atonement – you shall have the trumpet sounded throughout all your land. And you shall hallow the fiftieth year and you shall proclaim liberty throughout the land to all its inhabitants. It shall be a jubilee for you: you shall return, every one of you, to your property and every one of you to your family. That fiftieth year shall be a jubilee for you: you shall not sow, or reap the aftergrowth, or harvest the unpruned vines. For it is a jubilee; it shall be holy to you: you shall eat only what the field itself produces.   (Leviticus 25.8–12)

Jesus' hearers would have understood the Isaiah passage in this sense. They would have been eager to know how exactly he supposed these great prophecies would be fulfilled. As so often, however, Jesus' message seems to be that they *are* being fulfilled – but not in the way people had imagined. Yes, God is taking charge. Yes, the great jubilee year is dawning, the time of release, of forgiveness. But it won't work out the way they had expected. In a shocking reversal, amounting almost to a slap in the face to his hearers (including, we assume, his own family), Jesus declares that the people who will benefit from this great act of God will not, after all, be the people of Israel as they stand. This is what he says next to his hearers in the synagogue that day:

> Everyone remarked at him; they were astonished at the words coming out of his mouth – words of sheer grace.
>
> 'Isn't this Joseph's son?' they said.
>
> 'I know what you're going to say,' Jesus said. 'You're going to tell me the old riddle: "Heal yourself, doctor!" "We heard of great happenings in Capernaum; do things like that here, in your own country!"
>
> 'Let me tell you the truth,' he went on. 'Prophets never get accepted in their own country. This is the solemn truth: there were plenty of widows in Israel in the time of Elijah, when heaven was shut up for three years and six months, and there was a great famine over all the land. Elijah was sent to none of them, only to a widow in the Sidonian town of Zarephath.

'And there were plenty of people with virulent skin diseases in Israel in the time of Elisha the prophet, and none of them was healed – only Naaman, the Syrian.'

When they heard this, everyone in the synagogue flew into a rage.

(Luke 4.22–28)

The people who will benefit will be the outsiders, the wrong people, the foreigners. Even, perhaps, the commander of the enemy army. Naaman the Syrian, to whom Jesus refers as the one man who was healed by the prophet Elisha, was the commander of the army that, in the old story, had been attacking the Israelites (2 Kings 5).

Startling though this is, it fits with everything else we know about Jesus' public teaching. 'Love your enemies,' he told his followers (Matthew 5.44), and he elaborated the point from a dozen different angles. Forgiveness was at the heart of his message. This was a striking departure from the otherwise universal practice of Jewish martyrs, for whom it was a point of honour to call down heaven's curses upon their torturers and executioners. The grisly story of the torture and death of seven brothers and their mother in 2 Maccabees includes the threats they uttered against King Antiochus:

After him they brought forward the sixth [brother]. And when he was about to die, he said, 'Do not deceive yourself in vain. For we are suffering these things on our own account, because of our sins against our own God. Therefore astounding things have happened. But do not think that you will go unpunished for having tried to fight against God!' . . .

[The seventh brother said:] 'But you, unholy wretch, you most defiled of all mortals, do not be elated in vain and puffed up by uncertain hopes, when you raise your hand against the children of heaven. You have not yet escaped the judgement of the almighty, all-seeing God. For our brothers after enduring a brief suffering have drunk of ever-flowing life, under God's covenant; but you, by the judgement of God, will receive just punishment for your arrogance.' (7.18–19, 34–36)

By contrast, both Jesus himself and the first martyr, Stephen, prayed for God's mercy on their killers:

'Father,' said Jesus, 'forgive them! They don't know what they're doing!'

(Luke 23.34)

Then Stephen knelt down and shouted at the top of his voice, 'Lord, do not hold this sin against them.' Once he had said this, he fell asleep.

(Acts 7.60)

But, as we've just seen, when Jesus expanded on his own jubilee programme (Luke 4.24–27), he explained that this wasn't about God simply forgiving Israel its debts and punishing its ancient or contemporary enemies, the pagan nations all around. Rather, this was a message that would be good news – for those pagan nations themselves!

That went down like a lead balloon in his local synagogue. They all knew him and his family. Who did he think he was? Jesus was run out of town and lucky to escape with his life. Indeed, his final fate hovers over Luke's narrative from that point onwards. Somehow the message of forgiveness is doing more than simply reassuring God's people that they will be all right after all. In fact, it's not really doing that at all – it's warning them that they may *not* be all right after all. Their God isn't simply coming to endorse their national ambitions. He's doing what he said he would, but it won't work out the way they thought it would. That, over and over again, is the burden of Jesus' song.

'Your sins are forgiven'

We see it once more in the striking story of the woman who approaches Jesus, washes Jesus' feet with her tears, dries them with her hair, and anoints them with ointment. Jesus was, embarrassingly, having dinner with a Pharisee at the time. The Pharisees were a self-appointed pressure group who believed in keeping themselves as ritually pure as if they were in the Temple itself and who did their best to encourage other Jews to the same kind of rigorous piety, hoping thereby to speed the coming of God's kingdom. They thus shared Jesus' goal, but differed radically on the way to get there. This story perfectly illustrates the point:

A Pharisee asked Jesus to dine with him, and he went into the Pharisee's house and reclined at table. A woman from the town, a known bad character, discovered that he was there at table in the Pharisee's house.

She brought an alabaster jar of ointment. Then she stood behind Jesus' feet, crying, and began to wet his feet with her tears. She wiped them with her hair, kissed his feet, and anointed them with the ointment.

The Pharisee who had invited Jesus saw what was going on.

'If this fellow really was a prophet,' he said to himself, 'he'd know what sort of a woman this is who is touching him! She's a sinner!'

'Simon,' replied Jesus, 'I have something to say to you.'

'Go ahead, Teacher,' he replied.

'Once upon a time there was a moneylender who had two debtors. The first owed him five hundred dinars; the second a tenth of that. Neither of them could pay him, and he let them both off. So which of them will love him more?'

'The one he let off the more, I suppose,' replied Simon.

'Quite right,' said Jesus.

Then, turning towards the woman, he said to Simon, 'You see this woman? When I came into your house, you didn't give me water to wash my feet – but she has washed my feet with her tears, and wiped them with her hair. You didn't give me a kiss, but she hasn't stopped kissing my feet from the moment I came in. You didn't anoint my head with oil, but she has anointed my feet with ointment.

'So the conclusion I draw is this: she must have been forgiven many sins! Her great love proves it! But if someone has been forgiven only a little, they will love only a little.'

Then he said to the woman, 'Your sins are forgiven.'

'Who is this,' the other guests began to say among themselves, 'who even forgives sins?'

'Your faith has saved you,' said Jesus to the woman. 'Go in peace.'

(Luke 7.36–50)

There are many interesting features to the passage – notice, for instance, the way in which Simon, the Pharisee, is mentally criticizing Jesus for not knowing what sort of a woman this is, whereupon Jesus shows that he knows what's going on, not only in the woman's heart, but in Simon's too. But we focus here on forgiveness itself.

Jesus, as usual, tells a story to explain what he is doing. This time it's about a man who had two debtors, one owing him a huge sum and the other a small sum. Neither could pay, so he forgave them both. So, he asks his host, which of the two will love him the more?

Clearly, comes the answer, the one for whom he forgave the greater debt. Precisely so, says Jesus, explaining that this is why this woman had poured out love so richly upon him – unlike the host, who hadn't even begun to show Jesus any love at all. In other words, Jesus is saying, you can tell that this woman has been forgiven, has indeed been forgiven a great deal. She knows, deep inside herself, that she's been forgiven. That's why there's so much love coming out of her. And if she's a forgiveness person, perhaps that shows that she is already enjoying the fact that God is becoming king, whereas people who aren't forgiveness people don't believe it.

These stories, and others like them, resonate not only with the sense of a long-awaited jubilee, a much-anticipated rescue from a sin-caused exile, but also with a sense that another aspect of the great Exodus story is being invoked. Both times when Jesus declares that someone's sins are forgiven, there are mutterings about his doing so. Those in the Pharisee's house ask, 'Who is this who even forgives sins?' and the legal experts observing the paralytic man point out that forgiving sins is something only God can do (Mark 2.7). We shouldn't skip the stages in that implicit argument. How does God normally forgive sins within Israel? Why, through the Temple and the sacrifices that take place there. *Jesus seems to be claiming that God is doing, up close and personal through him, something that you'd normally expect to happen at the Temple.* And the Temple – the successor to the tabernacle in the desert – was, as we saw, the place where heaven and earth met. It was the place where God lived. Or, more precisely, the place on earth where God's presence intersected with human, this-worldly reality.

The Temple was also the place where the high priest had supreme authority. Already we can see what we should have expected if it was indeed true that Jesus was going around telling people that a new government was taking over, that God was in charge from now on. His healings, his celebrations, his forgiving of those in dire need of it – all these were the up-close-and-personal versions of the larger picture he knew his hearers would pick up on whenever he spoke of God becoming king. These actions and sayings were ramming home the point, dangerous though it was, that the present rulers were being called to account and were indeed being replaced. This was the time for God to take charge, to fix and mend things, to make everything right. Starting with *you* here, and *this person* there. Whether or not the authorities liked it. Whether or not the self-appointed pressure groups approved.

John and Herod

If the Temple, and by implication the high priest, were standing in the background when Jesus was forgiving sins, the other local authority was moving into the foreground. Jesus' own cousin, John the Baptist, sent a message to him – from prison. His own fearless preaching, not least his attack on Herod Antipas, had brought about his arrest.

What had happened was this. Antipas was married to a foreign princess, but then fell in love with his own niece, Herodias, who was at the time married to Antipas's half brother Philip. (Anyone who wants to understand the Herodian family tree should be prepared to take a long weekend, a very large sheet of paper, and an ice pack.) The foreign princess was sent back home, and Antipas and Herodias became husband and wife.

John the Baptist publicly denounced this arrangement. I don't think he was simply concerned with Antipas's immoral behaviour, though that was flagrant enough. I think the point was, more tellingly, that anyone who behaved in that way could not possibly, not ever, not in a million years, be regarded as the true 'king of the Jews'. John was expecting a true 'king of the Jews'; Antipas had just demonstrated his utter unsuitability for the position. John pointed this out. Not surprisingly, then, John ended up in one of Antipas's dungeons.

But John believed that Jesus, his cousin, *was* the coming king! He was the one through whose work God would at last become king – would at last break the power of tyrants and set his people free! If that was going to happen, surely John himself was a case in point? After all, John's own public career had reached its climax in launching Jesus on his mission, in setting him up as the man for God's moment! So why wasn't Jesus doing something about John's plight?

> Meanwhile, John, who was in prison, heard about these messianic goings-on. He sent word through his followers.
>
> 'Are you the one who is coming?' he asked. 'Or should we be looking for someone else?'

'Go and tell John', replied Jesus, 'what you've seen and heard. Blind people are seeing! Lame people are walking! People with virulent skin diseases are being cleansed! Deaf people can hear again! The dead are being raised to life! And – the poor are hearing the good news! And God bless you if you're not upset by what I'm doing.'

As the messengers were going away, Jesus began to speak to the crowds about John.

'What were you expecting to see,' he asked, 'when you went out into the desert? A reed wobbling in the wind? No? Well, then, what were you expecting to see? Someone dressed in silks and satins? If you want to see people like that you'd have to go to somebody's royal palace. All right, so what *were* you expecting to see? A prophet? Ah, now we're getting there: yes indeed, and much more than a prophet! This is the one the Bible was talking about when it says,

> See, I'm sending my messenger ahead of you
> And he will clear your path before you.

'I'm telling you the truth: John the Baptist is the greatest mother's son there ever was. But even the least significant person in heaven's kingdom is greater than he is. From the time of John the Baptist until now the kingdom of heaven has been forcing its way in – and the men of force are trying to grab it! All the prophets and the law, you see, made their prophecies up to the time of John. In fact, if you'll believe it, he is Elijah, the one who was to come. If you've got ears, then listen!

'What picture shall I give you for this generation?' asked Jesus. 'It's like a bunch of children sitting in the town square, and singing songs to each other. This is how it goes:

> You didn't dance when we played the flute;
> You didn't cry when we sang the dirge!

'What do I mean? When John appeared, he didn't have any normal food or drink – and people said 'What's got into him, then? Some demon?' Then along comes the son of man, eating and drinking normally, and people say, "Ooh, look at him – guzzling and boozing, hanging around with tax-collectors and other riff-raff." But, you know, wisdom is as wisdom does – and wisdom will be vindicated!'

(Matthew 11.2–19)

It must have broken Jesus' heart to have to send the message back, but send it back he did. Yes, he said, the work he was doing really was the breaking in of God's kingdom. But no, sadly, it wasn't working out the way they would have liked. And when, days or weeks later, they brought him news that Antipas had had John beheaded on the whim of his alluring stepdaughter, I suspect that Jesus' sorrowful reaction (Matthew 14.13) was as much about this irony – the fact that he hadn't been able to do anything to help, to rescue John – as about his natural sorrow at his cousin's death, or his natural recognition that he himself might well be the next in line for the same treatment. Here again the shadow of the cross looms over the story of the kingdom.

So what was Jesus doing? What sense did it make then, and what sense might it make now, to see him as in some way inaugurating 'heaven's rule', or 'God's kingdom'? Why didn't it mean setting John free from prison? How might what he was doing and saying be seen, by any stretch of the imagination, as putting into practice a programme that said, 'This is what it looks like when God's in charge'? That's the question that must have been on many minds and hearts in revolution-hungry Galilee. Here was someone talking about God becoming king; well, they'd had a few of those before, so what was new? What was different? What did this man have to offer? Could they trust him? Was he a loyal Jew, obedient to God and his law, or was he leading Israel astray?

And when the explanation came – significantly, in the passage where Jesus is sending back a difficult answer to his imprisoned cousin John – it picks up a strand in the ancient Jewish expectation that had, all along, gone with the dream of the final battle, the rebuilding of the Temple, and the return of Israel's God to Zion. But it hadn't been featured in the programmes of the other would-be royal or kingdom-of-God movements – presumably because those at the head of them were not gifted with healing, while those in that world who did have such gifts (we have records of some such) did not see that as setting them on the track of a kingdom-of-God movement. Jesus, however, makes the connection. When he tells John's messengers that the blind see, the lame walk, the deaf hear, and so forth, he is quoting directly from Isaiah's vision of a 'return from exile' that would also be nothing short of a new creation:

Then the eyes of the blind shall be opened,
  and the ears of the deaf unstopped;
then the lame shall leap like a deer,
  and the tongue of the speechless sing for joy.
                                    (Isaiah 35.5–6)

Interestingly, similar language also shows up in a fragment of the Dead Sea Scrolls, showing that other Jews of roughly the same period were reading the Isaiah passage as a prediction of what the Messiah was to do:

For the heavens and the earth shall listen to his Messiah . . . for he will honour the devout on the throne of his everlasting kingdom, setting the prisoners free, opening the eyes of the blind, raising up those who are brought low . . . and the Lord shall do wonderful deeds which have not been done, as he said. For he shall heal those who are badly wounded, and raise up the dead, and send good news to the afflicted.
                              (4Q521, col. 2; my translation)

And then Jesus adds, as a warning, that if people want to understand what's going on they will have to do some thinking and be prepared for a dangerous political stance. 'And God bless you if you're not upset by what I'm doing.' In other words, they shouldn't look at his work and imagine that he must be a charlatan, out for his own ends, in league with the devil, or off on some fantasy trip that has nothing to do with Israel's aspirations, the ancient promises of God, or the hope of the world at large. They shouldn't look at all this and imagine it has nothing to do with God becoming king – with God taking over, calling the petty old tyrant up the road to account.

On the contrary. This is the sharp edge of what God is doing. Look at the texts and you'll see. When God does the big things, the little people get drawn in too. Human systems often forget that, but God doesn't. Read on in Isaiah 40: the God who comes in power and glory, who stretches out the heavens like a curtain, who glances down and sees the princes of the earth as so many grains of sand, is also the God who feeds his flock like a shepherd, gathers the lambs in his arms, and gently leads the mother sheep. Blessed are those who can see this, who can spot what's going on, who are prepared to go with

Jesus rather than with the princelings of the earth, even though what Jesus was doing wasn't what they had expected.

Tellingly, Jesus himself then goes on to *compare* John the Baptist and Herod Antipas. Jesus is too canny to do this directly; he refers to Antipas by means of the symbol Antipas himself had chosen for his coins. Jews weren't supposed to make pictures of human faces, so they chose symbols instead. Antipas's symbol was a particular kind of reed that grows beside the Sea of Galilee. So, asks Jesus, 'What were you expecting to see when you went out into the desert? A reed wobbling in the wind?' In other words, 'When you went off after John, were you looking for another ruler like the ones you've got already?' Surely not, he implies.

He then repeats the question, coming a shade more into the open. 'Well, then, what were you expecting to see? Someone dressed in silks and satins? If you want to see people like that you'd have to go to somebody's royal palace.'

Again, the expected answer is, 'No, we've got people like that already, and we're fed up with them. We want something else. We want God himself to be king.'

'So,' Jesus presses the question, 'what *were* you expecting to see? A prophet?' Someone announcing God's rule? 'Yes, and much more than a prophet.' He then quotes Malachi 3.1, where God promises to send his messenger ahead of him, to prepare the way. 'All right,' he seems to say, 'you were wanting God to be king – so you went looking for a prophet, hoping that he would be the one to tell you that it was happening at last. *And you were right – he was.* Since the time of John's brief work, God's kingdom has indeed been breaking in, even though the men of violence are trying to hijack it.' 'So,' he concludes, 'if you'll believe it, he is Elijah, the one who was to come' – another reference to Malachi, this time to 4.5, where the messenger-in-advance is said to be Elijah himself. And then he adds, characteristically, 'If you've got ears, then listen!'

What's going on? Why does he say it like that? Because *the campaign is already under way*, and if John is the 'preliminary messenger' of Malachi 3—4, this can only mean one thing. John had sent messengers to Jesus to ask if he was indeed 'the one who is to come', and the answer, given cryptically but plainly enough for those with ears to hear, is an emphatic yes. Jesus was well aware that what he was doing didn't fit with what people were expecting. But he believed that he was indeed launching God's kingdom-campaign. He was the one in whose presence, work and teaching Israel's God was indeed becoming king.

The campaign, you see, isn't about someone running for office as happens in our modern democracies. Jesus isn't going around trying to drum up support like today's politicians. He is much more like a rebel leader within a modern tyranny, setting up an alternative government, establishing his rule, making things happen in a new way. He chooses twelve of his closest followers and seems to set them apart as special associates. For anyone with eyes to see, this says clearly that he is reconstituting God's people, Israel, around himself. Israel hadn't had twelve tribes since the eighth century BC, when the Assyrians came and captured the northern kingdom, leaving only Benjamin and Judah ('the Jews') in the south, plus any Levites who remained with them. But some of the prophets had spoken of the day when all the tribes would be gathered again. Jesus' choice of the twelve seems to indicate, symbolically, that this is how he wanted his work to be seen. This is a campaign. It's a rebel movement, a risky movement, a would-be royal movement under the nose of the present would-be 'king of the Jews', Herod Antipas himself.

But before we can explore all this further, we must examine in more detail the stories Jesus was telling. What are they about? How do they explain this strange new announcement that God is in charge? How do they help the campaign move forward?

8

Stories that explain and a message that transforms

Jesus, as we saw, had one particular method of explaining what was going on. As part of his campaign, he told stories. Not just any old stories. These stories were, for the most part, not 'illustrations', preachers' tricks to decorate an abstract or difficult thought, to sugar-coat the pill of complicated teaching. If anything, they were the opposite. They were stories designed to tease, to clothe the shocking and revolutionary message of God's kingdom in garb that left the hearers wondering, trying to think it out, never quite able (until near the end) to pin Jesus down. They were stories that, eventually, caused some to decode his deep, rich message in such a way as to frame a charge against him, either of blasphemy, sedition or 'leading the people astray'.

The stories were full of echoes. They resonated with ancient scriptural promises; they reminded their hearers of Israel's future hopes and claimed by implication that these hopes were now being realized, even if not in the way they had imagined. These explanatory stories – the 'parables' – were not, as children are sometimes taught in Sunday school, 'earthly stories with heavenly meanings', though some of them may be that, as it were, by accident. Some, indeed, are heavenly stories, tales of other-worldly goings-on, with decidedly earthly meanings. That's exactly what we should expect if Jesus' kingdom-announcement was as we are describing it, with God's kingdom coming on earth as in heaven.

A good example is Luke 16.19–31, where the strange tale of two dead people inhabiting different worlds has as its punch line a warning about caring for the poor and the urgent need to repent:

'There was once a rich man,' said Jesus, 'who was dressed in purple and fine linen, and feasted in splendour every day. A poor man named

Lazarus, who was covered with sores, lay outside his gate. He longed to feed himself with the scraps that fell from the rich man's table. Even the dogs came and licked his sores.

'In due course the poor man died, and was carried by the angels into Abraham's bosom. The rich man also died, and was buried. As he was being tormented in Hades, he looked up and saw Abraham far away, and Lazarus in his bosom.

'"Father Abraham!" he called out. "Have pity on me! Send Lazarus to dip the tip of his finger in water and cool my tongue! I'm in agony in this fire!"

'"My child," replied Abraham, "remember that in your life you received good things, and in the same way Lazarus received evil. Now he is comforted here, and you are tormented. Besides that, there is a great chasm standing between us. People who want to cross over from here to you can't do so, nor can anyone get across from the far side to us."

'"Please, then, father," he said, "send him to my father's house. I've got five brothers. Let him tell them about it, so that they don't come into this torture-chamber."

'"They've got Moses and the prophets," replied Abraham. "Let them listen to them."

'"No, father Abraham," he replied, "but if someone went to them from the dead, they would repent!"

'"If they don't listen to Moses and the prophets," came the reply, "neither would they be convinced, even if someone rose from the dead."'

The message, then, remains very much about what ought to be happening here and now, on 'earth', not just in 'heaven'.

Many of Jesus' stories pick up Israel's stories from long before, stories about God and Israel, the Exodus, the creation itself, the trials and tribulations of God and God's people, and – not least – the horrible exile in Babylon and God's repeated promises to restore his people's fortunes at last. This, in particular, is the reason why some of Jesus' key parables were about seeds being sown. The idea of a farmer sowing a seed – to be sure, one of the most natural and common sights in an agricultural economy – had been used centuries before by the prophets to promise that Israel's God, having plucked up the plant that was Israel, would come back and sow once more the seeds that would bear fruit, fruit that this time would last (see e.g. Isaiah 1.9; 6.13; 37.31–32; Jeremiah 31.27; Ezra 9.2). Here is Matthew's parable of the Sower (parallels are in Mark 4.1–20 and Luke 8.4–15):

That very day Jesus went out of the house and sat down beside the sea. Large crowds gathered around him, so he got into a boat and sat down. The whole crowd was standing on the shore.

He had much to say to them, and he said it all in parables.

'Listen!' he said. 'Once there was a sower who went out to sow. As he sowed, some seed fell beside the path, and the birds came and ate it up. Some seed fell on rocky soil, where it didn't have much earth. It sprang up at once because it didn't have depth of soil. But when the sun was high it got scorched, and it withered because it didn't have any root. Other seed fell in among thorns, and the thorns grew up and choked it. And other seed fell into good soil, and produced a crop, some a hundred times over, some sixty, and some thirty times over. If you've got ears, then listen!'

His disciples came to him.

'Why are you speaking to them in parables?' they asked.

'You've been given the gift of knowing the secrets of the kingdom of heaven,' he replied, 'but they haven't been given it. Anyone who already has something will be given more, and they will have plenty. But anyone who has nothing – even what they have will be taken away! That's why I speak to them in parables, so that they may look but not see, and hear but not understand or take it in. Isaiah's prophecy is coming true in them:

You will listen and listen but won't understand,
you will look and look but not see.
This people's heart has gone flabby and fat,
their ears are muffled and dull,
their eyes are darkened and shut;
in order that they won't see with their eyes
or hear with their ears, or know in their heart,
or turn back again for me to restore them.

'But there's great news for *your* eyes: they can see! And for *your* ears: they can hear! I'm telling you the truth: many prophets and holy people longed to see what you see and didn't see it, and to hear what you hear and didn't hear it.

'All right, then,' Jesus continued, 'this is what the sower story is all about. When someone hears the word of the kingdom and doesn't understand it, the evil one comes and snatches away what was sown in their heart. This corresponds to what was sown beside the path. What was sown on rocky ground is the person who hears the word and immediately receives it with delight, but doesn't have any root of their own. Someone like that only lasts a short time; as soon as there's any trouble or persecution because of the word, they trip up at once. The one sown among thorns is the one who hears the word, but the world's worries and the seduction of wealth choke the word and it doesn't bear fruit. But the one sown on good soil is the one who hears the word and understands it. Someone like that will bear fruit: one will produce a hundred times over, another sixty, and another thirty times over.'

(13.1–23)

Jesus, telling stories about a sower sowing seeds, about weeds among the wheat (Matthew 23.24–30), about a seed growing secretly (Mark 4.26–29), and about a vineyard where the tenants refuse to give the owner the fruit (Mark 12.1–12), is allowing these ancient echoes to take root in the fertile and scripture-soaked minds of his hearers, to try to get through to them the message that what they have longed for is happening at last, but it doesn't look as they thought it would! God is at last doing the great new thing he's always promised for Israel – but the wrong people seem to be getting the message, and many of the right people are missing it entirely!

The parables, in fact, are told as kingdom-explanations for Jesus' kingdom-actions. They are saying: 'Don't be surprised, but *this* is what it looks like when God's in charge.' They are not 'abstract teaching', and indeed if we approach them like that, we won't understand them at all. Specialists who have studied the way in which Jesus' language works describe a 'speech-act' effect, whereby telling a story creates a new situation, a whole new world. That was indeed what Jesus was aiming to do, and by all accounts he was succeeding. But what such specialist studies do not always point out is what this new world actually was. It was the new world in which God was in charge at last, on earth as in heaven. God was fixing things, mending things, mending *people*, making new life happen. This was the new world in which the promises were coming true, in which new creation was happening, in which a real 'return from exile' was taking place in the hearts and minds and lives both of notorious sinners and of people long crippled by disease.

The famous parable of the Sower has another dimension too. We find first a story ('Once there was a sower . . .', vv. 1–9), then a question as to what it means ('Why are you speaking to them . . .', vv. 10–17), and then a point-by-point explanation ('This is what the sower story is all about . . .', vv. 18–23). Again, learned readers in our own day have shaken their heads. That's not how parables ought to work, they say. All you need is the story – the short bit at the front, in which the sower sows his seed. That extra explanation – that's an allegory, not a parable! Jesus, such scholars go on, couldn't or wouldn't have said it. After all, an explained parable is about as much use as an explained joke. Someone else, some flat-footed 'redactor', obviously added the 'explanation' at a later stage.

Again, that's an interesting point, but a wrong conclusion. Frequently, indeed, the main thrust of a parable must be left unsaid. The parable of the Prodigal Son, which we have already mentioned, is a case in point. The story ends without resolution, with the father remonstrating with the older son. We want to know what happens next, and presumably Jesus wanted his hearers to think it out and to apply what they were thinking to their own situation. Like a good advertisement, a parable may be much more powerful in what it doesn't say than in what it does. But with Matthew 13 (and the parallels) something else is going on. Here we are faced not so much with 'allegory' in some technical sense, but with something much more like *an apocalyptic vision*.

As often, the book of Daniel is important here. In Daniel 2, the king has a dream, and Daniel first tells him the dream and then, point by point, interprets it: four kingdoms will all come crashing down and be replaced by a great new kingdom that will last for ever. Another dream and its interpretation are provided in Daniel 4 (Nebuchadnezzar's madness); then another strange vision, with a point-by-point inter-pretation, in chapter 5 (Belshazzar's feast). Then, in chapter 7, we have the central vision of the book; only this time it's Daniel himself who has the dream and an angel who interprets it for him. Again there are four kingdoms, which are followed by a fifth, a very different one, which will judge all the others and rule the world.

These sharp, multicoloured stories are all about what the whole book of Daniel is all about: the kingdom of God and the kingdoms of the world. And guess what? That's what Jesus was talking about too. So we shouldn't be surprised if he uses similar techniques to get his point across. The book of Daniel was designed to be subversive, to act as 'resistance literature' to help the Jews as they faced persecution. Jesus seems to have designed his parables a bit like that too – though now to help his followers understand a deeper and stranger point, namely, that he was calling into being a renewed 'Israel' over against not only the might of pagan empire, but the official structures of Judaism itself (Herod, the chief priests, and so on).

The dreams or visions in Daniel follow exactly the pattern we have in Matthew 13 and parallels. First, a strange story; then a question about how to interpret it, about what it means; then, a point-by-point interpretation. And, before we get anywhere near the actual content, we must grasp a vital point if we are to understand the whole kingdom-picture in the gospels. Apocalyptic visions are not simply special divine revelations for their own sake. Nor, on the other hand, are they about the 'end of the world'. Apocalyptic visions of this sort are about *the coming of God's kingdom on earth as in heaven.* The point of 'apocalyptic' is that the seer, the visionary – Daniel, Jesus – is able to glimpse what is actually going on in heaven and, by means of this storytelling technique, the strange-story-plus-interpretation, is able to unveil, and therefore actually to set forward, the purposes of heaven on earth. The very *form* of the parable thus embodies the *content* it is trying to communicate: heaven appearing on earth.

The content too does not then disappoint. Here is a sower sowing seed. The wise first-century Jew, hearing this, may suspect that this is about God sowing Israel again after the time of tragedy, the sorrow of the exile. Yes, says Jesus, but see what heaven's perspective on this is going to be. Israel is indeed to be sown again. But there will be many who look and look, but never see, who hear and hear, but never understand. Many seeds will fall on the path, on rocky ground, and among thorns. Israel is not to be reaffirmed as it stands. John the Baptist got it right: you can't just say 'Abraham is our father', because the axe is laid to the roots of the tree (another scriptural metaphor for the judgment of Israel), and God can now raise up children for

Abraham from these stones (Matthew 3.9–10). Jesus echoes that elsewhere: many will come from east and west and sit down with Abraham,
Isaac and Jacob in the kingdom of heaven, while the children of the
kingdom – those who are presuming on ancestral heritage rather than
grasping the chance of the kingdom itself now that it's here – will be
cast out (Matthew 8.11–12). Jesus is telling his contemporaries what
heaven's verdict is right now, what heaven's action on earth looks like
now, and he is using the best possible medium for doing so, the
apocalyptic tradition of story-plus-interpretation, which allows the
bifocal vision of heaven and earth, the simultaneous translation from
the one language into the other, to take effect.

Not all the stories, of course, work in this way. Jesus is anything but
a wooden, stilted teacher, a one-string fiddle or a one-tune wonder.
Some of the stories amount to pithy sayings or extended metaphors
heavy with the hidden excitement of a new world waiting to be born.
Think of the wedding guests being unable to fast, because the bridegroom is there with them, or the new wine needing new wineskins:

> Then John's disciples came to him with a question.
> 'How come,' they asked, 'we and the Pharisees fast a good deal, but
> your disciples don't fast at all?'
> 'Wedding guests can't fast, can they,' replied Jesus, 'as long as the
> bridegroom is with them? But sooner or later the bridegroom will be
> taken away from them. They'll fast then all right.
> 'No one,' he went on, 'sews a patch of unshrunk cloth onto an old
> coat. The patch will simply pull away from the coat, and you'll have a
> worse hole than you started with. People don't put new wine into old
> wineskins, otherwise the skins will split; then the wine will be lost, and
> the skins will be ruined. They put new wine into new skins, and then
> both are fine.'   (Matthew 9.14–17)

Other stories are heavy in a different way, with the sorrowful realization that Israel as a whole simply isn't interested in Jesus' kingdom-
vision, indeed is violently rejecting it, because violence has become
its way of life. Then the sequence of four moves, ending with the
crucial one, comes again, but this time in the form of the rejected
prophets and the rejected son. The rejected prophets correspond to
the seed that falls on the wrong kind of soil, while the son corresponds
to the seed that produces a large harvest:

'Listen to another parable,' Jesus went on. 'Once upon a time there was a householder who planted a vineyard, built a wall for it, dug out a wine-press in it, and built a tower. Then he let it out to tenant farmers and went away on a journey.

'When harvest time arrived, he sent his slaves to the farmers to collect his produce. The farmers seized his slaves; they beat one, killed another, and stoned another. Again he sent other slaves, more than before, and they treated them in the same way. Finally he sent his son to them.

'"They'll respect my son," he said.

'But the farmers saw the son.

'"This fellow's the heir!" they said among themselves. "Come on, let's kill him, and then we can take over the property!"

'So they seized him, threw him out of the vineyard, and killed him.

'Now then: when the vineyard-owner returns, what will he do to those farmers?'

'He'll kill them brutally, the wretches!' they said. 'And he'll lease the vineyard to other farmers who'll give him the produce at the right time.'

'Did you never read what the Bible says?' said Jesus to them:

> The stone the builders threw away
> is now atop the corner;
> it's from the Lord, all this, they say
> and we looked on in wonder.

'So then let me tell you this: God's kingdom is going to be taken away from you and given to a nation that will produce the goods. Anyone who falls on this stone will be smashed to pieces, and anyone it falls on will be crushed.'

When the chief priests and the Pharisees heard his parables, they knew he was talking about them. They tried to arrest him, but they were afraid of the crowds, who regarded him as a prophet.   (Matthew 21.33–46)

The crowds understood that one all right, without any further explanation. So did the chief priests and the Pharisees, who rightly saw that the story had been told against them.

'Don't miss it'

Jesus' stories build to a crescendo, keeping pace with the wider narrative of his brief public career. The kingdom is coming, on earth as in heaven; but the people of the kingdom, 'the children of the kingdom', are missing out on it! Everything is coming right at last – and everything is going wrong at the same time. There is a dark twist in the way God's plans are working out, in the way that Israel's destiny is being fulfilled. All suggestions that Jesus was simply a 'great religious teacher' telling his contemporaries about a new pattern of spirituality or even a new scheme of salvation must be set aside (unless, of course, we are to rewrite the gospels wholesale, which is what many have done in their efforts to domesticate Jesus and his message). Jesus' parables, never mind for the moment anything else about him, tell us in their form alone, but also in their repeated and increasingly direct content, that the purposes of heaven are indeed coming true on earth, but that the people who in theory have been longing for that to happen are turning their backs on it now that it is actually knocking on their door:

> Jesus spoke to them once again in parables.
>
> 'The kingdom of heaven,' he said, 'is like a king who made a wedding feast for his son. He sent his slaves to call the invited guests to the wedding, and they didn't want to come.
>
> 'Again he sent other slaves, with these instructions: "Say to the guests, Look! I've got my dinner ready; my bulls and fatted calves have been killed; everything is prepared. Come to the wedding!"
>
> 'But they didn't take any notice. They went off, one to his own farm, another to see to his business. The others laid hands on his slaves, abused them, and killed them. (The king was angry, and sent his soldiers to destroy those murderers and burn down their city.) Then he said to his slaves, "The wedding is ready, but the guests didn't deserve it. So go to the roads leading out of town, and invite everyone you find to the wedding." The slaves went off into the streets and rounded up everyone they found, bad and good alike. And the wedding was filled with partygoers.
>
> 'But when the king came in to look at the guests, he saw there a man who wasn't wearing a wedding suit.
>
> '"My friend," he said to him, "how did you get in here without a wedding suit?" And he was speechless. Then the king said to the servants, "Tie him up, hands and feet, and throw him into the darkness outside, where people weep and grind their teeth."
>
> 'Many are called, you see, but few are chosen.'   (Matthew 22.1–14)

'So, you see,' he went on, 'the kingdom of heaven is like a king who wanted to settle up accounts with his servants. As he was beginning to sort it all out, one man was brought before him who owed ten thousand talents. He had no means of paying it back, so the master ordered him to be sold, with his wife and children and everything he possessed, and payment to be made.

'So the servant fell down and prostrated himself before the master.

'"Be patient with me," he said, "and I'll pay you everything!"

'The master was very sorry for the servant, and let him off. He forgave him the loan.

'But that servant went out and found one of his fellow servants who owed him a hundred dinars. He seized him and began to throttle him. "Pay me back what you owe me!" he said.

'The colleague fell down and begged him, "Be patient with me, and I'll pay you!"

'But he refused, and went and threw him into prison until he could pay the debt. So when his fellow-servants saw what had happened, they were very upset. They went and informed their master about the whole affair. Then his master summoned him.

'"You're a scoundrel of a servant!" he said to him. "I let you off the whole debt, because you begged me to. Shouldn't you have taken pity on your colleague, like I took pity on you?"

'His master was angry, and handed him over to the torturers, until he had paid the whole debt. And that's what my heavenly father will do to you, unless each of you forgives your brother or sister from your heart.'   (Matthew 18.23–35)

Even the story of the great wedding party to which all and sundry are invited carries within it a dark note of warning: don't think you can come into God's party without putting on the proper clothes. Even the great story of spectacular forgiveness is turned back against itself when the servant who had been forgiven a huge sum refused to forgive his fellow servant a tiny sum. If this is what it looks like when God's kingdom comes on earth as in heaven – if this is what it looks like when God's in charge – then there must have been more wrong with 'earth' than anyone had supposed.

That, indeed, is the conclusion we are forced to draw at every turn. It isn't that God, coming to rule on earth, is picky or grouchy, deter-mined to find fault. It is, rather, that the patient is deathly sick, and the doctor must prescribe an appropriately drastic course of treatment. It is that the sheep are in danger of being totally lost, since they appear to have no shepherd at all. Jesus speaks of himself, more than once, as a doctor; also, more than once, as a shepherd (Mark 2.17; Luke 4.23; Matthew 9.36; John 10.11; Mark 14.27).

But there are other doctors out there prescribing other remedies. There are other shepherds (the word was often used, as we saw in Chapter 5, to designate Israel's kings or other rulers), and they are failing in their tasks, or worse. The idea of Herod Antipas, the debauched and degenerate son of a warlord father, as the true shepherd of Israel is laughable. The same could be said for the fake 'aristocracy' in Jerusalem, the 'chief priests' and 'Sadducees', who were kept in power by the Romans because they were rich and successful (the Romans, as we saw, preferred to rule through existing 'elites') rather than because they really represented or taught the true, ancient traditions of Israel. Jesus was up against it. If God was to become king it would be – it could only be – by some kind of a confrontation with these forces, or rather with the forces that stood behind them.

Jesus' campaign was never going to be a smooth, easy ride to power. He knew that only too well, even if his followers were hoping that he would wave a magic wand and do to their political and social arrangements what he was doing for people's bodies, minds and spirits.

Which is all the more relevant, because what Jesus was doing at that level was itself extremely challenging. Jesus had grasped that, if God was to become king on earth as in heaven, something deeper than outward reformation would be required. It wouldn't do simply to tighten up existing laws and regulations and enforce them more strictly. That's what the Pharisees wanted to do; they were a popular pressure group urging a moral reformation as part of their own vision of how God might become king. But Jesus had a different sort of 'moral reformation' in mind.

Hearts transformed

In two remarkable passages, Mark 7.1–23 and 10.1–12 (with parallels in Matthew 15.1–20 and 19.1–12), Jesus picks up another of the themes of Israel's ancient promises. What will it look like when God becomes king? *Hearts will be transformed.* So it is with the first of the relevant passages:

The Pharisees gathered around Jesus, together with some legal experts from Jerusalem. They saw that some of his disciples were eating their food with unclean (that is, unwashed) hands.

(The Pharisees, you see – and indeed all the Jews – don't eat unless they first carefully wash their hands. This is to maintain the tradition of the elders. When they come in from the market, they never eat without washing. There are many other traditions which they keep: washings of cups, pots and bronze dishes.)

Anyway, the Pharisees and legal experts asked Jesus, "Why don't your disciples follow the tradition of the elders? Why do they eat their food with unwashed hands?"

'Isaiah summed you up just right,' Jesus replied. 'Hypocrites, the lot of you! What he said was this:

> With their lips this people honour me,
> but with their hearts they turn away from me;
> all in vain they think to worship me;
> all they teach is human commands.

'You abandon God's commands, and keep human tradition!

'So,' he went on, 'you have a fine way of setting aside God's command so as to maintain your tradition. Here's an example: Moses said, "Honour your father and your mother," and, "Anyone who slanders father or mother should die." But you say, "If someone says to their father or mother, 'What you might get from me – it's Korban!'" (which means 'given-to-God'), you don't let them do anything else for their father or mother! The net result is that you invalidate God's word through this tradition which you hand on. And there are lots more things like that which you do.'

Jesus summoned the crowd again.

'Listen to me, all of you,' he said, 'and get this straight. What goes into you from outside can't make you unclean. What makes you unclean is what comes out from inside.'

When they got back into the house, away from the crowd, his disciples asked him about the parable.

'You didn't get it either?' he asked. 'Don't you see that whatever goes into someone from outside can't make them unclean? It doesn't go into the heart; it only goes into the stomach, and then carries on, out down the drain.' (Result: all foods are clean.)

> 'What makes someone unclean,' he went on, 'is what comes out of them. Evil intentions come from inside, out of people's hearts – sexual immorality, theft, murder, adultery, greed, wickedness, treachery, debauchery, envy, slander, pride, stupidity. These evil things all come from inside. They are what make someone unclean.' (Mark 7.1–23)

The story begins as a controversy about whether Jesus and his followers are keeping the detailed regulations of the law in regard to how they prepare to eat. The question of food – what you eat, who you eat it with, and how clean you have to be to eat it – was one of the major symbols of Jewish identity in this period. As the story continues, though, Jesus goes to the deep root of the problem. It isn't what goes into you that defiles you, he declares; it's what comes out of you that defiles you.

That isn't just cryptic. (What is he talking about? Excrement?) It's positively subversive. That's why it's only when Jesus and his followers go back into the house, away from the crowds, that he explains what he means. The purity rules on which Judaism thrived then and, for the most part, thrives still today are (he says) irrelevant. (Pause for sharp intake of breath from those of his hearers, i.e. most of them, who knew the stories of the Maccabean martyrs being tortured and killed for refusing to eat pork.) What goes into you from the outside merely passes through and out the other end. The real uncleanness comes from the heart. That's where thoughts leading to all kinds of evil – murder, adultery, immorality, theft, lying, slander – are lurking. That's the source from which they come bubbling out, unbidden, into actual deeds and words. That's the thing that really makes you 'unclean', not eating with unwashed hands or indeed eating 'unclean' food.

So what is Jesus saying? That some people are simply permanently unclean – namely, all those who find these things bubbling up in their hearts? Hardly. There wouldn't be too many 'clean' people around if that were his point. No, his point is that *when God becomes king, he provides a cure for uncleanness of heart.* Again and again it comes, in the Sermon on the Mount (Matthew 5—7), on the edge of one remark after another. When God becomes king, he will come with a message of forgiveness and healing, and this is designed not just to remove old guilt or to cure old disease, but to renew the whole person from the inside out. *This is the point at which Jesus' whole agenda embraces the 'vocation' aspect of the ancient Exodus story.*

Exactly this point emerges again, though again it's cryptic, in Mark 10.1–12:

> Jesus left the region, and went to the districts of Judaea across the Jordan. A large crowd gathered around him, and once more, as his custom was, he taught them.
>
> Some Pharisees approached him with a question. 'Is it permitted', they asked, 'for a man to divorce his wife?' They said this to trap him.
>
> 'Well,' answered Jesus, 'what did Moses command you?'
>
> 'Moses permitted us', they replied, 'to write a notice of separation and so to complete the divorce.'
>
> 'He gave you that command', said Jesus, 'because you are hardhearted. But from the beginning of creation
>
>> male and female he made them; and that's why
>> the man must leave his father and his mother
>> and cleave unto his wife; so that the two
>> become one flesh.
>
> 'There you are, then: they are no longer two, but one flesh. What God has joined, humans must not split up.'
>
> When they were back indoors, the disciples asked him about this.
>
> 'Anyone who divorces his wife', said Jesus, 'and marries someone else commits adultery against her. And if she divorces her husband and marries someone else she commits adultery.'

To begin with, you might suppose that this is simply a discussion of a particular point of family ethics, namely, the question of divorce. But – remember Herod Antipas and the reason John the Baptist got into trouble! – it can never be merely that. The question turns out to be powerfully loaded, to carry all the baggage of the question of what it will look like when God becomes king.

Jesus' interlocutors remind him that Moses gave permission for divorce. Yes, says Jesus, but that wasn't how it was meant to be from the beginning. Jesus goes back to the story of creation itself, in which man and woman are to be joined permanently, as 'one flesh'. Within the story of Genesis itself, of course, this is powerfully symbolic: the coming together of man and woman is the sign of the belonging together of heaven and earth themselves, of the integration of God's astonishingly variegated creation. What Jesus is claiming is that when God becomes king creation itself is renewed, so that the rule within the kingdom is the rule of what creation was meant to be. And that includes lifelong, faithful monogamous marriage.

This is, no doubt, as much of a challenge today as it was to Jesus' first hearers (Matthew 19.10). But the underlying point comes in Jesus' response to the Pharisees when they ask why, if God intended lifelong marriage, Moses gave permission for divorce. 'It was because of your hard hearts,' replies Jesus, sending them back again to the beginning, to the creation story in Genesis 1—2, for the real standard. So what is he saying? That he is going to force this new agenda on people, even though their hearts are still hard? No. Putting this together with all the other passages about the heart, we can say with confidence that Jesus' point was this. When God becomes king, on earth as in heaven, *he will provide a cure for hardness of heart.* The healing that Jesus offered for sick bodies was to penetrate to the very depths of one's being. Transformed lives, healed from the inside out, are to be the order of the day when God becomes king.

In neither of these cases is there any chance of this teaching collapsing into a private piety. One cannot conclude from these passages that Jesus is 'really' teaching about a 'religion of the heart', which has nothing to do with public life. To take the first passage (Mark 7.1–23; Matthew 15.1–20), the question of whether Jesus and his followers are being loyal to Israel's law is a question about whether Jesus is a true teacher or a false one. The law is quite specific (at least, as interpreted by the stricter minds of the day); if Jesus and his followers are transgressing it, that shows that they are on the wrong track, and that Jesus' claim to be announcing and indeed spearheading God's kingdom-movement must be false, deluded, or perhaps even demonic. This is a decidedly political as well as a religious charge. And this in turn explains once more why Jesus only gives a cryptic answer in public and waits until he is in private before saying the truly explosive thing – that what you eat is irrelevant for genuine purity. That is tantamount to burning a flag or spray-painting a revolutionary slogan on a palace wall. No wonder he had to say it in private.

In the second case too (Mark 10.1–12; Matthew 19.1–12), the stakes are high. The question of divorce is no abstract ethical problem. I remember once being asked by a reporter for my views on marriage and divorce – at just about the same time that Prince Charles was getting a divorce from Princess Diana. I remember thinking at the time that an 'innocent' question about divorce and remarriage posed by a journalist to a churchman in the middle 1990s was no more 'innocent' than the Pharisees' question to Jesus. Mark and Matthew both locate the incident in question in 'the districts of Judaea across the Jordan'. Memories are stirred. That was where John had been baptizing. That was where John had denounced Herod Antipas for taking his brother's wife. To ask the question about divorce in that setting was no mere theoretical enquiry. It was inviting Jesus to incriminate himself, to say something that might lead Antipas to do to Jesus what he'd done to John.

Jesus sticks to scripture, which they can hardly fault. But in doing so he demonstrates that he is speaking from a world in which God, becoming king on earth as in heaven, is transforming the very hearts of human beings as part of his project of new creation. Jesus' hearers, thinking from within a world where the legislation for the hard-hearted still applies, cannot even recognize the kingdom when it is breaking in right there in their midst.

Many other passages point in the same direction. In particular, some of the discourses in John's gospel, climaxing in the so-called high-priestly prayer of John 17, explore at much greater depth the many-sided transformation Jesus seems to have believed would happen when people followed him and discovered what it meant for God to become king. This was, it seems, a major part of Jesus' whole programme.

Just as a politician today needs to have a coherent set of policies about apparently quite different issues (immigration, foreign policy, the economy, education, and so on), so Jesus' campaign for the kingdom seems to have included all the elements we have so far described – healings, celebrations, forgiveness, the renewed heart – and much more besides. But what then must we say about Jesus' vision of the kingdom itself? Did he think it was already here, or was it still in the future? Or was it in some sense both, and if so how?

9

The kingdom present and future

When Jesus healed people, when he celebrated parties with all and sundry, when he offered forgiveness freely to people as if he were replacing the Temple itself with his own work – in all these ways it was clear, and he intended it to be clear, that this wasn't just a foretaste of a future reality. This *was* reality itself. This was what it looked like when God was in charge. God's kingdom was coming, as he taught his followers to pray, 'on earth as in heaven'. On one occasion, indeed, Jesus said sharply to those who were accusing him of being in league with the devil that, if it was indeed by God's own Spirit that he was casting out demons, 'then God's kingdom has come upon [them]' (Luke 11.20). A great deal of what Jesus was doing and saying only makes sense on the assumption that he really did believe that God was already becoming king in the new way he had promised. It was happening, and this is what it would look like.

But there are constant hints, throughout Jesus' public career, that the coming of the kingdom would depend on future events yet to be realized. He speaks again and again of a coming cataclysm – a great disaster, a judgment, terrible events that would turn the world upside down. He speaks, in a famous passage, of the sun and the moon being darkened and the stars falling from heaven (Matthew 24.29, quoting Isaiah 13.10). He speaks, notoriously, of the 'coming of the son of man' (Matthew 24.30, quoting Daniel 7.13). So how can the kingdom be both present and future? What was Jesus trying to say? How does this affect our view of the 'campaign' we have seen him carrying on to this point?

In order to answer this, we must come forward from our earlier glance at the stories of ancient Israel and look very briefly at four men, two before Jesus and two after, whose careers embody something of the same present-and-future tension. That will clear the way to a fresh understanding of what Jesus was really all about.

Judah the Hammer

First, there was 'Judah the Hammer', or Judas Maccabaeus, as he is more regularly known. He came to prominence during the crisis of the 160s BC, almost exactly two hundred years before the public career of Jesus of Nazareth. As with Jesus, the crucial part of his career was a three-year campaign ending in a triumphant entry into Jerusalem and a 'cleansing' of the Temple (see the table). But there the parallel stops.

Judah the Hammer		Jesus of Nazareth	
167/6 BC	Starts revolution	AD 27/8	Starts 'kingdom' movement
164	Cleanses Temple	30	Cleanses Temple

In Judah's day, it was Syria, immediately to the north, that had taken over Jerusalem. The Syrian king, Antiochus Epiphanes (i.e. Antiochus 'the divine appearance'), desecrated the Temple, rededicating it to the pagan god Zeus, and was trying to smash the resistant spirit of the Jews by forcing them to break their holy law by eating pork. The resistance was led by one family, whose figurehead, Judah the Hammer, waged a three-year guerrilla campaign, at the end of which he cleansed the Temple of pagan elements. This is the event still commemorated annually in the Jewish festival of Hanukkah. Judah and his family celebrated their success by parading about singing hymns and, significantly for our story, carrying palm branches.

Judah's victory, consolidated later by his brothers, was enough to establish his family in the roles of high priest and king of the Jews, even though they didn't come from the right families to hold either of these offices. Equally important, they sharpened up the ancient story line: the wicked tyrant oppressing God's people, the noble and heroic leader risking all, fighting the key battle, cleansing the Temple, and setting Israel free to follow God and his law once more. This was the story of Moses, Egypt and the Exodus. It was the story of David, Solomon, the Philistines and the Temple. It was the story of Babylon overthrown, of return from exile.

The book that picks this up most explicitly is Daniel. It tells the story of the Jewish heroes, Daniel and his friends, resisting pagan kings and being vindicated by God. As we have seen, this is the book that, in strange, lurid imagery, speaks of the power of pagan kingdoms reaching their horrible height, of God's own people suffering at their hands, and then of God doing a new thing, setting up his own sovereign rule once and for all. In terms of the image we used earlier on, it's the story of the gale, the high-pressure system and the hurricane: the build-up of pagan power, the hope of Israel and the victory of God. It's the story of the Exodus turned in a new direction. It's the story of David, only now in a new dimension. It's the story of exile and restoration, but now with a new destination. Some people believed it had all come true in and through Judah and his brothers.

In particular, the book of Daniel sets up its own cryptic puzzle. How long, asks the prophet, will the exile last? How long will we have to wait before God performs the final great rescue operation? Will it be seventy years (as others had foretold)? No, comes the answer, it will be seventy times seven – that is, 490 years (Daniel 9.24). Nobody quite knew when you should start the counting and hence when the great moment would finally arrive, but many people during the centuries on either side of Jesus of Nazareth were eager to find out. Different theories were advanced. Each generation hoped that the divine arithmetic would work in their favour.

The problem with the story of Judah the Hammer only gradually dawned on people in the next generation. It was that, despite the early excitement and the continuing enthusiasm of some, it became apparent that the prophecies had still not been fulfilled. Utopia had not arrived. The Hasmoneans, Judah's family, were themselves far from perfect rulers. Pressure groups arose to try to force the issue. The most famous came to be known as the Pharisees, who, as we've seen, were a populist movement deeply loyal to the ancient traditions as they understood them, fervently expecting their God to act once more. But the point is that the great story had been etched into their minds and into their scripture-reading habits: the wicked rulers, the people's suffering, the hero, the battle, the victory, the rule over surrounding nations, the establishment of God's dwelling. This was what people were praying for, hoping for, waiting for when Jesus of Nazareth came on the scene.

Simon the Star

Before we come back to Jesus himself, we need to jump forward, past his day, to another movement that tells us a good deal about how people were telling the story and trying to live it out. We turn from Judah the Hammer to Simon the Star. Or rather, Simon Son-of-the-Star. The year is AD 132, almost exactly a hundred years after the public career of Jesus of Nazareth and hence almost exactly three hundred years after Judah the Hammer (see the chronology below).

Chronology of Simon Son-of-the-Star

AD 115–17	Unsuccessful Jewish revolts against Rome in Egypt, Cyrene, Cyprus
117	Hadrian becomes emperor
132	Hadrian institutes anti-Jewish legislation, builds temple of Jupiter in Jerusalem
133	Start of bar-Kochba rebellion; Rabbi Akiba hails bar-Kochba as the Messiah
133	Coins with 'year 1'
134	Coins with 'year 2'
135	Coins with 'year 3'
135	Rome crushes rebellion; bar-Kochba and Akiba killed

The story starts off the same. Another wicked king; another time of intense suffering; and another new hero emerges, winning (it seems) some initial victories. Another three-year campaign. The aim was the same: defeat the pagan enemy, re-establish the Temple, liberate the Judaeans, and establish a new king as master in his own realm, and perhaps more widely.

The wicked king this time was the Roman emperor Hadrian. We still know him of course from the wall he built on one of his northern borders, more than two thousand miles from Jerusalem, to keep his empire safe from the wild tribes of Scotland. Like many other successful emperors, Hadrian was brilliant and ruthless. Two of his predecessors,

Vespasian and Titus, had defeated the Jewish rebels in a famous and bitter war, culminating in the burning of the Temple in AD 70. Now Hadrian, perhaps spurred on by the possibility of further Jewish uprisings, decided on drastic measures. Like Antiochus Epiphanes, he transformed Jerusalem into a pagan city, giving it a new name, Aelia Capitolina. Antiochus, we recall, had attacked the major symbols of Jewish life and tradition, not least the food laws (by trying to force people to eat pork). Hadrian likewise attacked the Jewish symbols, with a particular focus being his ban on the practice of circumcision.

Other factors too led to revolt. Rome had hinted at one point that the Judaeans might be allowed to rebuild the Temple, so when, instead, the city was turned into a pagan centre, there would have been a toxic mixture of disappointment and righteous indignation. Heavy taxation may have added fuel to the fire. There may also have been a perceived timetable. Jerusalem had been destroyed in AD 70; Jeremiah had spoken of seventy years of desolation, followed by restoration; perhaps after all God was intending to liberate his people in or around AD 140. It is noticeable that the previous great revolt, in AD 66, was nearly seventy years after the original establishment of Roman rule in Judaea. Rebels will often strike at the moment of regime change, when they perceive a potential power vacuum. But rebels who believe God has revealed his plan to them may choose to strike at the time when, according to that revelation, God has promised to act. Perhaps, they may have thought, the best way to make this happen, to get things ready for God to act, would be to launch a liberation movement a few years in advance.

Some or all of these factors contributed to the readiness of people to risk all and sign on when a new leader emerged. The new leader, Simon bar-Kosiba ('Simon, Kosiba's son'), was hailed as bar-Kochba, 'son of the Star', echoing an ancient prophecy:

> A star shall come out of Jacob,
>   and a sceptre shall rise out of Israel;
> it shall crush the borderlands of Moab,
>   and the territory of all the Shethites . . .
> One out of Jacob shall rule,
>   and destroy the survivors of Ir.
>
> (Numbers 24.17–19)

It didn't take much imagination to transfer those ancient victories over Moab, the Shethites and 'the survivors of Ir' to the world of the second century. Simon was the man to do it! Some said he performed miracles; others, later, that he proclaimed himself to be 'a great heavenly light'. One tradition says that the greatest Jewish teacher of the time, Rabbi Akiba himself, declared that Simon was indeed the Messiah, Israel's long-awaited king.

We actually have first-hand remains from bar-Kochba, making him one of the very few leaders of any ancient country for whom we have that kind of information. He wrote letters, some of which have survived. He was both strictly devout in the Jewish tradition and fierce in his demand for allegiance and obedience. He also minted coins, which tell their own powerful story. Like the French Revolutionaries, he restarted the calendar: the first issue of coins bear the year '1', the second '2', and the third '3'. They speak of the coming 'freedom of Jerusalem'. One of them has a picture of the Temple, which was not, of course, standing at the time; this was a statement of intent. The agenda is by now familiar. God would provide a great victory and set his people free; the Temple would be rebuilt; and bar-Kochba himself would be established as the true king. It's the same set of themes that we have heard before, rooted in the same ancient scriptures.

The numbering of the coins, in particular, tells us something about the way this great story worked. Bar-Kochba wasn't waiting for the final events before making it clear that the new age had already begun. He had established his rule, even though the great victory was still to come and the Temple was still to be rebuilt. The three years of his rule were thus a kind of interim period: the new day had dawned, and the new day was about to dawn! Once we think in terms of the real politics of the time, that makes a lot of sense. In the language we used earlier on, this was both *retrospective eschatology* and *prospective eschatology*: a long story had *already* reached its climax (the king was already here!), and the same long story was *about* to reach its climax (the king was on the way to his great victory!). To deny that the new day had dawned would be to deny that he, bar-Kochba, really was the Messiah. But to imagine that, because the new day had dawned, there was nothing more to be done would be to miss the point. This was a time for planning the great victory, for keeping holy and saying fervent prayers, for organizing the continuing anti-Roman revolt, and for developing the design for rebuilding the Temple. Bar-Kochba's coins speak of a period of history that began with a bang, but that needed to be completed with further decisive actions, if that beginning was to be consolidated and validated.

It came to nothing – or rather it came to even greater suffering. Simon the Star seems to have won some early victories and to have established an administration over at least part of the ancient Jewish homeland. He was in charge – for a while and over some territory. But the Romans closed in with massive force, compelling him and his followers to retreat, and then pursued them into caves and other hiding places. Archaeology has uncovered enough from those caves for us to realize how horrible the end must have been for Simon and many others.

Later Jewish writings sometimes speak of Simon not as bar-Kochba, 'son of the Star', or by his proper name, bar-Kosiba, 'son of Kosiba', but by a different pun: bar-Koziba, 'son of the lie'. He was, they believed, a false messiah.

Indeed, many then drew the conclusion that it was false to expect a messiah at all. There were, in any case, no more Jewish uprisings. From then on, the Jews were content to live out their obedience to their God and his law in private and to let other people run the world if they so wished. Some Jewish teachers had been advocating this policy for quite a while. Now it was adopted without further question.

The story of Simon the Star, coming three hundred years after Judah the Hammer, indicates a remarkable common pattern, even though the end results were so different. The story line is once more the same, echoing the Exodus, David and Solomon, and the return from Babylon: the wicked pagan king, suffering and persecution, the emergence of a hero, victories, the cleansing and restoration of the Temple, and the establishment of the new regime. In Judah's case, all went according to plan. It was only gradually, in the years that followed, that people began to doubt whether this had been after all the long-awaited divine liberation. In Simon's case, all went according to plan for three years; then, instead of the final victory and rebuilding, there occurred a disaster so great that for many generations it was spoken of, if at all, with a shudder. The great gale of Roman imperial power had quenched the high-pressure system of Jewish aspiration, leaving a disturbing question mark over the third element: what was Israel's God up to? But the story in which Simon and his followers had lived was the same story. It was, they believed, the scriptural story, the story in which the scriptural promises would be fulfilled. It was the story that was in the heads and the hearts of those who first heard Jesus of Nazareth speaking about God finally becoming king. It was the story that they turned into song as he rode into Jerusalem.

Before we can come back to Jesus himself, though, we need to look at two other kings. Both failed, though for quite different reasons.

Herod the Great

When you take a guided tour in the Holy Land today, you are likely to be struck by one name that comes up again and again. I have heard tourists complain that they came to find out about Jesus and ended up learning more about Herod. Herod the Great (the notorious Herod who, according to Matthew's gospel, killed all the babies in Bethlehem in a vain attempt to get rid of a potential rival to his throne) was indeed a famous leader in his own day and remained thereafter a name to conjure with. If anyone was 'king of the Jews' around the time of Jesus, it was Herod.

Herod the Great fulfilled at least some of the story we have been tracking. He began his career as a successful warlord. A century or so after the time of Judah the Hammer, there was once again a power vacuum in the Middle East. The Hasmonean royal house was in disarray. The Romans were gaining power, and their famous general Pompey captured Jerusalem in 63 BC. As we saw earlier, the Romans preferred, where possible, to rule their subject nations through local elites, so they allowed the Hasmonean family to carry on as high priests.

But the Roman world was about to be plunged into chaos. Pompey was killed in 48 BC. Julius Caesar was assassinated in 44, bringing on the civil wars from which, as we saw, Caesar's adopted son, Octavian, would emerge as the first actual Roman emperor. Meanwhile Rome's old enemy, Parthia (corresponding roughly to modern Iraq, Iran and Afghanistan), seized the moment to invade Roman possessions in the Middle East, including Jerusalem. Long Jewish memories of Assyria, Babylon, Persia and Syria meant that Parthia was bound to be seen by the Jews as the new wicked kingdom. And Herod the Great, the most effective military leader of the moment, already recognized by Rome as 'king of the Jews' on purely pragmatic grounds, defeated the Parthians and recaptured Jerusalem – on behalf of Rome. He knew which side his bread was buttered on.

Herod's chronology

44 BC	Death of Julius Caesar; civil wars break out in the Roman world
40	Parthians invade Syria/Judaea, installing a puppet 'king' in Jerusalem
40	Rome declares Herod to be 'King of Judaea'
37	Herod retakes Jerusalem for Rome after Parthian invasion
31	Octavian ('Augustus') defeats Antony at Actium, ending the civil war; Augustus confirms Herod (previously a supporter of Antony) as king of Judaea
19	Herod starts to rebuild the Temple in Jerusalem
9	New Temple consecrated (though building continues; completed in AD 63)

Already we glimpse the same pattern in the chronology above. The victory over the foreign power, the recapture of the holy city – Herod the Great was starting down a familiar track. True, he needed Roman backing to gain and maintain power, but he was good at fancy political footwork and got the authorization he wanted. This launched him on a great career of public building works, which is why tourists see so many signs of him to this day. He was constantly drumming up support from Jewish communities around the world. And, at the heart of the whole project, he began to rebuild the Temple itself. Now, at last, it would regain the glory it had had in the days of Solomon, a thousand years before! And now, at last, this would legitimate Herod and his family as the true kings of the Jews. Not merely Roman puppets, but the real thing.

Herod the Great had no family tree to back up this claim. He wasn't descended from David. He wasn't even fully Jewish, being half Idumaean. But he married into the (then) royal family, taking as one of his many wives Mariamne, a princess from the Hasmonean house. And he maintained his rule – no mean feat in itself – for over thirty years. Judah the Hammer managed seven years; Simon the Star, only three.

Herod's career, which began brilliantly, gradually went into decline. Our sources tell a sad but typical tale of a man who, having gained absolute power, used it increasingly not to make life better for his subjects, but to make life safer for himself. He killed several members of his own family, including his beloved Mariamne, on suspicion of plotting against him. On his own deathbed, guessing that nobody would mourn his passing, he gave orders for leading citizens to be killed at the same time, to guarantee weeping and wailing at his funeral. Fortunately, the order was not carried out.

Herod the Great is important for our story not just because he provides a backdrop to the life of Jesus, but because he shows, admittedly in an almost caricatured fashion, what it might have meant for someone at the time to be 'king of the Jews'. It meant victory; it meant Temple; it meant establishing the Jewish people in peace and prosperity. Herod tried to set his sails by the great high-pressure system of ancient Jewish narrative, while cleverly trimming them so as to avoid the impact of the gale blowing increasingly from Rome. However much his aspirations had shrunk, by the time of his death, to a thin, shrivelled little parody of his original hopes, we can still see in Herod a glimpse of the story that might make sense of it all, the story that stretched back to the ancient scriptures and on into a future that, to the eye of faith and hope, might yet produce the true king who would succeed where others had failed.

Simon bar-Giora

The other failed king was Simon bar-Giora. He appeared at yet another time of social and political chaos, near the start of the great revolt against Roman rule that lasted from AD 66 to 70 and that ended with total catastrophe and the Temple's destruction. There were plenty of other would-be leaders, prophets and so on at the time, some emerging from families long associated with anti-Roman activity. But it was Simon who was ruling Jerusalem as the Romans closed in.

Simon gained popular support, and then actual power, by announcing freedom for slaves. That was always a good move, not only in itself, but because the ancient memory of being set free from slavery in Egypt has always been central to Jewish self-understanding. Faced with other warlords and troublemakers, many of the leading men in Jerusalem were happy to give Simon power and to line up behind him. He instituted martial law, executing and imprisoning people he suspected might be traitors. Anyone who has tried to make sense of what was going on in Jerusalem in those years knows that it was a highly confusing period, and if that is so for us as historians, it must have been even more so for the people there at the time. Simon's agenda, clearly, would have been the usual one: defeat the enemy, cleanse the Temple and establish his own kingdom.

But Simon did none of these things. Instead, as the Romans destroyed the Temple and defeat became inevitable, he surrendered in spectacular fashion. He dressed himself in white, with a purple cloak on top, and emerged from hiding all of a sudden on the Temple Mount. Whether he was hoping to frighten people and make his escape or whether he was just putting on a final show of bravado, we cannot tell. He was taken in chains to Titus, the victorious general, and then shipped off to Rome along with thousands of other captives and boatloads of booty, which you can still see in carved pictures on the Arch of Titus, at the top of the Forum in Rome. According to the Roman custom, Titus was given a 'triumph', a spectacular procession through the streets of Rome, demonstrating to the citizens (in the days before television and photography could prove it by other methods) how great a victory he had won. The prisoners were led behind him, a bedraggled and sorry crew; and last of all came Simon. He was whipped as he walked along, until he arrived at the prison where the death sentence was carried out. Once again, the gale overcame the high-pressure system. Titus, and all Rome with him, celebrated this victory over the 'king of the Jews'. Once again, the Jewish people, crushed and dismayed, wondered what had happened to the divine hurricane that was supposed to come to their aid.

It takes little imagination to see that Jesus of Nazareth, nailed to a Roman cross with the words 'king of the Jews' over his head, must have been seen by many in exactly the same way as Simon bar-Giora. Here is a would-be rebel king, and this is what the Romans always do to such people. Subsequent Jewish tradition came to regard Jesus too as a liar who had deceived God's people, leading them astray with false hopes.

Between two moments

This detour into the history of would-be royal movements in the centuries on either side of Jesus is designed to make two points that will, I hope, clarify various things about his public career. First, there was a well-recognized set of expectations for a 'king of the Jews', with roots extending all the way back to the Exodus. The recitation of expectations has become almost monotonous with repetition; victory over the pagans and cleansing or rebuilding the Temple were high on the list. Second, it was to be expected that any such campaign would have (at least) two key 'moments': first, the time when the flag was raised, the initial proclamation was made and the movement was launched, and then the moment when the final battle was won and the Temple rebuilt. Such movements would expect to live between these two moments, between an initial announcement and a final victory.

Think for a minute about what that means. As soon as the initial announcement had been made, as we saw particularly with Simon the Star, it would have been tantamount to treason to suggest that the kingdom, the new rule of God, was not already present. If the true king is here and people are starting to do what he says, the kingdom has begun! Equally, however, there was a major task still to be performed. The pagans had to be beaten. The Temple had to be rebuilt. Until that had happened, the kingdom would not be complete.

Think even of King David himself, a thousand years before. David was anointed by Samuel quite some time before he was finally enthroned. Was he king during that period? Well, yes, from one point of view. But, from another point of view, no; Saul was still king, and David in consequence had a price on his head. It is not insignificant, as we have seen already, that Jesus at one point likens himself to David at exactly this stage of his career (Mark 2.25–28). Once we learn to think the way Jews of the time thought and indeed take into consideration the real political situation (rather than just a set of religious ideas or beliefs), the idea of a kingdom that is *both* emphatically present *and* emphatically future is not a problem. It is just what we should expect.

So what were Jesus' aims for the future? What was he hoping to achieve? What would be, for him, the equivalent of the battle to be fought and the cleansing or rebuilding of the Temple? To what extent did he share the aspirations of the kings and would-be kings before and after his day?

That is undoubtedly the right question to ask, but answering it is not straightforward. As with everything else Jesus did, it seems that he quite deliberately remodelled first-century Jewish expectations around himself. And, not least, around his own fresh reading of Israel's scriptures. What we shall then find is that, as with some of those other 'royal' movements, though with highly significant variations of his own, he believed *both* that God's kingdom was already a present reality *and* that it would be settled by a great event that would shortly happen.

To see how all this works in practice, we need to explore some more themes. All four of the fascinating characters we have looked at in this chapter had two major parts to their kingdom-agenda: the battle(s) they fought or intended to fight, and the Temple they cleansed, rebuilt, or wanted to rebuild and defend. What did Jesus do with those great interlocking themes of the battle and the victory, on the one hand, and the building or cleansing of the Temple, of the place of God's presence, on the other?

10

Battle and Temple

First, the battle. Whether we look at the Sermon on the Mount in Matthew 5—7 or the Nazareth Manifesto in Luke 4; whether we look at the strange language about 'binding the strong man' in Matthew 12 or the even stranger language about the 'coming of the son of man'; wherever we look, it appears that Jesus was aware of a great battle in which he was already involved and that would, before too long, reach some kind of climax.

This was not, it seems, the battle that his contemporaries, including his own followers, expected him to fight. It wasn't even the same *sort* of battle – though Jesus used the language of battle to describe it. Indeed, as the Sermon on the Mount seems to indicate, fighting itself, in the normal physical sense, was precisely what he was not going to do. There was a different kind of battle in the offing, a battle that had already begun. In this battle, it was by no means as clear as those around Jesus would have liked who was on which side, or indeed whether 'sides' was the right way to look at things. The battle in question was a different sort of thing, because it had a different sort of enemy.

The Bible is never very precise about the identity of the figure known as 'the satan'. The Hebrew word means 'the accuser', and at times the satan seems to be a member of YHWH's heavenly council, with special responsibility as director of prosecutions (1 Chronicles 21.1; Job 1—2; Zechariah 3.1–2). However, the term becomes identified variously with the serpent of the Garden of Eden (Genesis 3.1–15) and with the rebellious daystar cast out of heaven (Isaiah 14.12–13) and was seen by many Jews as the quasi-personal source of evil standing behind both human wickedness and large-scale injustice, sometimes operating through semi-independent 'demons'. By Jesus' time various words were used to denote this figure, including Beelzebul/b (lit., 'Lord of the Flies') and simply 'the evil one'; Jesus warned his followers against the deceits this figure could perpetrate. His opponents accused him of being in league with the satan, but the early Christians believed that Jesus in fact defeated it in his own struggles with temptation (Matthew 4; Luke 4), his exorcisms of demons, and his death (1 Corinthians 2.8; Colossians 2.15). Final victory over this ultimate enemy is thus assured (Revelation 20), though the struggle can still be fierce for Christians (Ephesians 6.10–20).

Battling the satan

The battle Jesus was fighting was against the satan. Whatever we think of this theme, it was clearly centrally important for all the gospel writers, and we have every reason to suppose it was central for Jesus as well:

He was in the desert for forty days, and the satan tested him there.
(Mark 1.13)

'What's this? New teaching – with real authority! He even tells the unclean spirits what to do, and they do it!' (Mark 1.27)

He didn't allow the demons to speak, because they knew him.
(Mark 1.34)

Whenever the unclean spirits saw him, they fell down in front of him and yelled out, 'You are the son of God!' He gave them strict orders not to reveal his identity. (Mark 3.11–12)

Experts . . . were saying, 'He is possessed by Beelzebul!'
Jesus . . . spoke to them. 'How can the Accuser cast out the Accuser? If a kingdom splits into two factions, it can't last . . . But remember: no one can get into a strong man's house and steal his property unless first they tie up the strong man; then they can plunder his house.'
(Mark 3.22–27)

They were suddenly confronted by a man with an unclean spirit . . . Jesus was saying to him, 'Unclean spirit, come out of him!'
'What's your name?' Jesus asked him.
'Legion,' he replied. 'That's my name – there are lots of us!' . . .
The unclean spirits came out and went into the [herd of] pigs. The herd rushed down the steep slope into the sea – about two thousand of them! – and were drowned. (Mark 5.2b, 7, 9, 13b)

'I saw the satan fall like lightning from heaven.'   (Luke 10.18)

'And isn't it right that this daughter of Abraham, tied up by the satan for these eighteen years, should be untied from her chains on the sabbath day?'   (Luke 13.16)

'The satan demanded to have you [Peter]. He wanted to shake you into bits like wheat.'   (Luke 22.31)

The devil had already put the idea of betraying him into the heart of Judas, son of Simon Iscariot . . . After the bread, the satan entered into him.   (John 13.2, 27)

Many modern writers, understandably, have tried to marginalize this theme, but we can't expect to push aside such a central part of the tradition and make serious progress. It is, of course, difficult for most people in the modern Western world to know what to make of it at all; that's one of the points on which the strong wind of modern scepticism has done its work well, and the shrill retort from 'traditionalists', insisting on seeing everything in terms of 'supernatural' issues, hardly helps either. As C. S. Lewis points out in the introduction to his famous *Screwtape Letters*, the modern world divides into those who are obsessed with demonic powers and those who mock them as outdated rubbish. Neither approach, Lewis insists, does justice to the reality. I'm with Lewis on this. Despite the caricatures, the obsessions and the sheer muddle that people often get themselves into on this subject, there is such a thing as a dark force that seems to take over people, movements and sometimes whole countries, a force or (as it sometimes seems) a set of forces that can make people do things they would never normally do.

You might have thought the history of the twentieth century would provide plenty of examples of this, but many still choose to resist the conclusion – despite the increasing use in public life of the language of 'force' (economic 'forces', political 'forces', peer 'pressure', and so on). In recent scholarship, Walter Wink in particular has offered a sharp and compelling analysis of 'the powers' and the way they function in today's world as much as in yesterday's. The psychotherapist Scott Peck wrote a book, *People of the Lie*, about the small but significant number of his clients who had, it seemed, bought so deeply into unreality that they appeared to have been taken over by dark forces beyond themselves. The post-Enlightenment idea that such language reeks of medieval superstition is too simplistic by half. Granted the split-level world of Enlightenment thought, we should perhaps expect that we wouldn't have very good language for talking about a reality that is neither divine nor reducible to terms of the ordinary material world. But this should not stop us trying to come to grips with the reality in question.

Without the perspective that sees evil as a dark force that stands *behind* human reality, the issue of 'good' and 'bad' in our world is easy to decipher. It is fatally easy, and I mean fatally easy, to typecast 'people like us' as basically good and 'people like them' as basically evil. This is a danger we in our day should be aware of, after the disastrous attempts by some Western leaders to speak about an 'axis of evil' and then to go to war to obliterate it. We turn ourselves into angels and 'the other lot' into demons; we 'demonize' our opponents. This is a convenient tool for avoiding having to think, but it is disastrous for both our thinking and our behaviour.

But when you take seriously the existence and malevolence of non-human forces that are capable of using 'us' as well as 'them' in the service of evil, the focus shifts. As the hazy and shadowy realities come into view, what we thought was clear and straightforward becomes blurred. Life becomes more complex, but arguably more realistic. The traditional lines of friend and foe are not so easy to draw. You can no longer assume that 'that lot' are simply agents of the devil and 'this lot' – us and our friends – are automatically on God's side. If there is an enemy at work, it is a subtle, cunning enemy, much too clever to allow itself to be identified simply with one person, one group or one nation. Only twice in the gospel story does Jesus address 'the satan' directly by that title: once when rebuking him in the temptation narrative (Matthew 4.10), and again when he is rebuking his closest associate (Mark 8.33) for resisting God's strange plan. The line between good and evil is clear at the level of God, on the one hand, and the satan, on the other. It is much, much less clear as it passes through human beings, individually and collectively.

This is precisely the kind of redefinition that was going on in Jesus' Nazareth Manifesto. Traditional enemies were suddenly brought, at least in principle, within the reach of the blessing of God's great jubilee. And traditional friends – those who might have thought that they were automatically on the right side – had to be looked at again. Perhaps one can no longer simply identify 'our people' as on the side of the angels and 'those people' as agents of the satan. That's why Jesus was run out of town and nearly killed. He had suggested that foes could become friends and by implication was warning that the 'good people' – Israel as the people of God – might become enemies. Ironically, his own townsfolk proceeded to prove the point by their reaction.

Later, as we just noticed, he even warned his closest supporter, Simon Peter, of precisely this, calling him 'Satan' when he tried to dissuade him from his vocation to suffer and die (Mark 8.33) and warning him, later again, that the satan had wanted to work him over violently (Luke 22.31). Jesus sees the satan at work among his hearers, snatching away the word of the kingdom, so that it won't take root (Mark 4.15), and sowing weeds among the wheat (Matthew 13.39); and again at work in the dehumanizing and deforming ailments that have crippled an old woman (Luke 13.16). He recognizes that one of his own followers is an 'accuser' (John 6.70), and the gospel writers pick up this point, seeing the satan at work in the 'accusing' role of Judas Iscariot (Luke 22.3; John 13.2, 27). Tragically, even the people of God themselves, focused on the Temple in Jerusalem, are to be seen now as children of the devil (John 8.44).

All this comes to a crunch in one particular confrontation:

> They brought to Jesus a man who was possessed by a demon that made him unable to see or speak. Jesus healed him, so that the sick man was able to talk and see. All the crowds were astonished.
>
> 'He can't be David's Son, can he?' they said.
>
> The Pharisees heard this.
>
> 'This fellow can only cast out demons', they said, 'because he's in league with Beelzebul, the prince of demons!'
>
> Jesus knew their thoughts.
>
> 'Suppose a kingdom is split down the middle,' he said to them. 'It'll go to rack and ruin! If a city or a household is split down the middle, it's doomed! And if the satan drives out the satan, he's split down the middle – so how can his kingdom stay standing?

'What's more, if I cast out demons by Beelzebul, whose power are your people in league with when they cast them out? Yes, they'll tell you what's what! But if I'm casting out demons because I'm in league with God's spirit – well, then, God's kingdom has arrived on your doorstep!

'Look at it like this. Suppose you want to break into a strong man's house and steal his belongings. How are you going to do that unless you first tie up the strong man? Then you can plunder his house to your heart's content. If you're not with me, you're against me. Unless you're gathering the flock with me, you're scattering it.

'So let me tell you this: people will be forgiven for every sin and blasphemy; but blasphemy against the spirit will not be forgiven. If anyone speaks a word against the son of man, it will be forgiven. But if anyone speaks a word against the holy spirit, it won't be forgiven, either in the present age or in the age to come.' (Matthew 12.22–32)

It would be easy for us, anxious as we are to keep up our profile as sophisticated children of the Enlightenment, to dismiss all this as standard first-century religious polemic. Certainly that is one element in the package, as we can see when Jesus' own accusers (note the irony) accuse him of being in league with the Accuser. Jesus' answer shows his own remarkable perspective on what's going on, on what is really involved when God's kingdom comes on earth as in heaven. It's a clash of kingdoms: the satan has his kingdom, God has his, and sooner or later the battle between them will be joined. It is, once again, fatally easy to misunderstand, to draw the lines wrong, to see 'our present system' as automatically good, so that anyone who disturbs it – as Jesus was disturbing the system of the scribes and Pharisees – must be 'satanic', must be from the dark side. That road leads to the 'war of the sons of light against the sons of darkness', as at Qumran: the overbright light of an overrealized eschatology, enabling 'us' to see ourselves as 'children of light', casting a surreal, overdramatized shadow over 'them', the 'children of darkness'.

Jesus will have none of it. First, it makes no sense to imagine the satan working against himself. Jesus is casting out demons, but why would the satan want to do that, destroying his own power base? Second, there are only two options at this point: if it isn't the power of the satan that Jesus is drawing on to do what he's doing, he must be doing it through the power of God. But that means that God's kingdom, God's sovereign and saving rule, really is breaking in, on earth as in heaven. Third, however, the victories Jesus is winning here and now, up close and personal, are signs that *an initial victory has already been won*. The 'strong man' has already been 'tied up', which is why Jesus can now plunder his house (Matthew 12.29; Luke 11.21–22). Jesus declares that he has already seen the satan falling like lightning from heaven (Luke 10.18). These strands within Jesus' teaching are all over the place. If we want to understand what he thought he was up to, we have to take them seriously and see the role they play in the whole picture.

But if there had been an earlier 'victory', when did it take place? Matthew, Mark and Luke all supply the answer: at the beginning of Jesus' public career, during his forty-day fast in the desert, when the satan tried to distract him, to persuade him to grasp the right goal by the wrong means, and so to bring him over to his side (Matthew 4.1–11; Mark 1.12–13; Luke 4.1–13). Jesus won that battle, which was why he could then announce that God's kingdom was now beginning to happen. But the battle clearly isn't over yet. The great initial victory, won in Jesus' own intense private struggle, has created a space in which God's kingdom can now make inroads, much as the early victory of Judah the Hammer created space for the Temple to be cleansed, the early victory of the rebels in AD 66 for a short-lived sense of triumph, and the initial victories of Simon the Star for a few brief moments of freedom and Jewish self-rule. But this same kingdom, God's kingdom, can only be finally established through the final battle. The enemy troops will mass again, close in, and do their worst to repair the earlier damage.

What is the final battle that Jesus envisages? It is no longer, clearly, a military battle against Rome or even a revolt against Herod and the chief priests, an attempt (perhaps) to take over the Temple or Jerusalem itself. It is no longer the traditional freedom fight of pious Jews fed up with pagan rule – and with corrupt local rulers colluding with that rule, and so becoming no better than pagans themselves. It goes much deeper. It is the battle against the satan himself. And, though the satan no doubt uses Rome, uses Herod, uses even the chief priests themselves, Jesus keeps his eye on the fact that the satan is not identified with any of these, and that to make such an identification is already to give up, and so to lose the real battle.

'Your moment has come,' he said to the chief priests, the officers of the Temple police, and the elders who had come out to arrest him. 'Your moment has come at last, and so has the power of darkness' (Luke 22.53). The darkness, it seems, had to be allowed to do its worst in order to be defeated. And the dark powers that put Jesus on the cross continued to the last with their mocking questions: 'Save yourself, if you're God's son! Come down from the cross!' (Matthew 27.40), echoing the same voice in the desert, 'If you really are God's son, tell these stones to become bread!' (Matthew 4.3). Somehow it appears that Jesus' battle with the satan, which was the battle for God's kingdom to be established on earth as in heaven, reached its climax in his death. This is a strange, dark and powerful theme to which we shall return. For the moment the point is clear: Jesus is indeed fighting what he takes to be the battle against the real enemies of the people of God, but it is not the battle his followers or the wider group of onlookers were expecting him to fight. Jesus has redefined the royal task around his own vision of where the real problem lies. And he has thereby redefined his own vocation, which he takes to be the true vocation of Israel's king: to fight and win the key battle, the battle that will set his people free and establish God's sovereign and saving rule, through his own suffering and death.

Cleansing the Temple

The same is true when we consider the other great 'royal' aspiration: to cleanse or rebuild the Temple. We regularly refer to the striking action Jesus performed in the Temple as his 'cleansing of the Temple'. We don't, perhaps, always realize that any such action was staking an implicitly royal claim: it was kings, real or aspiring, who had authority over the Temple. It was Israel's kings or would-be kings who planned it (David), built it (Solomon), cleansed it (Hezekiah, Josiah, Judah the Hammer), rebuilt it (Zerubbabel, Herod the Great), and hoped to defend it (Simon bar-Giora) or to rebuild it once more (Simon the Star). In each case, of course, building the Temple was associated with the larger story of victory over enemies, liberation for the people, and so on. It was the Exodus narrative, in other words, the Passover narrative, all over again; and we shouldn't forget that a key element in the Passover narrative was always the presence of Israel's God himself with his people, in the pillar of cloud and fire and then, apparently more permanently, in the tabernacle. Passover implies Presence.

Jesus, as we have seen, chose the Passover season as the moment to ride into Jerusalem on a donkey, deliberately awakening in the onlookers' minds the powerful prophecy of Zechariah 9.9–11:

> Rejoice greatly, O daughter Zion!
>> Shout aloud, O daughter Jerusalem!
> Lo, your king comes to you;
>> triumphant and victorious is he,
> humble and riding on a donkey,
>> on a colt, the foal of a donkey.
> He will cut off the chariot from Ephraim
>> and the warhorse from Jerusalem;
> and the battle-bow shall be cut off,
>> and he shall command peace to the nations;
> his dominion shall be from sea to sea,
>> and from the River to the ends of the earth.
> As for you also, because of the blood of my covenant with you,
>> I will set your prisoners free from the waterless pit.

So many themes come rushing together at this point, both in Zechariah itself (which draws on images from many earlier texts) and in Jesus' own dramatic acting out of the prophecy. Imagine an experienced naval commander seeing a ship approaching. If it were me, I would have to think about several things which would present themselves, to my inexperienced eye, as completely separate issues: the ship's speed and size, its type and make, its nationality and fire power, and the likely threat it might pose. Only then might I be able to think through what was going on and take appropriate action. The experienced commander, however, takes all this in at a single glance and makes decisions instantly.

In the same way, as we read the stories of Jesus, especially the stories of his final days, it takes us quite an effort to assemble in our minds the various themes that came together at that moment and to think of them as a single, coherent whole. But those who saw Jesus ride into Jerusalem that day, as the city prepared for Passover, were in the position of the experienced commander. Jesus' action, the prophecy it evoked, the multiple themes of Passover (victory over the tyrant, freeing of slaves, sacrifice, the presence of God) would without difficulty form a single, coherent, though deeply challenging whole. What we, unschooled in their worldview, their controlling narrative, are bound (at least to begin with) to see as separate elements would have appeared to people in Jerusalem at the time as a single rich, dense event. They would have taken it in at a glance, meanings and all.

So what was its 'meaning'? For a start, this was an emphatically royal action, a claim to be Israel's true king. But Zechariah's prophecy also makes it clear that this king will come as a man of *peace*. As we have just seen, Jesus redefined the great coming battle, so that it would no longer be a military battle of 'us' against 'them', of the forces of light fighting with literal weapons against the forces of darkness. Nevertheless, the arrival of this peaceable king will mean the establishment of his worldwide rule; as in the Psalms and Isaiah, Israel's true king will be the king of the whole world, 'from sea to sea'. The result will be the establishment of God's covenant with his people, a covenant sealed in blood and resulting (think once more of Egypt, of the Exodus, of Passover) in prisoners being set free. And, as often in Zechariah and in other prophecies of the time, if this great event were to happen, it could only mean that Israel's God was at last coming back. His glorious Presence was once again to appear. All this, I suggest, Jesus' followers and the watching people of Jerusalem would have taken in right away, with no particular mental effort. Their minds were already in tune with the various elements and with the controlling drama within which they made sense. And if that's what it all meant for them, it can hardly have meant any less for Jesus himself.

So when Jesus came into the Temple and performed another dramatic action, driving out the money changers and the dealers selling animals for sacrifice, this too would have been seen within a web of prophetic allusion and symbolism. Jeremiah, after all, had famously smashed a pot at the same place (Jeremiah 19), symbolizing the coming judgment. But what was Jesus intending to communicate? What did he mean by his action?

Like many others, I have become convinced that Jesus' dramatic action was a way of declaring that the Temple was under God's judgment and would, before too long, be destroyed for ever. That is certainly how the gospel writers saw it. Matthew, Mark and Luke follow the incident with a string of discussions that all turn on the question of whether Jesus has the right to do this kind of thing, what he means by it, what sort of a revolution he has in mind, and so on, all of which lead readers into the long discourse in which Jesus solemnly declares that the Temple is to be destroyed within a generation (Matthew 24; Mark 13; Luke 21). John, who describes Jesus' action in the Temple much earlier in his gospel, has Jesus saying something cryptic about the Temple being destroyed and then rebuilt in three days – a saying that then turns up in the other gospels, in garbled form, when Jesus is on trial before the chief priests (John 2.19; Matthew 26.61; 27.40).

It looks as though everyone knew that Jesus was in some sense or other pronouncing God's judgment on the Temple itself – and, by implication, on the present regime that was running it. Jesus would not have been the only first-century Jew to express such warnings. After all, when Jesus stopped the changing of money (you were only allowed to use the official Temple coinage) and the selling of sacrificial animals, he was effectively stopping the sacrificial system itself, for a brief but symbolic moment. And if you stop the regular flow of sacrifices, you bring the Temple to a shuddering halt. It no longer has a purpose. And if you do that, within the setting of first-century Judaism, it can only be because you think Israel's God is now acting in a new way. If the Temple isn't the centre of everything, the place where heaven and earth meet, the building in which God and his people come together, then what is?

This is the point at which we must again take a deep breath and plunge into the deep and (to us) dark waters of the way in which most first-century Jews saw the world. The often noted 'peril of modernizing Jesus' is precisely that. Faced with Jesus' dramatic sayings and actions, we assume that they meant then what they would mean within our world. We should resist this assumption. But the only way forward is then to think about very, very basic elements of how people see reality.

This means that we must pause and ask some extremely foundational questions. We have been looking at the *what* question – what Jesus did, his characteristic actions, and the way he spoke about them. We are still postponing the question of *why* – why he did it, and what it all meant. We are closing in on the *who* question – who Jesus thought he was. But before we can get any farther with these, we need to think about three other great questions: *where, when* and *how*. In other words, we need to think about space, time and matter. How, at this deep level, did first-century Jews, Jesus included, think about these vital but often hidden questions?

11

Space, time and matter

The one thing we can be sure of is that inhabitants of first-century Palestine didn't think of space, time and matter in quite the way that we do. If we're going to understand Jesus, it's vital to grasp the difference between his world and ours.

Most people in the Western world today think of geography as simply places on a map. The sense of 'sacred space' or even a sense of 'place' is gone; territory is just property to be developed, exploited, bought and sold. We are brought up short when confronted with the worldviews of different groups (say, the indigenous populations of America or Australia) who persist in regarding 'their land' as 'special' in a way that transcends mere ownership and cultural memory.

In the same way, we have in my generation watched the erosion of special time. When I was growing up, Sunday was certainly special, and certain other days such as Good Friday were too. But now virtually all days are alike. Many people still work from Monday to Friday, but many more find their working week reaches its climax on Saturday and Sunday. The same is true for seasons and years. Few people now know when it's Advent or Lent, and even those who do know don't do much about them. And apart from the millennium, one year is pretty much like another one too (and even with the millennium we couldn't agree which year it was, 2000 or 2001).

As for 'matter', the physical stuff of which we and the world are made – well, it's just that to most people: stuff. If we can use it or make something out of it, fine. If we can't, it has no point. The thought that certain bits of 'matter' – certain lumps of 'stuff' – might be filled with new meaning and identity, might be the carriers of energy and meaning from elsewhere – well, for most people today that's just an old bit of superstitious nonsense.

But if we come to the stories about Jesus with this modern Western view of space, time and matter, we will never understand what he was about. We need to take a deep breath and explore the way in which people in his world would have thought about these three vital elements.

Redefining where God dwells

Space! We have already seen that for many centuries mapmakers put Jerusalem at the middle of the earth. That corresponds to what most Jews in the first century believed about the city, and particularly about the Temple. It was the heart of everything, the holiest spot on earth. It was the focal point of the holy land. Its decoration symbolized the larger creation, the world we read about in Genesis 1. It wasn't, as sacred buildings have been in some other traditions, a retreat from the world. It was a bridgehead *into* the world. It was the sign that the creator God was claiming the whole world, claiming it back for himself, establishing his domain in the middle of it.

It was, in particular, the place where God himself had promised to come and live. This was where God's glory, his tabernacling presence, his Shekinah, had come to rest. That's what the Bible had said, and some fortunate, though frightened, individuals had glimpsed it and lived to tell the tale. But God lived, by definition, in heaven. Nobody, however, supposed that God lived most of the time in heaven, a long way away, and then, as though for an occasional holiday or royal visitation, went to live in the Temple in Jerusalem instead. Somehow, in a way most modern people find extraordinary to the point of being almost unbelievable, the Temple was not only the centre of the world. *It was the place where heaven and earth met.* This isn't, then, just a way of saying, 'Well, the Jews were very attached to their land and their capital city.' It was the vital expression of a worldview in which 'heaven' and 'earth' are not far apart, as most people today assume, but actually overlap and interlock, as shown in the diagram on page 131.

And Jesus, as we have already seen, had been going about saying that this God, Israel's God, was right now becoming king, was taking charge, was establishing his long-awaited saving and healing rule on earth as in heaven. Heaven and earth were being joined up – but no longer in the Temple in Jerusalem. The joining place was visible where the healings were taking place, where the party was going on (remember

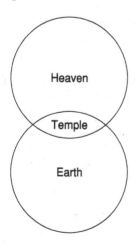

the angels celebrating in heaven and people joining in on earth?), where forgiveness was happening. In other words, the joining place, the overlapping circle, was taking place *where Jesus was and in what he was doing.* Jesus was, as it were, a walking Temple. A living, breathing place-where-Israel's-God-was-living.

As many people will see at once, this is the very heart of what later theologians would call the doctrine of the incarnation. But it looks quite different from how many people imagine that doctrine to work. Judaism already had a massive 'incarnational' symbol, the Temple. Jesus was behaving as if he *were* the Temple, in person. He was talking about Israel's God taking charge. And he was doing things that put that God-in-chargeness into practice. It all starts to make sense. In particular, it answers the old criticism that 'Jesus talked about God, but the church talked about Jesus' – as though Jesus would have been shocked to have his pure, God-centred message corrupted in that way. This sneer fails to take account of the fact that, yes, Jesus talked about God, but he talked about God *precisely in order to explain the things that he himself was doing.*

So we shouldn't be surprised at Jesus' action in the Temple. The Temple had, as it were, been a great signpost pointing forward to another reality that had lain unnoticed for generations, like the vital clue in a detective story that is only recognized as such in the final chapter. Remember the promise to David – that God would build him a 'house', a family, founded on the son of David who would be the son of God? David had wanted to build a house for God, and God had replied that *he* would build *David* a 'house'. David's coming son is the ultimate reality; the Temple in Jerusalem is the advance signpost *to* that reality. Now that the reality is here, the signpost isn't needed any more.

But it isn't just that the signpost had become redundant with the arrival of the reality. The Temple, as many other first-century Jews recognized, was in the wrong hands and had come to symbolize the wrong things. It was, for a start, a place that for many Jews stank of commercial oppression. This is an additional rather obvious overtone of Jesus' action in driving out the money changers and the traders. But it gets worse. The Temple was the centre of the banking system. It was where the records of debts were kept; the first thing the rebels did when they took over the Temple in the great revolt was to burn those records. That tells you quite a lot about how people saw the Temple. I had a letter today from the tax man, politely asking me for my annual contribution to government finances. If I don't answer it, the next one won't be so polite. Now imagine letters and records building up, detailing all the debts of ordinary people in Jerusalem, while the chief priests, who ran the system, lived in their fine mansions in the nice part of town and went about in their smart clothes. If you were an ordinary, hard-working resident of Jerusalem or the surrounding area, what would you think of the building that was supposed to be God's house, but that stored the records of your debts, while the rich rulers who performed the religious rituals marched by with their noses in the air on their way to put on their splendid vestments and chant their elaborate prayers? Yes, that's exactly how many people saw the Temple.

It gets worse again. The Temple had come to symbolize the nationalist movement that had led many Jews to revolt against pagan oppression in the past and would lead them to do so once more. As we see graphically throughout the history of Israel, and not least in the first century, the Temple was the sign that Israel's God, the world's creator, was with his people and would defend them against all comers. Battle and Temple had gone together for a thousand years, from David himself through to Judah the Hammer to Simon the Star. And Jesus had come as the Prince of Peace. 'If only you'd known,' he sobbed out through his tears, 'on this day – even you! – what peace meant. But now it's hidden, and you can't see it.' Enemies will come, he said. 'They won't leave one single stone on another, because you didn't know the moment when God was visiting you' (Luke 19.42–44).

Israel's God was coming back at last, and they couldn't see it. Why not? Because they were looking in entirely the wrong direction. The Temple, and the city of which the Temple was the focal point, had come to symbolize violent national revolution. Instead of being the light of the world, the city on the hill that should let its light shine out to the nations, it was determined to keep the light for itself. The Temple was not just redundant; not just a place of economic oppression. It had become a symbol of Israel's violent ambition, a sign that Israel's ancient vocation had been turned inside out. In Luke's gospel, the scene of Jesus arriving in Jerusalem balances the scene near the start in which Jesus goes to Nazareth and risks his neck by declaring God's blessing on the pagan nations. Then it was the synagogue; now it's the Temple. It also balances the scene even earlier, when the twelve-year-old Jesus stays back in Jerusalem, to his parents' alarm, at the end of a Passover celebration – and is finally discovered sitting in the Temple with the teachers, listening to them, quizzing them in turn, and explaining that he had to be getting involved with his father's work (2.49). Now here he is, back again, involved up to the neck in his father's work, astonishing the Jerusalem authorities for a different reason. This is the climax of his father's work, and that work is now focused on Jesus himself, not the Temple.

If Jesus is acting out a vision – astonishing, risky and, one might say, crazy – in which he is behaving as if he is the Temple, redefining sacred space around himself, something equally strange and risky is taking place in the realm of time.

Time fulfilled

Time! Jews in Jesus' day and Jews in our own day have a very special sense of time. Time is moving forward in a linear fashion, with a beginning, a middle and an end – unlike some other visions of time, in which everything is cyclical, going round and round and constantly returning to the same point. The Jewish view of time is part of the Jewish view of God and creation: God has a purpose for his good creation, a purpose to be worked out in time. Indeed, the Jewish people think of themselves as living within the long story of how that purpose is to be worked out.

But already, in the opening of the Bible, there is another feature. When God made the world, he 'rested' on the seventh day. This doesn't just mean that God took a day off. It means that in the previous six days God was making a world – heaven and earth together – for his own use. Like someone building a home, God finished the job and then went in to take up residence, to enjoy what he had built. Creation was itself a temple, *the* Temple, the heaven-and-earth structure built for God to live in. And the seventh-day 'rest' was therefore a sign pointing forward into successive ages of time, a forward-looking signpost that said that one day, when God's purposes for creation were accomplished, there would be a moment of ultimate completion, a moment when the work would finally be done, and God, with his people, would take his rest, would enjoy what he had accomplished.

One of the few things that ancient pagans knew about the Jewish people was that, from the pagans' point of view, they had a lazy day once a week. From the Jewish point of view, it wasn't laziness; it was the chance to celebrate time in a different mode. The sabbath was the day when human time and God's time met, when the day-to-day succession of tasks and sorrows was set aside and one entered a different sort of time, celebrating the original sabbath and looking forward to the ultimate one. This was the natural moment to celebrate, to worship, to pray, to study God's law. The sabbath was the moment during which one sensed the onward movement of history from its first foundations to its ultimate resolution. If the Temple was the *space* in which God's sphere and the human sphere met, the sabbath was the *time* when God's time and human time coincided. Sabbath was to time what Temple was to space.

This sense of looking forward was heightened by the larger sabbatical scheme in which the seventh year was a year of agricultural rest and the seven-times-seventh year the year of jubilee, the time for slaves to be freed, for debts to be cancelled, for life to get back on track. As we have already seen in this book, the theme of jubilee ties in closely and naturally with the great all-encompassing theme of the Exodus. The jubilee was, as it were, the once-in-a-lifetime 'exodus' that everyone could experience. We don't know whether or to what extent the jubilee as set forth in Leviticus 25 was actually practised in Jesus' day. But it remained in the scriptures as a reminder that God's time was being marked out week by week, seven years by seven years, half century by half century. Matthew hints at all this in his own way, right at the start of his gospel, by arranging Jesus' genealogy in three groups of fourteen generations (that is, six sevens), so that Jesus appears at the start of the sabbath-of-sabbaths moment. And, as we have seen, people in Jesus' day were pondering, calculating and longing for the greatest superjubilee of them all, the 'seventy weeks' (that is, seventy times seven years) of Daniel 9.24. The great sabbath was coming! Soon they would be free!

Now, and only now, do we see what Jesus meant when he said *the time is fulfilled*. That was part of his announcement right at the start of his public career (Mark 1.15). Only this, I believe, will enable us to understand his extraordinary behaviour immediately afterwards. He seems to have gone out of his way to flout the normal sabbath regulations. Most people in the modern church have imagined that this was because the sabbath had become 'legalistic', a kind of observance designed to boost one's sense of moral achievement, and that Jesus had come to sweep all that away in a burst of libertarian, antilegalistic enthusiasm. That, though commonplace, is a trivial misunderstanding. It is too 'modern' by half. Rather, the sabbath was the regular signpost pointing forward to God's promised future, *and Jesus was announcing that the future to which the signpost had been pointing had now arrived in the present*. In his own career. He was doing the 'God's-in-charge' things. He was explaining what *he* was doing by talking about what *God* was doing. The time was fulfilled, and God's kingdom was arriving.

In particular, Jesus came to Nazareth and announced the jubilee. This was the time – the *time!* – when all the sevens, all the sabbaths, would rush together. This was the moment Israel and the world had been waiting for. When you reach your destination, you don't expect to see signposts any more. Nobody needs a signpost saying 'London' in Piccadilly Circus. You don't need the sabbath when the time is fulfilled. It was completely consistent with Jesus' vision of his own vocation that he would do things that said, again and again from one angle after another, that the time had arrived, that the future, the new creation, was already here, and that one no longer needed the sabbath. The sabbath law was not, then, a stupid rule that could now be abolished (though some of the detailed sabbath regulations, as Jesus pointed out, had led to absurd extremes, so that you were allowed to pull a donkey out of a well on the sabbath, but not to heal the sick). It was a signpost whose purpose had now been accomplished. It was a marker of time pointing forward to the time when time would be fulfilled; and that was now happening.

Notice how this theme then ties in with others we have already observed. If the sabbath now has a purpose, it won't be for rest from the work of creation, but rather for celebrating God's victory over the satan: 'And isn't it right', asks Jesus, 'that this daughter of Abraham, tied up by the satan for these eighteen years, should be untied from her chains on the sabbath day?' (Luke 13.16). Victory in the real battle is closely connected with the healings that reveal that God is in charge. 'My father is going on working,' declares Jesus, 'and so am I' (John 5.17). And these things happen, of course, in the moment when the time is fulfilled. If Jesus is a walking, living, breathing Temple, he is also the walking, celebrating, victorious sabbath.

But this means that *the time of Jesus' public career*, taken as a whole, also acquires a special significance. He spoke about this special significance when he insisted that the wedding guests can't fast while the bridegroom is still at the party. Something new is happening; a new time has been launched; different things are now appropriate. Jesus has a sense of a rhythm to his work, a short rhythm in which he will launch God's kingdom, the God's-in-charge project, and complete it in the most shocking and dramatic symbolic act of all. 'Look here,' he says to those who have warned him that Herod wants to kill him, 'I'm casting out demons today and tomorrow, and completing my healings. I'll be finished by the third day. But I have to continue my travels today, tomorrow and the day after that! It couldn't happen that a prophet would perish except in Jerusalem' (Luke 13.32–33).

This follows hard on the heels of some sharp little sayings about God's kingdom. It's like mustard seed, which starts small and grows to a great shrub for the birds to nest in; it's like yeast mixed into dough, transforming the whole lump. And, in a solemn warning that resonates with many similar ones, Jesus warns his hearers that they may one day see Abraham, Isaac, Jacob and all the prophets – and people from east and west, from north and south! – sitting down to eat in the kingdom of God, while they themselves will be thrown out (Luke 13.18–30). The time of Jesus' public career is the time of fulfilment, the time through which God's new creation, his earth-as-in-heaven new reality, is being launched, up close and personal. But this means it is possible to miss the boat, to lose the one chance. That is the warning that goes with the note of fulfilment.

A new creation

The theme of new creation that bubbles up from these stories emerges in our third category: matter. Reality. The physical world in all its complexity and glory. Here today's readers of the New Testament have to take an even deeper breath than before. We have been schooled to believe, as a bedrock principle in our worldview, that the material world is relentlessly and reductively subject to the laws of physics, chemistry and the more specific sciences of astronomy, biology, zoology, botany and the rest. But as with geography (space) and chronology (time), so here also the Jewish worldview begs to differ.

The world of matter, no less than those of space and time, was made by the creator God. It was made not only to display his beauty and power, but also as a vessel for his glory. Again and again the prophets and Psalms hint at what we might conceivably have guessed from the story of creation itself: the material world was made to be filled with God's glory. 'The earth will be filled with the knowledge of the glory of YHWH, as the waters cover the sea' (Habakkuk 2.14). Suppose that isn't just an extravagant way of speaking? Suppose it means what it says?

What prevents us from thinking in these terms, I believe, is the long and often unrecognized triumph of the movement called Deism – a modern version of the ancient philosophy called Epicureanism. As long as we are thinking in that way, with God or the gods a long way away and earth trundling on entirely under its own steam, we will never glimpse that vision. As long as we are still in awe of the great Scottish philosopher David Hume, who declared that miracles don't happen because they can't happen, we will not only find it difficult to *believe* in the ancient Jewish worldview. We will find it difficult even *to understand what it was about.* If we do try to believe it, we will be forced to treat it simply as fantasy, a pretty idea rather than rock-bottom reality. That is the curse of the false either/or that has been wished on scholarship these many years: either robust scepticism or grit-your-teeth conservatism. Back to our first perfect storm. It's time for both of those false reactions to be confronted by first-century reality.

Space, time and now matter. In this last respect too the prophetic visions of the ancient scriptures suddenly acquire new dimensions. Jesus' announcement that God is now in charge, that God is becoming king on earth as in heaven, means that we can glimpse, fitfully and in flashes, something of what this prophetic vision might mean – where Jesus is and what he is doing. We can see *the material world itself* being transformed by the presence and power of Israel's God, the creator.

We see it already, to be sure, in the healing stories. In them the physical matter of someone's body is being transformed by a strange power, which, in one telling scene, Jesus feels going out of him (Mark 5.30). But then, to the astonishment of the first onlookers and the scornful scepticism of Epicureans ancient or modern, we see creation, as it were, under new management. The professional fishermen who caught nothing during the night are overwhelmed with the catch they get when Jesus tells them where to cast the net. Jesus not only heals the sick; he raises the dead. He feeds a hungry crowd with a few loaves and a couple of fish. Something new is happening, and it's happening to the material world itself. He commands the raging storm to be quiet, and it obeys. Then, worse still, he walks on the lake and invites Peter to do it too.

As with the resurrection itself, which forms the climax to this whole sequence, it is no use trying to rationalize these events. Disbelieve them if you will; retain the Epicurean detachment, the belief that if there is a God he (or she, or it) is a long way away and doesn't get involved with this world. But at least see what is being claimed. These 'miracles' make little or no sense within the present world of creation, where matter is finite, humans do not walk on water, and storms do what storms will do, no matter who, Canute-like, tries to tell them not to.

But suppose, just suppose, that the ancient prophetic dream had glimpsed a deeper truth. Suppose there *were* a god like Israel's God. Suppose this God did after all make the world. And suppose he were to claim, at long last, his sovereign rights over that world, not to destroy it (another philosophical mistake) or merely to 'intervene' in it from time to time (a kind of soggy compromise position), but to fill it with his glory, to allow it to enter a new mode in which it would reflect his love, his generosity, his desire to make it over anew. Perhaps these stories are not, after all, the sort of bizarre things that people invent in retrospect to boost the image of the dead hero. Perhaps they are not even evidence of the kind of 'interventionist', miracle-working, 'supernatural' divinity of some 'conservative' speculation. Perhaps they are, instead, the sort of things that might just be characteristic of *the new creation*, of the fulfilled time, of what happens when heaven and earth come together.

Perhaps, after all, the attempts to cut them down to size are themselves part of a different agenda-driven process of invention that yields a world where such things don't happen because they shouldn't, they couldn't. Because if they did, it might mean that a living God really had established his sovereign rule on earth as in heaven and was intending to let this rule grow from a small seed into a large shrub, putting an end to the fantasy of human sovereignty, of being the master of one's own fate and the captain of one's own soul, of humans organizing the world as though they were responsible to nobody but themselves. Perhaps the real challenge of Jesus' transformations within the material world is what they would imply both personally and politically. If they are about God becoming king on earth as in heaven, the chances are he's not going to stop with storms on lakes. There will be bigger fish to catch. And to fry.

At the heart of the story told by Matthew, Mark and Luke – and suffused through the whole narrative of John – we have the most striking example of all:

After six days Jesus took Peter, James, and James's brother John, and led them off up a high mountain by themselves. There he was transformed in front of them. His face shone like the sun, and his clothes became as white as light. Then, astonishingly, Moses and Elijah appeared to them. They were talking with Jesus.

Peter just had to say something. 'Master,' he said to Jesus, 'it's wonderful for us to be here! If you want, I'll make three shelters here – one for you, one for Moses, and one for Elijah!'

While he was still speaking, a bright cloud overshadowed them. Then there came a voice out of the cloud. 'This is my dear son,' said the voice, 'and I'm delighted with him. Pay attention to him.'

When the disciples heard this, they fell on their faces and were scared out of their wits. Jesus came up and touched them.

'Get up,' he said, 'and don't be afraid.'

When they raised their eyes, they saw nobody except Jesus, all by himself.   (Matthew 17.1–8)

Suppose that, after all, the ancient Jewish story of a God making the world, calling a people, meeting with them on a mountain – suppose this story were true. And suppose this God had a purpose for his world and his people that had now reached the moment of fulfilment. Suppose, moreover, that this purpose had taken human form and that the person concerned was going about doing the things that spoke of God's kingdom coming on earth as in heaven, of God's space and human space coming together at last, of God's time and human time meeting and merging for a short, intense period, and of God's new creation and the present creation somehow knocking unexpected sparks off one another. The earth shall be filled, said the prophet, with the knowledge of the glory of the Lord as the waters cover the sea. It is within some such set of suppositions that we might make sense of the strangest moment of all, at the heart of the narrative, when the glory of God comes down not to the Temple in Jerusalem, not to the top of Mount Sinai, but onto and into Jesus himself, shining in splendour, talking with Moses and Elijah, drawing the Law and the Prophets together into the time of fulfilment. The transfiguration, as we call it, is the central moment. This is when what happens to space in the Temple and to time on the sabbath happens, within the life of Jesus, to the material world itself or rather, more specifically, to Jesus' physical body itself.

So what does this story mean? What, if anything, does it 'prove'? Consider another transfiguration story, from a different time and place. Nicholas Motovilov (1809–32) visited Seraphim of Sarov (1754–1833), a well-known saintly hermit, and asked him how one could know that the Spirit of God was really present. It was a cloudy day, and they were sitting on tree stumps in the woods. He describes what followed:

> Then Father Seraphim gripped me firmly by the shoulders and said: 'My friend, both of us, at this moment, are in the Holy Spirit, you and I. Why won't you look at me?'
>
> 'I can't look at you, Father, because the light flashing from your eyes and face is brighter than the sun and I'm dazzled!'
>
> 'Don't be afraid, friend of God, you yourself are shining just like I am; you too are now in the fullness of the grace of the Holy Spirit, otherwise you wouldn't be able to see me as you do.'
>
> Then I looked at the holy man and was panic-stricken. Picture, in the sun's orb, in the most dazzling brightness of its noon-day shining, the face of a man who is talking to you. You see his lips moving, the expression in his eyes, you hear his voice, you feel his arms round your shoulders, and yet you see neither his arms, nor his body, nor his face, you lose all sense of yourself, you can see only the blinding light which spreads everywhere, lighting up the layer of snow covering the glade, and igniting the flakes that are falling on us both like white powder.
>
> 'What do you feel?' asked Father Seraphim.
>
> 'An amazing well-being!' I replied . . .
>
> 'I feel a great calm in my soul, a peace which no words can express . . . A strange, unknown delight . . . An amazing happiness . . . I'm amazingly warm . . . There's no scent in all the world like this one!'
>
> 'I know,' said Father Seraphim, smiling. 'This is as it should be, for divine grace comes to live in our hearts, within us.'[1]

One can, of course, doubt stories like this as well, but there are enough of them to suggest that we should rather keep an open mind. But if this suggests that we should be wary of dismissing them out of hand, it is also a reminder that the transfiguration of Jesus is not, as it stands, a 'proof' of his 'divinity'. Moses and Elijah were 'transfigured' too. So, in this nineteenth-century story, were the Russian mystic and his disciple.

What the story of Jesus on the mountain demonstrates, for those with eyes to see or ears to hear, is that, just as Jesus seems to be the place where God's world and ours meet, where God's time and ours meet, so he is also the place where, so to speak, God's matter – God's new creation – intersects with ours. As with everything else in the gospel narrative, the moment is extraordinary, but soon over. It forms part of a new set of signposts, Jesus-shaped signposts, indicating what is to come: a whole new creation, starting with Jesus himself as the seed that is sown in the earth and then rises to become the beginning of that new world. Something similar seems to have been going on, as we shall see later, in the Upper Room on the night when Jesus was betrayed.

God's space and ours, God's time and ours, God's matter and ours. These three dimensions of the story of Jesus demonstrate the complete inadequacy of three ways of looking at Jesus that, however popular they have been, must be set aside at this point before we can proceed with yet more dimensions of this most extraordinary of stories.

A new kind of revolution

First, it will not do to suppose that Jesus came to teach people 'how to get to heaven'. That view has been immensely popular in Western Christianity for many generations, but it simply won't do. The whole point of Jesus' public career was not to tell people that God was in heaven and that, at death, they could leave 'earth' behind and go to be with him there. It was to tell them that God was now taking charge, right here on 'earth'; that they should pray for this to happen; that they should recognize, in his own work, the signs that it was happening indeed; and that when he completed his work, it would become reality.

In particular, we must be clear what is and isn't meant when Jesus, in Matthew's gospel, speaks about the 'kingdom of heaven'. Many have wrongly assumed that he was referring to a 'kingdom' in the sense of a place called 'heaven' – in other words, a heavenly realm to which people might aspire to go once their time on 'earth' was over. That is simply not what the phrase meant in the first century – though, sadly, it doesn't seem to have taken very long within the early church for the misunderstanding to creep in, doubtless because within a century or two the original Jewish meanings of Jesus' words were being forgotten. Within Jesus' world, the word 'heaven' could be a reverent way of saying 'God'; and in any case, part of the point of 'heaven' is that it wasn't detached, wasn't a long way off, but was always the place from which 'earth' was to be run. When, in the book of Daniel, people speak about 'the God of heaven', the point is that this God is in charge on earth, not that he's a long way away and unconcerned about it. 'The God of heaven' is precisely the one who organizes things on earth (Daniel 2.37) and will eventually set up his own kingdom there (2.44; see also 4.37; 5.23).

Second, was Jesus, then, mounting some kind of quasi-military revolution? Some have thought so. Many, fed up with the way contemporary churches have colluded with corrupt and wicked establishments, have been eager to find in Jesus a different dream, a dream that perches uncomfortably halfway between the Sermon on the Mount and the sermons of Karl Marx. Attempts have then been made to ward off this proposal by insisting that Jesus' message was 'spiritual' rather than 'political'. This has been, in my view, another dialogue of the deaf.

The case for seeing Jesus as a would-be revolutionary bent on overthrowing the Roman order (and the Jewish aristocrats who functioned as Rome's local puppets) and establishing himself and his followers as rulers in their place rests on one very solid foundation: Jesus' announcement of God's kingdom. As we saw earlier, first-century Jewish revolutionary movements used 'God's kingdom' as one of their major slogans. They didn't want other rulers; they just wanted God himself to be king. From some points of view, Jesus does indeed look a bit like Judah the Hammer, going around with his little band of loyal followers, gathering support, managing to stay out of trouble, and eventually going up to Jerusalem, palm branches waving, to 'cleanse the Temple'. From some points of view, Jesus even looks a bit like Simon the Star, mounting a three-year kingdom-movement in which the 'kingdom' had indeed already begun (remember the year 1 on Simon's coins!), while the great battle and the proper rebuilding of the Temple remained in the future. Jesus, like Simon, seems to have practised and taught a severe way of life in which Israel's ancient law was intensified; for Jesus, anger and lust were as much off limits as murder and adultery. And there are some signs in the gospels that people were eyeing Jesus, during his public ministry, to compare him with Herod Antipas. The sources suggest that he was giving his followers instructions on how to behave now that they were living under his rule. There are enough analogies there for us to say that Jesus really does belong on the map of those kingdom-movements.

The parallel with Simon the Star is particularly striking, showing how easy and natural it was in that climate to speak of something having already been well and truly inaugurated – the coins, again – and also of something that had yet to be accomplished. Jesus' way of combining present and future sayings about God's kingdom has long baffled scholars who were trying to understand him without reference to his Jewish context. Once we put him back in that world, the problem simply vanishes. Of course he believed that God's kingdom had already begun. Of course he believed that it would take another great act to complete the job. These are not in tension. They belong together quite naturally. The combination comes with the territory.

We can of course see why, faced with the Jesus-the-Marxist theory, many scholars and preachers have reacted in horror. It wasn't just their possible right-wing sympathies, though those may have come into play as well. It was that the whole thrust of Jesus' public career, insofar as we can reconstruct it from passage after passage in the gospels, seemed to be going in a very different direction. Whatever else he was, he wasn't a violent revolutionary. We have already studied his commands to love and forgive and we have set them in their first-century political context. He warned at one point that, if God's kingdom was breaking into the world, the men of violence were trying to muscle their way into the act (Matthew 11.12; Luke 16.16). He just wasn't the sort of freedom fighter we have come to know rather well in the last hundred years or so.

It won't do, then, to suppose that what Jesus was doing was simply advancing a kind of human revolution, a proto-Marxist movement in which the poor would overthrow the rich. Jesus has plenty of harsh words for the rich – far more than for anyone else, in fact. But, just as, to the dismay of his own imprisoned cousin, he showed no sign of launching a movement to oust Herod Antipas and set his prisoners free, so he showed no sign either of joining one of the various already

existing resistance movements or of starting his own. Those movements, clearly, were using the same language as he was, since they too
spoke about God becoming king. But what Jesus meant by that, acted
out in a hundred vivid demonstrations of God's sovereign power, and
explained in a hundred parables that told the ancient stories in a new
way, was quite different from what the ordinary revolutionaries had
in mind.

Nor does that mean, of course – in the light of the first point we
have just made – that Jesus was saying, 'Forget revolution. Go to
heaven instead.' It was about giving up the ordinary kind of revolution, in which violent change produces violent regimes, which are
eventually toppled by further violent change, *and discovering an
entirely different way instead.* 'Don't resist evil,' he said, and the words
he used didn't mean, 'Lie down and let people walk all over you.' They
meant, 'Don't join the normal "resistance" movements.' The Marxist
or quasi-Marxist option simply has too many elements of the story
running against it. Clearly, Jesus was not apolitical – how could he
be, talking about God becoming king in first-century Palestine? – but
his 'politics' don't seem to fit the moulds into which many have tried
to squash him.

Nor was Jesus simply advocating a clever, philosophically savvy way
of living courageously within the present evil world, a way by which
his followers might be able to attain some kind of detachment. After
the failure of earlier attempts to make Jesus into a Marxist hero, we
have seen more subtle attempts to make him a Cynic hero, looking
out on the follies and failings of the world with an ironic smile and
teaching his followers how to rise above it all. No doubt there are
echoes of Cynic sayings and attitudes here and there in Jesus' words,
just as his voicing of the Golden Rule ('Whatever you want people to
do to you, do that to them,' Luke 6.31) is echoed in many cultures
and traditions. But he wasn't teaching his followers how to rise above
the mess of the world. He was training them to be kingdom-bringers.
As Marx himself said, the point is not to understand the world, but
to change it.

Third, and most important, we must avoid jumping to the conclusion, from all that has been said above, that Jesus was doing things
that 'proved his divinity' – or that the main point he was trying to

get across was that he was the 'son of God' in the sense of the second person of the Trinity. Here we must be careful. I have already hinted strongly enough, I think, that Jesus saw his own work, his own public career, his own very person, as the reality to which Temple, sabbath and creation itself were pointing. That is, or ought to be, a clear indication that, in terms of the 'God' of first-century Jews, Jesus understood himself to be embodying this God, doing things whose best explanation was that this was what God was doing, and so on. My problem with 'proofs of divinity' is that all too often, when people have spoken or written like that, it isn't entirely clear that they have the right 'God' in mind. What seems to be being 'proved' is a semi-Deist type of Christianity – the type of thing a lot of Christians in the eighteenth century, and many since then, have thought they should be defending. In this sort of Christianity, 'God' is in heaven and sends his divine second self, his 'Son', to 'demonstrate his divinity', so that people would worship him, be saved by his cross, and return with him to heaven. But in first-century Christianity, what mattered was not people going from earth into God's kingdom in heaven. What mattered, and what Jesus taught his followers to pray, was that God's kingdom would come on earth as in heaven.

Jesus' powerful acts of healing, then, together with all the other extraordinary things the gospels credit him with, are not done in order to 'prove' his 'divinity'. If you see them like that, they prove too much and too little. Too much: other people had, and still have, remarkable gifts of healing. That's always been a feature on the edge of religious movements, and sometimes in the centre of them. But it doesn't mean that the person doing the healing is 'God', just like that. Were that to be the case, there would be quite a lot of gods. Equally, too little: those who have seen Jesus' powerful acts as 'proofs of divinity' have often just stopped there, as though that was the main thing one was supposed to conclude from a reading of the gospels. They have then allowed the 'right' answer to the question about 'divinity' to shut down the question the gospels are urgently pressing upon us – is God becoming king?

A considerable amount of 'apologetics' to this day, in fact, has consisted of arguing for the 'right answers' to two questions. First, asks the apologist, did Jesus do these things? Yes! Second, what does it prove? That he was God! QED! And off goes the apologist in triumph, a day's work done.

And Matthew, Mark, Luke and John would call the apologist back. Sorry, but you've hit a six when you should have kicked a goal. You're playing the wrong game. The gospels are not about 'how Jesus turned out to be God'. They are about *how God became king on earth as in heaven*. The good is the enemy of the best. From one point of view it's good to see the intimate connection, throughout the gospels, of Jesus with Israel's God. If you're trying to score a point against a Deist opponent who sniffily suggests that Jesus couldn't possibly have been 'divine', because no sane human being could imagine that he was God incarnate, you may end up winning that game. But you may then lose the real one.

Plenty of Christians, alas, have imagined that a 'divine Jesus' had come to earth simply to reveal his divinity and save people away from earth for a distant 'heaven'. (Some have even imagined, absurdly, that the point of 'proving that Jesus really did all those things' is to show that the Bible is true – as though Jesus came to witness to the Bible rather than the other way round.) It has been all too possible to use the doctrine of the incarnation or even the doctrine of the inspiration of scripture as a way of protecting oneself and one's worldview and political agenda against having to face the far greater challenge of God taking charge, of God becoming king, on earth as in heaven. But that is what the stories in the Bible are all about. That's what the story of Jesus was, and is, all about. That is the real challenge, and sceptics aren't the only ones who find clever ways to avoid it.

Once we begin to see beyond these three distracting angles of vision, then, and grasp the story in its own terms, we find ourselves compelled forward into the narrative again. If the time is fulfilled, what will happen to bring even this fulfilled-time moment to its proper conclusion? If Jesus is behaving as though he were the Temple in person, what will this mean both for the existing Temple and for his followers? And if, through his work, new creation is breaking into the world, how is it going to make any headway against the apparently still all-powerful forces of corruption, evil and death itself?

12

At the heart of the storm

With all of this now on the table, we return to the perfect storm: to the build-up of pressure from the Roman Empire in one direction, the thousand-year hope of Israel from another direction, and the cyclone itself, the strange and powerful purposes of God, sweeping in from yet a third angle. The gale of imperial pressure was bearing down on the Middle East. Some Jews, long before, had seen the Romans as potential allies against more immediate and localized enemies, but most now recognized Rome as the latest and perhaps the nastiest in a long sequence of pagan overlords stretching back half a millennium to Babylon and, a millennium before that again, to Egypt. But that recognition simply increased the high-pressure system of Jewish hopes, since the great Exodus story, celebrated time and time again, reminded Israel that when the tyrants did their worst, God would win the victory, liberate his people and come to live among them once more.

How easy, then, to assume that the hurricane of divine purpose would swing around and simply reinforce the high-pressure system of Jewish hope, instead of coming into the picture from a worryingly oblique angle, as had happened all too often in the past. How convenient it would be if God, coming back at last to launch his kingdom on earth as in heaven, were simply to validate and fulfil the national hope as it stood! But one prophet after another, one Psalm after another, had indicated that things were not necessarily going to work quite that neatly, and indeed that they might not work that way at all. Israel had had, in the past, a bad habit of allowing national expectation and aspiration to get out of line with the divine purpose; perhaps that had happened again. Certainly John the Baptist had thought so. All the signs are that Jesus thought so too and had no hesitation in saying so. His kingdom-of-God movement was then aimed not only (like all kingdom-of-God movements) against the

148

might of pagan empire and the forces of greedy paganized behaviour within Israel itself; it was also aimed at subverting the way in which the national hope was being conceived and expressed. Jesus spoke for a divine hurricane that was approaching from quite a different angle to both the Roman gale and the Jewish high-pressure system.

He was therefore walking into the perfect storm. Rome was brooding in the background, its imperial needs and ambitions ready to enforce themselves in the usual way. Israel was celebrating yet another Passover, another freedom festival, and longing for national liberty and victory over paganism. And God, the God whom Jesus called 'Abba, father', was apparently sending him on a mission that was neither of the above, that would be opposed by both, and that would appear to end in abject and horrible failure. If we can hold this picture in our minds, we are well on the way to understanding who Jesus was and why he did what he did.

The best description of how this storm reached its height is, I think, the account in John 18—19 of what happens when Pontius Pilate, the Roman governor, engages in conversation with Jesus. It seems to be, in theory, a kind of judicial hearing, but the conversation constantly threatens to lapse into a sharp-edged discussion about worldviews, with the chief priests looking on and giving their point of view as well. That gives us the three-angled picture I am talking about. But before we can come back to that, we must look at two other pictures. First, in the present chapter, we must examine the key places in Israel's scriptures where the perfect storm seems to be anticipated or even predicted. Second, in the next chapter, we must look at Jesus' own actions over the course of the last few days before his execution.

Isaiah's servant

First, then, the scriptures. We remind ourselves that the backdrop to all of this was the Exodus, with its seven themes: the tyrant, the leader, the divine victory, sacrifice, vocation, the divine presence and the promised inheritance. These themes were reworked at the time of the Babylonian exile and afterwards, producing several key texts. Three of these stand out in particular. They are linked in many complex ways, but for our present purposes we shall treat them separately.

The situation of all three is broadly the same and in each case echoes those seven Exodus themes. In the beginning the wicked tyrant is Babylon; then it shifts to other pagan regimes through to Antiochus Epiphanes and, beyond him, the Romans. The leader varies from book to book, and the situation is complicated. God's victory is assured – the victory over Babylon (or its successors), the victory that will set God's people free. The sacrifice, like the leader, is complicated, and we must return to it later. The vocation of Israel, consequent upon deliverance, is clear: new covenant, new creation. The divine presence is manifest throughout: Israel's God will return to Zion, will come back to judge and to rescue. And the inheritance will be not only the holy land, but the entire world.

The three books (or parts of books) I believe Jesus had in mind are Isaiah 40—66, Daniel and Zechariah. Behind and around these stand other books in which similar themes emerge, particularly Ezekiel, with its striking picture of covenant renewal, the restoration of Israel after the exile, and the return of Israel's God to the restored Temple. But, though Ezekiel was clearly important for the early church, Jesus himself does not seem to have made Ezekiel thematic for his work in the way he did with these other three. There are also, of course, the Psalms, resonating day by day in the large echo chamber of corporate Jewish memory and etched in particular into the mind and heart of Jesus himself.

Isaiah 40—66 is, incontestably, one of the greatest pieces of poetic writing in all history. A message of comfort and hope for God's people in the hopelessness of exile, it constantly stresses the greatness and sovereignty of the one true God over against the idols of Babylon and those who follow them, including those who seem to be great kings and tyrants on the earth. But it also repeatedly plays off the power and faithfulness of YHWH against the folly and failings of Israel itself; Israel has not only given up hope, but seems to have abandoned faith as well. But, flanked by the wickedness of Babylon, on the one hand, and the failure of Israel, on the other, a third figure emerges, bearing the divine purposes into the heart of the storm. The 'servant of YHWH' is a strange, much discussed character, to whom we are introduced in 42.1–9 and whose work – of bringing to fulfilment the rescue operation God has in mind – is then brought into sharper and sharper focus in three subsequent sub-poems embedded firmly within the larger narrative flow of the whole section.

The identity of the 'servant' has been widely discussed. It is clear that, from one point of view, the servant is 'Israel, in whom I will be glorified' (49.3) – the people of God through whom God's justice will spread to the nations (42.1) and his light shine to the ends of the earth (49.6). But throughout the larger poem it is equally clear that the nation as a whole is not up to this task, indeed has failed dismally in it. At the same time, those in Israel who remain faithful are described as those who 'obey the voice of the servant' (50.10), so that the servant cannot simply be identified with the faithful remnant. Somehow, the servant is a kind of true Israel figure, doing Israel's job on behalf of the Israel that has failed. *And doing God's job on behalf of God himself.*

In the three subsequent poems (49.1–7; 50.4–9; 52.13—53.12) it becomes clear how the servant will complete God's rescue operation. He will do it through his own obedient suffering, ultimately through his own humble, shameful, and even sacrificial death. This final poem follows directly on from one of the clearest brief statements of the whole kingdom-of-God agenda anywhere in the Old Testament, in 52.7–12:

> How beautiful upon the mountains
>> are the feet of the messenger who announces peace,
> who brings good news,
>> who announces salvation,
>> who says to Zion, 'Your God reigns' [i.e. 'Your God is king'].
> Listen! Your sentinels lift up their voices,
>> together they sing for joy;
> For in plain sight they see
>> the return of YHWH to Zion.
> Break forth together into singing,
>> you ruins of Jerusalem;
> For YHWH has comforted his people,
>> he has redeemed Jerusalem.
> YHWH has bared his holy arm
>> before the eyes of all the nations;
> And all the ends of the earth shall see
>> the salvation of our God.

Depart, depart, go out from there!
   Touch no unclean thing;
go out from the midst of it, purify yourselves,
   you who carry the vessels of YHWH.
For you shall not go out in haste,
   and you shall not go in flight;
For YHWH will go before you,
   and the God of Israel will be your rearguard.

The entire flow of thought of Isaiah 40—55 as a whole leaves us in little doubt that this kingdom-agenda, this rescue project, this return of YHWH to Zion, will be accomplished through the work, and now specifically the death, of the servant. This is why I said that the question of the 'leader' within this picture, and then also the question of the 'sacrifice', are complicated. In Isaiah's picture, there is no question but that YHWH himself is the 'leader'. But the servant's work is crucial. It is through his suffering and death, described here in terms of sacrifice (53.10), that the sins of the people find atonement and forgiveness. Throughout Isaiah 40—55, this 'forgiveness' means, quite explicitly, return from exile; exile had been the punishment for the people's sins, and their return is the embodiment of their forgiveness.

A full picture of the servant appears in the fourth poem, Isaiah 52.13—53.12:

See, my servant shall prosper;
   he shall be exalted and lifted up,
   and shall be very high.
Just as there were many who were astonished at him
   – so marred was his appearance, beyond human semblance,
   and his form beyond that of mortals –
so he shall startle many nations;
   kings shall shut their mouths because of him;
for that which had not been told them they shall see,
   and that which they had not heard they shall contemplate.
Who has believed what we have heard?
   And to whom has the arm of YHWH been revealed?
For he grew up before him like a young plant,
   and like a root out of dry ground;
he had no form or majesty that we should look at him,
   nothing in his appearance that we should desire him.

At the heart of the storm

He was despised and rejected by others;
> a man of suffering and acquainted with infirmity;
and as one from whom others hide their faces
> he was despised, and we held him of no account.

Surely he has borne our infirmities
> and carried our diseases;
yet we accounted him stricken,
> struck down by God, and afflicted.
But he was wounded for our transgressions,
> crushed for our iniquities;
upon him was the punishment that made us whole,
> and by his bruises we are healed.
All we like sheep have gone astray;
> we have all turned to our own way,
and YHWH has laid on him
> the iniquity of us all.

He was oppressed, and he was afflicted,
> yet he did not open his mouth;
like a lamb that is led to the slaughter,
> and like a sheep that before its shearers is silent,
> so he did not open his mouth.
By a perversion of justice he was taken away.
> Who could have imagined his future?
For he was cut off from the land of the living,
> stricken for the transgression of my people.
They made his grave with the wicked
> and his tomb with the rich,
although he had done no violence,
> and there was no deceit in his mouth.

Yet it was the will of YHWH to crush him with pain.
When you make his life an offering for sin,
> he shall see his offspring, and shall prolong his days;
through him the will of YHWH shall prosper.
> Out of his anguish he shall see light;
he shall find satisfaction through his knowledge.
> The righteous one, my servant, shall make many righteous,
> and he shall bear their iniquities.
Therefore I will allot him a portion with the great,
> and he shall divide the spoil with the strong;

because he poured out himself to death,
    and was numbered with the transgressors;
yet he bore the sin of many,
    and made intercession for the transgressors.

The result, in the great prophetic poem, is the new covenant (Isaiah 54) and the new creation (Isaiah 55). The book then moves into a new mode in the last eleven chapters (56—66), focused on the coming glory of Zion, though here again highlighting the work of a strange figure, part salvation bringer, part rescuer, part judge (61.1–7; 63.1–6). And now it becomes more and more explicit that the work of bringing salvation is YHWH's own work. He watched and saw that there was nobody else to do it, so 'his own arm brought him victory, and his righteousness upheld him' (59.16). Israel's God himself must do what needs to be done, as at the time of the Exodus: 'It was no messenger or angel but his presence that saved them' (63.9).

But this sense of a rescue job to do and only YHWH to perform it may undergird the 'servant' poems in the central section of the book as well. One of the prophet's regular ways of talking about 'God in action' is to speak of 'the arm of YHWH', echoing other scriptural passages all the way back to the song of Moses and Miriam in Exodus 15 (Isaiah 40.10; 48.14; 51.9; 52.10; 53.1; 59.16; 63.5; echoing Exodus 6.6; 15.16; Deuteronomy 5.15; and frequently Psalms 77.15; 89.10; 98.1). But at the start of the second section of the final servant poem, it appears that the servant is himself 'the arm of YHWH', albeit heavily disguised:

Who has believed what we have heard?
    And to whom has the arm of YHWH been revealed?
For he grew up before him like a young plant,
    and like a root out of dry ground;
he had no form or majesty that we should look at him,
    nothing in his appearance that we should desire him.
                    (53.1–2)

The return of YHWH to Zion, on the one hand, and the suffering of the servant, on the other, turn out to be – almost unbelievably, as the prophet realizes – two ways of saying the same thing. And the overall point, we remind ourselves, is that this is where the power of pagan

Babylon and the failure of God's people Israel are met with the sovereign, saving, kingdom-establishing rule of YHWH himself. This is Isaiah's version of Jesus' perfect storm: the gale of pagan tyranny, the high-pressure system of Israel's national life, and the hurricane of the divine purposes. It's important to keep these distinct, as the prophet clearly does. The fact that he is clearly denouncing Babylon doesn't mean he is underwriting Israel's ambitions, just as the fact that he is denouncing the failure of Israel as a whole doesn't mean he is siding with the Babylonians. He is announcing the coming of God, who will do in person what Israel has failed to do. In doing that, he will win the victory over the pagan power of Babylon and bring the people home to their land. The tyrant; the victory; the leader; the sacrifice; the vocation; the divine presence; and the promised inheritance. It's all there. This is the new Exodus.

Daniel's son of man

The second book in which these themes emerge, as once again the perfect storm ripped through the story of the people of God, is Daniel. Nowhere in scripture is it set out more clearly that the kingdom of the one true God stands over against the kingdoms of the world, judging them, calling them to account, condemning them, and vindicating God's people. Story after story in Daniel has that theme, whether it be the almost lighthearted dispute about eating (or not eating) pagan food (ch. 1), the terrifying ordeals of Daniel's friends (ch. 3), or Daniel himself in the den of lions (ch. 6). We know that this book was a favourite of many Jews in the time of Jesus. There is every sign that, as with Isaiah, it was a book Jesus himself drew on heavily for his understanding of what God was up to and what his own role might be within that drama.

Jesus was not the only person in the period who made Daniel 7 thematic in his vocation. A hundred years after his day, the great Rabbi Akiba hailed bar-Kochba, Simon Son-of-the-Star, as Messiah. Akiba is reputed to have explained his view with reference to the famous passage in Daniel 7. This chapter is very important, and we must look at it in a little more detail.

In this chapter, the prophet, who up to now has been able to interpret the dreams and visions of others, has a dream of his own. He sees a vision of four horrible monsters causing havoc on earth, climaxing in a terrible monster with a 'little horn' that grows up in place of some of its original ones; and the horn speaks arrogantly against God and his people. But then the vision changes:

> As I watched,
> thrones were set in place,
>   and an Ancient One took his throne;
> his clothing was white as snow,
>   and the hair of his head like pure wool;
> his throne was fiery flames,
>   and its wheels were burning fire . . .
> The court sat in judgement,
>   and the books were opened.

I watched then because of the noise of the arrogant words that the horn was speaking. And as I watched, the beast was put to death, and its body destroyed and given over to be burned with fire . . . As I watched in the night visions,

> I saw one like a son of man
>   coming with the clouds of heaven.
> And he came to the Ancient One
>   and was presented before him.
> To him was given dominion
>   and glory and kingship,
> that all peoples, nations, and languages
>   should serve him.
> His dominion is an everlasting dominion
>   that shall not pass away,
> And his kingship is one
>   that shall never be destroyed.
>   (7.9–11, 13–14)

The interpretation of the vision is given in a short form (7.15–18) and a longer version (7.19–27):

As for me, Daniel, my spirit was troubled within me, and the visions of my head terrified me. I approached one of the attendants to ask him the truth concerning all this. So he said that he would disclose to

me the interpretation of the matter: 'As for these four great beasts, four
kings shall arise out of the earth. But the holy ones of the Most High
shall receive the kingdom and possess the kingdom for ever – for ever
and ever.'   (7.15–18)

Then I desired to know the truth concerning the fourth beast, which
was different from all the rest, exceedingly terrifying, with its teeth of
iron and claws of bronze, and which devoured and broke in pieces,
and stamped what was left with its feet; and concerning the ten horns
that were on its head, and concerning the other horn, which came up
and to make room for which three of them fell out – the horn that had
eyes and a mouth that spoke arrogantly, and that seemed greater than
the others. As I looked, this horn made war with the holy ones and was
prevailing over them, until the Ancient One came; then judgement was
given for the holy ones of the Most High, and the time arrived when
the holy ones gained possession of the kingdom.

   This is what he said: 'As for the fourth beast,

> there shall be a fourth kingdom on earth
>   that shall be different from all the other kingdoms;
> it shall devour the whole earth,
>   and trample it down, and break it to pieces.
> As for the ten horns,
> out of this kingdom ten kings shall arise
>   and another shall arise after them.
> This one shall be different from the former ones,
>   and shall put down three kings.
> He shall speak words against the Most High,
>   shall wear out the holy ones of the Most High,
>   and shall attempt to change the sacred seasons and the law;
> and they shall be given into his power
>   for a time, two times, and half a time.
> Then the court shall sit in judgement
>   and his dominion shall be taken away,
>   to be consumed and totally destroyed.
> The kingship and dominion
>   and the greatness of the kingdoms under the whole heaven
>   shall be given to the people of the holy ones of the Most High;
> their kingdom shall be an everlasting kingdom,
>   and all dominions shall serve and obey them.'
>   (7.19–27)

From these it becomes clear, in case it wasn't already, that the 'monsters' or 'beasts' are pagan kingdoms, who – especially the final king of the final kingdom – will rage against God's people. But then, in a great heavenly court scene, God will take his seat and pronounce judgment, which will result in God's people, 'the holy ones of the Most High', being vindicated and themselves being given 'the kingdom' (7.18, 22, 27). The figure who is seen, in the original vision, as 'one like a son of man' – one, in other words, like a human being – is to be interpreted as a symbol for the whole faithful people of God, the people who will be rescued and vindicated.

But how will this happen? How will this vindication take place? Akiba, in the second century, thought that the 'one like a son of man' referred to the Messiah, the representative of the whole people of God. Akiba then picked up the word 'thrones' in verse 9. There are at least two thrones; the Ancient One sits on one of them, *and it seems as though the 'one like a son of man' is to sit on the other one.* This interpretation was shocking at the time, partly no doubt because Akiba had a candidate in mind: he saw bar-Kochba as the 'one like a son of man', embodying God's people, winning God's victory over the pagan nations (the 'monsters'). When God becomes king and (as in Psalm 2) the wicked nations are finally put in their place, this will be done through the human figure who represents God's faithful people, who will thus sit on a throne next to God himself. We thus have, a hundred years after the time of Jesus, an example of a would-be royal and prophetic movement that drew together the theme of God's kingdom with the theme of a messianic kingdom and rooted these in a prophecy that, as we know from other writings, had been important throughout the period.

Like the 'servant' in Isaiah, the phrase 'son of man' – or, more properly, 'one like a son of man' – has been endlessly discussed and debated in itself as well as in relation to the sayings attributed to Jesus. I have taken what seems to me the commonsense view of the chapter as a whole: that the vision and interpretations of chapter 7 are telling substantially the same story as chapters 1—6, namely, the story of pagan empire reaching its height and Israel's God then stepping in to call 'time' on the whole sequence, to bring arrogant paganism to judgment, and to establish instead his own kingdom in and through his faithful people. This is the story, in other words, of *how God becomes king*, overcoming the kingdoms of the world and establishing, through his faithful people, his own sovereign rule over the whole world instead. Exactly as in Isaiah, we should expect (rather than be surprised by) a certain fluidity between the people of Israel and a single representative.

I have taken too what seems to me the commonsense view of the fresh use of Daniel 7 in the gospel accounts of Jesus. The parallel between the sequence of events in Daniel 7 and the very similar sequence in Daniel 2, where it is the 'stone' that becomes the new, God-given kingdom, enables us to link this reading of Daniel quite closely with Jesus of Nazareth, who not only spoke repeatedly of the 'son of man', but also used the figure of the 'stone' to describe his own role, his own fate, and his own coming kingdom at the end of a not dissimilar story of several stages of wickedness ending in a moment of judgment. When the 'wicked tenants' kill the 'son' and throw him out of the vineyard, the owner will come and take vengeance on them; and this will fulfil the text from Psalm 118.22, which declares that 'the stone that the builders rejected has become the chief cornerstone' (Mark 12.10–11). The rejected and vindicated stone, the rejected and vindicated 'son', and the suffering and vindicated 'son of man' – it's all of a piece, all resonating within the same overall scriptural narrative.

This does not mean that every time Jesus is reported to have used the phrase 'son of man' he was intending a coded reference to Daniel 7. The phrase, by itself, is cryptic and could simply mean 'I' or 'someone like me'. But when we find on Jesus' lips actual quotations of the chapter in question (Mark 13.26; 14.62), we should be prepared to interpret them, and the phrase 'son of man' itself, in the light of Daniel 7 and of the book of Daniel as a whole. We should think of Jesus tapping directly into this, one of the most central and vivid prophetic accounts of the 'perfect storm', of Israel's God sweeping in like a cyclone where the pagans were doing their worst and Israel was unable to rescue itself. This is a vision of the kingdom of God, the kingdom in which God's people 'come' to the Ancient One (the 'coming', we note, is in an upward, not a downward, direction) in vindication after intense suffering. But the kingdom, the authority, the supreme power that is then given to the 'one like a son of man' is, remarkably, something Jesus already claimed during his short public career (Mark 2.10). Along with Isaiah, Daniel was one of the key elements in Jesus' understanding of how the 'perfect storm' would work out.

Zechariah's king

The third book, more mysterious though still very important, is Zechariah. Unlike Daniel, there is no steady sequence of oracles here to enable us to get a quick and clear sense of what the prophecy as a whole is about. Israel, clearly, is still in trouble, even though the geographical exile in Babylon is over. There are promises of a great future under the leadership of the Messiah, 'my servant the Branch' (3.8), echoing Isaiah 4.2; 11.1 and Jeremiah 23.5; 33.15 as well as the servant theme of Isaiah 42. This royal 'Branch' will, as we should have guessed by now, rebuild the Temple (Zechariah 6.12–13). When that happens, the days of fasting for the various desolations of Israel will be turned into feastings (8.18–19), a theme echoed by Jesus in his refusal to fast on the normal occasions (Mark 2.18–20).

But it is in the second half of the book, chapters 9—14, that we find the material drawn on by Jesus as he himself went to meet the ultimate perfect storm. We have already seen the oracle about the king coming on a donkey (9.9–10). There follow promises of God's coming in person to rescue his people (9.11–17). But then there are warnings: Israel's shepherds have led the people astray, and God will act to punish them (10.3; 11.3–17). As in Ezekiel 34, we are to understand the 'shepherds' to be the official leaders of the people, specifically the priests and the aristocracy. The picture then widens, and we glimpse the nations of the world coming to fight against the Jewish people, with God winning a victory over them (12.1–9). But this will also be a time of mourning, mourning in the royal house of David, mourning as for a firstborn child, though concluding with a promise of cleansing from sin (12.10—13.1). The prophets will then join the other leaders in being ashamed for the lies they have spoken (13.2–6). And, before God can purify and refine his true people, they must first be scattered as their shepherd goes to his death:

'Awake, O sword, against my shepherd,
    against the man who is my associate,' says YHWH of hosts.
Strike the shepherd, that the sheep may be scattered;
    I will turn my hand against the little ones.

(13.7)

This strange picture then broadens once again. All the nations will come to fight against Jerusalem, but as the battle reaches its height 'YHWH my God will come, and all the holy ones with him' (14.5). This will be the great moment of renewal, when, as in Ezekiel, living waters will flow out from Jerusalem, this time not only down to the Dead Sea, but also westward to the Mediterranean (14.8). And then, the climax of it all:

And YHWH will become king over all the earth; on that day YHWH will be one and his name one. (14.9)

The book then closes with warnings to the nations, if they wage war against Jerusalem, or if they then do not come and take part appropriately in the festivals. But at the centre of it all is the renewal of holiness in the Temple itself. 'There shall no longer be traders in the house of YHWH of hosts on that day' (14.21).

Putting together this strange, apparently jerky and disjointed set of oracles, we begin to see a pattern emerging. Israel's exile is to be reversed under the rule of the anointed king, who will end up ruling the whole world. The pagan nations will do their worst, but God himself will come to fight against them, and he will be king over all the earth. Meanwhile, however, Israel's official rulers and guardians, the 'shepherds', have failed hopelessly in their task. But YHWH's own 'shepherd' is to be killed and the sheep scattered in order that some-how – the prophet doesn't explain how – the victory can be won.

All of this seems to have helped to shape Jesus' own sense of voca-tion. His actions in Jerusalem – riding in on a donkey and then driving the traders out of the Temple – seem to hold together Zechariah 9.9–10 and 14.21. He seems then to have applied the passage about the shepherds both to his own critique of Israel's leadership and, more strikingly still, to his own forthcoming fate. For our purposes, the main thing to notice here is that Zechariah, like Isaiah and Daniel, envisages the same three lines all converging: the wicked pagan nations who fight against God and his people; the failed Jewish leadership; and God himself coming to do what nobody else can do. These are the three elements that, as seen by Jesus himself, constituted the perfect storm into which he rode, sorrowful but determined, for that final Passover in Jerusalem.

I said there were three main scriptural passages that seem to have contributed to Jesus' sense of vocation as he undertook this final journey. I mentioned then, and now recall, a fourth element we should factor in as well: the Psalms. We should assume that Jesus knew the Psalms as well as anyone and that they formed his natural prayer book and, as such, played a major role in shaping his worldview. And it is in the Psalms that we find, once more, the major themes of YHWH becoming king, installing his Messiah – his 'son'! – in Jerusalem, and bidding the surrounding nations pay him homage (e.g. Psalms 2; 72). But it is in the Psalms too that we find, even in a Psalm that speaks so powerfully of God's kingdom coming, the sense of utter desolation, of being abandoned by God to horrible and shameful suffering and death (Psalm 22). These themes come together in many different ways in these ancient poems, and we are on utterly safe ground in assuming that Jesus not only knew them and reflected on them, but made them the very stuff of his vocation. He found himself in them and determined to act accordingly.

All of this means that we can at last approach the central questions of who, what and why. Who did Jesus think he was, what was he intending to do, and why? What did he think it would all accomplish? What did he think it would all mean?

13

Why did the Messiah have to die?

Layer upon layer it comes, dense and rich within the texts, echo upon echo, allusion and resonance tumbling over one another, so that for those with ears to hear it becomes unmissable, a crescendo of questions to which in the end there can be only one answer. Why are you speaking like this? Are you the one who is to come? Can anything good come out of Nazareth? What sign can you show us? Why does he eat with tax-collectors and sinners? Where did this man get all this wisdom? How can this man give us his flesh to eat? Who are you? Why do you not follow the traditions? Do the authorities think he's the Messiah? Can the Messiah come from Galilee? Why are you behaving unlawfully? Who then is this? Aren't we right to say that you're a Samaritan and have a demon? What do you say about him? By what right are you doing these things? Who is this son of man? Should we pay tribute to Caesar? And climactically: Are you the king of the Jews? What is truth? Where are you from? *Are you the Messiah, the son of the Blessed One?* Then finally, too late for answers, but not too late for irony: Aren't you the Messiah? Save yourself and us! If you're the Messiah, why don't you come down from that cross?

Whatever we say about Jesus, there can be no doubt that his actions and his teaching raised these questions wherever he went. And Jesus had his own questions. Who do you say I am? Do you believe in the son of man? Can you drink the cup I'm going to drink? How do the scribes say that the Messiah is David's son? Couldn't you keep watch with me for a single hour? And finally and horribly: My God, my God, why did you abandon me?

The answers come too in more or less equal profusion. But, like all the best answers to the hardest questions, they come themselves as a set of sparkling puzzles, as though to remind people both ancient and modern that the questions are questions precisely because something is going on that demands a collapse of categories, a breaking of boundaries, a widening of worldview to the point where the new thing, whatever it is, will make the sense it does. The reason there were so many questions, in both directions, was that – as historians have concluded for many years now – Jesus fitted no ready-made categories.

To be sure, the categories were themselves flexible. They were flexible enough to allow significantly different visions of kings and prophets, as we see both from the relevant texts and from the actual movements of the period. But, even at their most flexible, Jesus both fitted and didn't fit.

Messiah? Well, Jesus wasn't doing the things you would expect a messiah to do, and yet so much of what he did and said seemed irresistibly messianic.

Rabbi? Clearly, he wasn't simply a rabbi with a different message, and yet he was a teacher, interpreting and expounding the scriptures and applying them urgently to what he believed was their moment of ultimate fulfilment.

Priest? Well, priests taught people the law, and Jesus was doing that in a sense, though it wasn't like anything they'd heard before. And priests also went up to Jerusalem to serve their turn in the Temple. Jesus was going up to Jerusalem, but, as we have seen, his deeds and words indicated that he was going to upstage the Temple, to do something that would make it redundant and leave it to its fate.

Prophet? Yes, indeed, he spoke and acted as a prophet, but, however cryptically, he described his cousin as 'more than a prophet' and clearly believed that he was bringing something greater again. Prophets characteristically pointed away from themselves to God and what God was doing and would do, but Jesus, as we have seen, spoke about God *in order to explain what he himself was doing and was about to do*. It was as though he filled the existing categories, flexible as they were, so full that they all overflowed, and in that overflow he overwhelmed his followers, his hearers, the enthusiastic and the suspicious alike, and ultimately those who were attempting to put him on trial, both Jews and pagans.

The story, as we have it in the different gospels, is punctuated with moments of clarity, moments that steer the narrative away from the banal attempt that readers have made from time to time to squash

Jesus into this or that box. Instead, these moments open the story up to the possibility that maybe, after all, heaven and earth would come together, God's time and human time would coincide, and the physical reality of this world might indeed become the bearer of the fresh reality of God's new creation. There are certain moments in the life of Jesus and indeed certain geographical locations that were already heavy with symbolic meaning. Think of the great Jewish festivals, particularly Passover, or the great Jewish landmarks, particularly the river Jordan and Jerusalem itself.

At these moments and in these places, repeated throughout our sources, we find three strands meeting up, not now like the elements of a perfect storm, but more like three great rivers that had been travelling in separate valleys and now come together, as though through an earthquake or a landslip, merging with a swirl and a rush, a gigantic and powerful confluence. The great river of *messiahship*, of Israel's long and chequered history of monarchy, comes crashing together with the dark flow of the *servant*, and both together are swept up in the longer, darker and still more powerful current of the belief that Israel's *God* would return at last to his people. The best historical analysis we can offer of what we can only call Jesus' 'vocation' is that he believed, through his prayerful study of the scriptures and his reading of what he himself called the 'signs of the times', that the full force of this great combined river would accomplish the purposes for which Israel itself had been called in the first place; and that it would do so in him, in his willing obedience to this vast and terrifying purpose. Israel's God had promised to return and establish his kingdom. He would do this in and as the Messiah, the servant. In and as Jesus of Nazareth.

Jesus must have known that to believe something like this about oneself, about one's own vocation, was to court the charge of madness or of blasphemy. These charges were duly made against him – by, among others, members of his own family. It is highly unlikely that the early church made such things up. Jesus really did speak and act as though he believed he was called to bring these three great rivers of historic purpose into one. It must have been clear from early on that they would carry him over a final great waterfall into an abyss never previously imagined. Every other way of bringing God's kingdom had been tried and failed. This one was where the scriptures seemed to point and where his own prayerful awareness of vocation was pointing with them. He went ahead.

The baptism

It is indeed by a river, Israel's principal river, that we glimpse the first of these moments of triple vocation. John, Jesus' cousin, was baptizing people in the river Jordan, the place (it cannot have been accidental) where the Exodus story reached its goal and the people their inheritance. Jesus joins the crowds, and, as he is baptized, his vocation is confirmed and sharpened by a voice from the heavens: 'You are my son! You are the one I love! You make me very glad' (Mark 1.11). That voice, a sudden audible joining of heaven and earth, also provides a sudden joining of the royal vocation of the Messiah, who will rule the nations from his throne in Jerusalem (Psalm 2), and the servant (Isaiah 42—53), who will bring God's justice to the nations through his own obedient suffering. Everything we know about the public career of Jesus indicates that he took that double role as the crucial shaping of his own sense of vocation. All the signs are that Jesus understood his baptism as the moment when he was 'anointed', like Israel's kings long ago, for this task. Israel's God was acting through him, in him, *as* him. The baptism confirmed what Jesus had intuited long before and gave him the moment and the platform from which to launch the kingdom-movement through which the saving plan would be accomplished.

Bringing together these three ideas, up to now quite separate, was breathtaking. A royal figure? Yes, people believed that such a figure would rule, bring God's justice to the whole world, and smash the pagans with a rod of iron. The servant? Yes, the servant would suffer and die; the servant people would bear a heavy load, leading not least to martyrdom. And God himself? Israel's God would come back to dwell with his people; devout Jews believed it. That was why it was so important to rebuild or cleanse the Temple.

Up to this point, though, the three themes had been separate. Jews who had studied Isaiah 53 had thought of the servant *either* as a suffering figure, but not a messiah, *or* as a messiah, but not a suffering one. If they thought of the servant as the Messiah, the suffering was reversed, since it was the Messiah's task to inflict suffering on God's enemies, not to suffer it himself. If they went with the natural flow of the text and saw the servant as a suffering figure, they concluded that he couldn't be the Messiah. He would be, whether individually or (more likely) corporately, the martyr people of God who would in the end be vindicated (e.g. Daniel 12). And, though the scriptures were taken to indicate that Israel's God would work his salvation through these figures, we have no evidence prior to the time of Jesus that anyone supposed that when God returned to his people he would return *as* the Messiah or as the servant.

But Jesus brought these vocations together. When he submitted to John's baptism, expressing the repentance necessary before the great coming restoration and symbolically re-enacting the crossing of the Jordan and the entry into the promised land, he identified with his people in their humiliation and penitence, in their longing for God's kingdom. This double strand of meaning (sorrow for sin, on the one hand, launching the kingdom, on the other) points directly to the double meaning of the voice from heaven. The servant vocation and the royal vocation became fused together in his mind and heart. This was what he had to do, and this was the time at which he had to do it. He became, in a new and deeper way, what he already was, much as a king's firstborn son, born to rule after his father, would still be anointed for the task when the time came. 'You are my son! You are the one I love!': the lifelong sense of intimate closeness to the one he called 'Abba, father' took shape with a new clarity, a new sense of direction, a new God-given energy.

It was this newly shaped vision that was tested in the desert. What sort of a messiah should he be? He knew the stories as well as anyone, but he wouldn't follow the line of David or Solomon or indeed of Judah the Hammer or Herod the Great. His secret wilderness victory, however, played the same role in his career that David's killing of Goliath played in his. It indicated that the anointing at his baptism, like David's anointing by Samuel, had been real, had not been a fantasy or an empty gesture. The initial victory pointed ahead to the tasks that now had to be accomplished.

Sure enough, we see the same battle quickly joined as Jesus' public career generated opposition and even plots against his life. People sometimes try to read the early days of Jesus' public career as successful, popular, carrying all before him, but then posit a change, a decline in popularity, and the embracing of a Plan B that included suffering. The texts know nothing of such a mid-course change. Danger, threat and challenge are there from the beginning. Jesus behaves from the start *both* with the sovereign authority of one who knows himself charged with the responsibility to inaugurate God's kingdom *and* with the recognition that this task will only be completed through his suffering and death.

The disciples, however, don't see it like that. When Peter acts as spokesman for the group, declaring that, as far as they're concerned, Jesus is 'the Messiah, . . . the son of the living God' (Matthew 16.16), he is of course echoing the voice at the baptism. Jesus acknowledges that what Peter has said is, like that voice, heaven-sent. But his attempts to explain to the disciples what his particular messianic vocation involves are met with horror and incomprehension. The disciples, we may assume, were still working on the assumption of a more or less standard messianic model, the model that had allowed the family of Judah the Hammer to become kings following military triumph and the cleansing of the Temple, the model that would animate Simon bar-Giora in the 60s and Simon the Star in the 130s. They were expecting Jesus to march on Jerusalem and, by whatever means, to overthrow the wicked Jewish leadership and the hated Romans. All the signs are that they thought he was going to be king in the normal, obvious sense and that they would form his immediate circle. James and John were still agitating for the top jobs as they made their way to Jerusalem (Mark 10.35–40). The thought of combining this model with the powerful biblical theme of the suffering and martyred people of God made no sense to them. Nor had they even glimpsed, so far as we can tell, the possibility that the Jesus they were following on the road to Jerusalem might be the living embodiment of Israel's God, returning at last as he had promised.

What Jesus had done, it seems, was not only to combine Psalm 2 with Isaiah 42, but more specifically to combine Isaiah 52.7–12 with Isaiah 52.13—53.12, the announcement of God's kingdom and his return to Zion with the accomplishment of the Suffering Servant.

This combination was a small step exegetically, but a giant leap theologically, politically and vocationally. The first passage held out the hope of God's kingdom: 'Your God reigns' – resulting in the overthrow of Babylon and the rescue of God's people from slavery. The second held out, apparently as the means by which this would be accomplished, the suffering of the servant. Nobody, so far as we know, had dreamed of combining these ideas in this way before. Nor had anyone suggested that when the prophet spoke of 'the arm of YHWH' (53.1) – YHWH himself rolling up his sleeves, as it were, to come to the rescue – this personification might actually refer to the same person, to the wounded and bleeding servant.

All this was, however, dramatically confirmed immediately after Peter's confession, with the second echo of the baptismal voice. At the transfiguration, the voice is heard once more: 'This is my son, my chosen one: listen to him' (Luke 9.35). As we saw, this is another explicit heaven-and-earth moment. Luke suggests that when Jesus was talking with Moses and Elijah, the subject of their conversation was 'his departure, which he was going to fulfil in Jerusalem' (9.31; the word for 'departure' is 'exodus', and Luke undoubtedly intended us to hear all the overtones that word would generate). This dovetails with Luke's consistent emphasis on the divine plan that 'must' be fulfilled, the plan that would send Jesus not to a throne, but to a cross – or, rather, as all four gospel writers insist, a cross that is to be seen as a throne. This, they all say, is how Jesus is enthroned as 'King of the Jews'. *Jesus' vocation to be Israel's Messiah and his vocation to suffer and die belong intimately together.*

What is more, they are *together* the means by which, he believed, Israel's God would decisively launch his kingdom on earth as in heaven. The disciples wanted a kingdom without a cross. Many would-be 'orthodox' or 'conservative' Christians in our world have wanted a cross without a kingdom, an abstract 'atonement' that would have nothing to do with this world except to provide the means of escaping it. Many too have wanted a 'divine' Jesus as a kind of 'superman' figure, a heavenly hero come to rescue them, but not to act as Israel's Messiah, establishing God's kingdom on earth as in heaven. Jesus' shocking combination of scriptural models into a single vocation makes excellent historical sense; that is, it explains at a stroke why he did and said what he did and said. But, as we shall see, it remains as challenging in our world, and indeed in our churches, as it was in Jesus' own day.

The new Exodus

It was this fresh vocation that demanded that Jesus should redraw the messianic themes of battle and Temple into a radical new configuration around himself. Following through this train of thought enables us both to root what he was doing back into the Exodus story, which he himself chose as the grid of interpretation for his death, and to begin to understand how it was that his forthcoming death would mean what he meant it to mean.

Think back to those messianic themes. Jesus would indeed fight the battle, but it would be against the forces of evil, corruption and death itself. And, like the Maccabean martyrs, who went to their deaths confident that God would raise them from the dead to new bodily life, Jesus came to believe that the only way one could defeat death itself, and thereby launch the new creation for which Israel and the world had longed, was to take on death itself, like David taking on Goliath in mortal combat, trusting that Israel's God, the creator of life itself, would enable victory to be won. And, since death was seen in the scriptures as the ultimate result of human rebellion against God and the failure to obey him, if death were to be defeated, then idolatry, rebellion, disobedience and sin would be defeated along with it. Death, like a great ugly giant, would do its worst, and pour out its full weight upon him. And the creator God would overcome it, showing it up as a defeated enemy.

In human terms, as we have already seen, this was the craziest vocation one could imagine. The disciples knew that, and Jesus must have known it too. Nothing could have brought him to conceive of his vocation in these terms except his unshakeable faith in Israel's God as the creator and his deep awareness of Israel's scriptures as marking out the course he had to tread. Jesus really does seem to have believed not only that this was indeed the way to fight the battle, but that this was also the way to rebuild, to reconstitute, the Temple. This was the way in which Israel's God would come back to his people as the rescuer, the deliverer, overthrowing the powers of the world, overcoming the folly and frailty of Israel itself. This was how, when the perfect storm had done its worst, Israel's God would establish a new community, a people in whom the promises would be fulfilled, in whom the living God would come to dwell as in the Temple, revealing his glory to the world.

This would, in other words, be the new Exodus. Work through the seven themes once more. The tyrant would be not the Jerusalem leaders (though they, in love with their own wealth and prestige, were in league with the dark powers), not even Rome (though Rome would nail him to the cross), but all the powers of the Accuser, up to and including death itself. The leader would be, of course, Jesus himself. The sacrifice, likewise, would be Jesus himself; that, we must assume, is why he chose to make his decisive move at Passover-time, knowing that it would lead to the death of the firstborn, the beloved son, a hint he dropped in one of his last parables (Mark 12.6–8). The vocation would be the vocation he had marked out for Israel in the Sermon on the Mount: going the second mile, turning the other cheek, loving enemies, and praying for them even as they nailed him to the cross. The inheritance would not, now, be a restored holy land, but the whole world, the uttermost parts of the earth, which had been promised to the Messiah as his inheritance and then promised again to the servant as the realm to which he, through his suffering, would bring God's justice.

And the presence of Israel's God would be the presence of Jesus himself, coming to Jerusalem as the embodiment of Israel's returning God, the fulfilment of Isaiah 40 and 52. This, Jesus believed, is what it would look like when Israel's God came back to Zion. It would not be the three men visiting Abraham, not the burning bush, not the pillar of cloud and fire, not Isaiah's smoky, seraphim-surrounded vision, not Ezekiel's whirling wheels, but a young man on a donkey, in tears, announcing God's judgment on the city and Temple that stood on the cosmic fault lines, establishing his own still incomprehending followers as its surprising replacement, and then going off to take upon himself the full weight of evil, the concentrated calamity of the cosmos, so that its force would be annulled and the new world would be born.

This way of looking at the climax of Jesus' story is not, to be sure, the standard, traditional, 'orthodox', 'conservative' reading, though it highlights from a new angle the 'traditional' dogmas of 'incarnation' and 'atonement'. My contention is that it enables us to understand the original, historical reality for which those dogmas are later, often dehistoricized, abstract summaries. Nor, of course, is this way of telling the story the standard 'modern' or 'radical' reconstruction, in which Jesus comes to Jerusalem to continue his programme of moral or social teaching and gets overtaken accidentally in a death his later followers would cunningly reinterpret, but to which he gave neither forethought nor meaning. My contention is that this modernist tour de force does no justice to the texts or the contexts and places on the earliest church a burden of invention it was totally unequipped to bear. Historically, all the lines point back not to a puzzled and saddened early church recovering its nerve and inventing such a Jesus out of thin air, but to Jesus himself, a completely credible first-century Jew who nevertheless burst the boundaries of all expectations and lived and died in the belief that he was embodying the returning, rescuing, royal mission of Israel's God.

Stepping into the storm

But this return, as Malachi had warned, would not be comfortable: 'Who can endure the day of his coming?' (3.2). Jesus came to pronounce, in sorrow, ultimate doom on the city and Temple that had corrupted and perverted its vocation to be the light of the world. Perhaps the most terrifying thing in the whole gospel story is the realization that Jesus' solemn warnings about the judgment that was to come upon Jerusalem and the Temple within a generation were drawn from biblical prophecies not simply of the destruction of Jerusalem, but of the destruction of *Babylon*. Somehow, Jerusalem had lost its way so drastically; somehow the leaders of the Jewish people had got things so wrong in their collusion with Rome and in their corruption, oppression and greed; somehow the Jewish people, Jesus' own people, had got things so wrong in their determination to bring God's victory to the world through military violence and armed rebellion – that the only word the last of the prophets can now speak is the word of judgment: 'Not one stone will be left standing upon another. All of them will be thrown down' (Matthew 24.2).

The terrifying warnings are sustained through the great discourse we know as Mark 13, Matthew 24 or Luke 21, using end-of-the-world language to demonstrate that with the fall of Jerusalem and the destruction of the Temple a world is indeed coming to an end, because a new world is being born. Jesus had come to his own, and his own had not received him; he had come to the place where God had promised to put his name, and the place had rejected him. He therefore invoked the language of the book of Daniel – against the very city and Temple for which Daniel had been so concerned. The 'abomination that desolates' would stand in the Temple (Daniel 9.27; Matthew 24.15) not as a prelude to the Temple being rescued, but rather as a prelude to the tumultuous event that would be like the fall of Babylon itself, an event for which the only appropriate language would be the darkening of sun and moon and the falling of the stars (Matthew 24.29; Isaiah 13.10). And in that terrible event, Jesus wanted his followers to see the sign of his own vindication. No longer would the Temple in Jerusalem be the place where heaven and earth met. From now on, heaven and earth would meet in the person and through the achievement of the 'one like a son of man', who after his suffering would be vindicated, who would be 'coming on the clouds of heaven' to be seated beside 'the Ancient One' (Matthew 24.30, quoting Daniel 7.13). The greatest empires of the world would do their worst, and Israel's representative would be enthroned as their Lord, establishing a kingdom that could never be shaken.

To say that this was not what anyone else in Israel at the time had imagined, let alone dreamed of or prayed for, was putting it mildly. The disciples themselves must have been shocked and dismayed. But this vision of judgment is not an extra bit of teaching tacked onto the end of a public career that was in all other respects about something else. The note of warning had been there throughout, from the Sermon on the Mount (think of the foolish man building his house on the sand!), to the Nazareth Manifesto (think of God's blessing bypassing God's people and going out to the foreigners!), to the solemn warnings in Luke 13, following reports of Jews being killed by Roman soldiers and by a falling tower in the south-east corner of Jerusalem, to repent or to perish in the same way. No wonder people thought Jesus was like Jeremiah, always warning that the enemy would come and destroy, and that when that happened it would be God's own wrath rather than simply a ghastly accident.

Then comes the twist. Jesus was not simply announcing God's judgment on his rebel people, warning like Jeremiah that Israel and its leaders had so badly misread God's vocation that they were now rushing down a steep slope to destruction. Jesus was speaking and acting in such a way as to imply that he was to go ahead of his people, to meet the powers of destruction in person, to take their full weight on himself, so as to make a way through, a way in which God's people could be renewed, could rediscover their vocation to be a light to the nations, could be rescued from their continuing slavery and exile.

Here too we discover that this was not a new thing, a sudden idea imported at the last minute. It is implicit in that heavenly voice at the baptism. It is there in the Sermon on the Mount. It is there, in particular, as Jesus speaks about the hen sheltering the chicks under her wings; his intention was to see the danger coming and to take its full force onto himself (Matthew 23.37; Luke 13.34). It is there again when he speaks of the 'cup' he himself had to drink; the allusions there are all to the 'cup of God's wrath', working through the destructive violence of the Roman Empire against what seemed to it to be rebel subjects and a rebel king (Matthew 20.22; 26.39). And it is there when, on his last bitter journey, he warns the weeping bystanders that what Rome is doing to a green tree it will do, far more, to a dry one. He is the green tree, not ready for the fire; the next generation of Jerusalemites will be the dry sticks, rebels who will court the great disaster until it comes upon them.

All the gospel writers draw this theme out, and it is perhaps Luke in particular who highlights it. Jesus is innocent, but he is dying the death of the guilty. He has not been advocating violent rebellion against Rome, but he is suffering the fate that Rome regularly inflicts on violent rebels. Jesus, having warned his people of what was to come, has gone to take it upon himself. His predictions of the destruction of the Temple and the city are matched, stride for stride, by his own vocation. That is part of the mystery of his crucifixion:

'wounded for our transgressions, crushed for our iniquity'. He cannot establish the new creation without allowing the poison in the old to have its full effect. He cannot launch God's kingdom of justice, truth and peace unless injustice, lies and violence do their worst and, like a hurricane, blow themselves out, exhausting their force on this one spot. He cannot begin the work of healing the world unless he provides the antidote to the infection that would otherwise destroy the project from within. This is the point at which we see how the early work of Jesus' public career, the healing, the celebrations, the forgiveness, the changed hearts, all look forward to this moment. This is what it looks like when Israel's God becomes king. This is what it looks like when Jesus is enthroned as king of the Jews. Those two statements sit side by side. But to get the full story you have to creep around beside them, in awe, and look through the first at the second, then move to the other side, in gratitude, and see the first through the lens of the second.

The crucifixion

How did Jesus prepare his followers for this gigantic, previously unimagined vision? Once again so many strands of story, symbol and meaning are woven together that it is hard for us to follow a single thread without realizing how tightly it belongs with the others as well. Jesus had tried, again and again, to explain to his closest followers that he was going to Jerusalem to fulfil his kingdom-work by being handed over to the pagans and dying a shameful death. On at least one occasion he tried to show them that this was the way in which the powers of the world would be called to account and that by giving 'his life as a ransom for many' (Mark 10.45, echoing Isaiah 53.11–12) he was putting into operation a different way of life entirely, a different way of *power*. But this was (not surprisingly) so far outside their worldview that they couldn't understand it. They didn't even appreciate the fact that when he spoke of his forthcoming death, he meant it in a literal, concrete sense. If they had, they might have decided not to follow him any farther. It is, perhaps, one explanation for the treachery of Judas that he did indeed understand it when Jesus, after his dramatic gesture in the Temple, failed to follow this up with some kind of full-scale assault, but contented himself with teaching and debating and waiting for Passover.

But when Passover approached – the exact chronology remains a matter of debate, but there is no doubt that Jesus intended his action to resonate with all those great Passover themes, those Exodus themes we have seen repeatedly – he no longer contented himself with telling his followers what was to happen and hinting at what it would mean. When he wanted fully to explain what his forthcoming death was all about, he didn't give them a theory. He didn't even give them a set of scriptural texts. He gave them a meal.

It was, undoubtedly, a Passover meal. But it was, undoubtedly, a Passover meal with a radical difference. Like everything else Jesus did, he filled the old vessels so full that they overflowed. He transformed the old mosaics into a new, three-dimensional design. Instead of Passover pointing *backward* to the great sacrifice by which God had rescued his people from slavery in Egypt, this meal pointed *forward* to the great sacrifice by which God was to rescue his people from their ultimate slavery, from death itself and all that contributed to it (evil, corruption and sin). This would be the real Exodus, the real 'return from exile'. This would be the establishment of the 'new covenant' spoken of by Jeremiah (31.31). This would be the means by which 'sins would be forgiven' – in other words, the means by which God would deal with the sin that had caused Israel's exile and shame and, beyond that, the sin because of which the whole world was under the power of death. This would be the great jubilee moment, completing the achievement outlined in Nazareth and at the price that was nearly demanded on that occasion. This would usher in the new era of blessing announced in the Sermon on the Mount and achieved by the same means that was explained on that occasion. Jesus, as the servant, turned the other cheek; Jesus, carrying his cross, went the extra mile at the behest of his Roman executioners; Jesus, finally, ended up enthroned, set on a hill, unable to be hidden, the light of the world shining out at the darkest moment in history.

Part of the point of the meal is that Jesus' followers would then be able to share in its benefits by sharing, in a new way, in his own life. The gifts of bread and wine, already heavy with symbolic meaning, acquire a new density: this is how the presence of Jesus is to be known among his followers. Sacrifice and presence. This is the new Temple, this strange gathering around a quasi-Passover table. Think through the Exodus themes once more. The tyrant is to be defeated: not Rome, now, but the dark power that stands behind that great, cruel empire. God's people are to be liberated: not Israel as it stands, with its corrupt, money-hungry leaders and its people bent on violence, but the reconstituted Israel for whom the Twelve are the founding symbol. The battle is to be won, the Red Sea crossed, not by force of arms, but by a different power, the power that John's gospel names most accurately: having loved his own who were in the world, Jesus loved them to the end (13.1).

Jesus thereby leads the way to a new vocation. Instead of the frantic pressure to defend the identity of people, land and Temple, Jesus' followers are, through the renewal of hearts and lives, to recover the initial vision of being a royal priesthood for the whole world, which is the Messiah's inheritance and now will become theirs as well. Behind it all is the sacrifice by which Jesus will offer the one he called 'Abba, father' the obedience in which Israel's vocational obedience, for so long in default, is at last made good. Jesus has taken Israel's destiny upon himself and will now take Israel's fate upon himself, so that Israel's vocation can be accomplished. Around and within it all is the presence, the presence of Israel's God himself, no longer in the pillar of cloud and fire, no longer in a wilderness tabernacle or an ornate stone-and-timber Temple, but in and as a human being, the Human Being, the Image-bearer, Jesus himself. This is where the glory of God is revealed, so that all flesh may see it together. Once you allow the Passover meal to speak in the way it should, these are the themes to which you will be led.

And it is John who draws out, in particular, the way in which all the lines converge into the perfect storm. Earlier in the gospel it has become clear, as it does in all the accounts, that the real and self-appointed leaders of the Jewish people are set on a course that is radically different from that of Jesus. The Pharisees are looking for an intensification of law-keeping in the hope that this will speed up the coming restoration of Israel. The chief priests are anxious to keep their own shaky power intact and are prepared to do whatever it takes to prevent the Romans from coming and destroying the city (11.48).

That, indeed, is what leads them to the conclusion, which John ironically endorses, that one man had better die for the nation (11.50–53).
The high-pressure system of Jewish hopes is at its greatest, but it is
not moving in the direction that Jesus knows he has to go. Meanwhile,
however, the great gale of Roman imperial power is gathering its
full force; a crisis in the Middle East is the last thing Rome wants,
and it will take all the steps it needs to crush anything that looks like
a rebel movement. And then the cyclone: Jesus arrives in Jerusalem
as the one through whose work God's glory has been and is being
revealed.

Many readers have managed to ignore this theme in the Fourth
Gospel, and have simply read John as a 'spiritual' or (in that sense)
'theological' tract, encouraging them into a personal spirituality and
the hope of an other-worldly salvation. But John is quite clear. When
the power of Rome and the betrayal of Israel's leaders meets the
love of God, the great whirlpool that results will bring about God's
kingly victory, the victory of the kingdom of God over the kingdoms
of the world.

Watch how John builds the sequence up. Some foreigners come
to see Jesus during the preparations for the Passover festival, and at
the heart of Jesus' answer to them is the remarkable promise: 'Now
comes the judgment of this world! Now this world's ruler is going to
be thrown out! And when I've been lifted up from the earth, I will
draw all people to myself' (12.31–32). Somehow, Jesus' forthcoming
death will constitute his victory, God's victory, over 'this world's ruler',
who seems to be not merely Caesar, but the power that stands behind
Caesar and uses him for its dark, destructive purposes.

Then, during the 'farewell discourses', which are John's way of
exploring the meaning of Jesus' final evening with his followers – his
unfolding, piece by piece, of what it means to say that to be with Jesus
is now to be the true Temple people – we find the same theme coming through again and again. 'I haven't got much more to say to you,'
says Jesus. 'The ruler of the world is coming. He has nothing to do
with me. But all this is happening so that the world may know that
I love the father, and that I'm doing what the father has told me to
do' (14.30–31). This is cryptic indeed, but the force of it is to say that
Jesus' forthcoming conflict with Caesar, and with the powers that

stand behind Caesar, will not take place because Caesar has wanted it, but because the Father has wanted it. What Jesus will now do is an act of obedience and love. The 'world' has hated him and will hate his followers too (15.18—16.4). But when the 'Advocate' comes, the spirit of truth, that spirit will prove the world wrong in three things, sin, righteousness and judgment. The 'ruler of this world' is to be judged, convicted, condemned (16.11).

These advance hints enable us to understand John's explanation, the fullest in any of our accounts, of what is at stake when Jesus stands before the Roman governor. The scene in John 18—19 has the hallmarks of the kind of hearing we might expect in a Roman provincial court, and it is this confrontation that lies at the heart of both the political and the theological meaning of the kingdom of God. Jesus has announced God's kingdom and has also embodied it in what he has been doing. But it is a different sort of kingdom from anything that Pilate has heard of or imagined: a kingdom without violence (18.36), a kingdom not *from* this world, but emphatically, through the work of Jesus, *for* this world. (The routine misunderstanding of the kingdom as 'other-worldly' has been generated by the translation 'My kingdom is not *of* this world'; but that is certainly not what John means, and it isn't what Jesus meant either.) The Judaean leaders have a small part; we are still in this three-angled perfect storm, and this is where it reaches its height. But the main confrontation is between Jesus, representing God's kingdom, and Pilate, representing the kingdoms of the world. The Judaean leaders, ultimately, cave in and accept the Roman way: 'We have no king except Caesar' (19.15). But Jesus tells Pilate, in the teeth of his imperial scepticism, that he has come to bear witness to the truth.

So Jesus is executed as the 'king of the Jews'. All four gospels report that this phrase was written out and nailed above his head on the cross. Just as condemned criminals in early modern Britain used to carry a placard telling the onlookers of their crime, so the Romans would put such a notice on the cross, as a warning to others. The gospel writers, of course, see the sign over Jesus' head as heavily ironic, charged with meaning of which the Roman governor and his soldiers were ignorant – just as John sees Caiaphas's statement about Jesus dying for the people (11.50). Pilate's words point, despite his cynical intention, to the reality: the 'king of the Jews' must complete his scripturally rooted vocation by giving his life for his people, for the world, expressing and embodying the saving, healing, sovereign love of Israel's God, the world's creator. He should die, say the Jewish leaders, because 'he made himself the son of God' (19.7), just as in Mark and elsewhere the bystanders at the cross mock Jesus and challenge him to come down from the cross if he is the son of God. But John's readers and Mark's readers know by now that it is because he is son of God that Jesus must go to the cross, that he must stay there, that he must drink the cup to the dregs. And he must do so not in order to rescue people from this world for a faraway heaven, but in order that God's kingdom may be established on earth as in heaven.

That is why, in John's account, the last words of Jesus are reported as being, 'It's all done' (19.30), in other words, 'It's accomplished' or 'It's completed.' The echo is of Genesis: at the end of the sixth day, God *completed* all the work that he had done. The point was not to rescue people *from* creation, but to rescue creation itself. With the death of Jesus, that work is complete. Now, and only now, and only in this way can new creation come about.

How then can we interpret Jesus' death? What models, what metaphors, what constructions can we find to do justice to it? It is, of course, easy to belittle it, to treat it as yet another example of a good man crushed by 'the system', another eager revolutionary who gave his life for the cause. There is, naturally, a sense in which that is true, but if we are to understand Jesus' own intentions, it is far from the whole truth.

Equally, it is easy to belittle Jesus' death theologically. This can be done by placing it solely within a framework that speaks of Jesus as the ultimate example of love – although why, without more of a framework, his death would be an act of love it is interestingly difficult to say. Or it can be done by making Jesus the representative model who goes through death to new life and thereby enables us to make the same journey 'in him' or 'through him'. Or, notoriously, it can be done by imagining a straightforward transaction in which a God who wanted to punish people was content to punish the innocent Jesus instead. This always, of course, leaves unanswered the question of how such a punishment could itself be just, let alone loving.

Each of these models, though, has its point to make. First, as I have argued above, there is undoubtedly a vital sense in which Jesus' death is exemplary. At every stage in the narrative we see, acted out in the small but vital human details, that sense of healing and forgiveness, that sense of a powerful love going out to rescue and restore, that we saw in the earlier details of Jesus' public career. He hasn't, in other words, stopped being the same kingdom-bringing Jesus; on the contrary, what he does on the cross is the culmination and retrospective explanation of all that earlier work.

Likewise, second, there is indeed a sense in which Jesus was 'representing' his people, and through them the whole world. He lived in a world of understanding in which it made sense to see the Messiah as standing in for Israel and Israel as standing in for the rest of humankind. But, important though this theme is not only in the gospels but in Paul and elsewhere, it will scarcely carry all the weight required.

There is too, third, a massive sense in which Jesus' death is penal. Jesus has announced God's imminent judgment on his rebel people, a judgment that would consist of devastation at the hands of Rome. He then goes ahead of his people to take precisely that judgment, literally, physically and historically upon himself. 'Not only in theological truth, but in historic fact, the one bore the sins of the many.'[1] This is both penal and substitutionary, but it is far bigger and less open to objection than some other expressions of that theory. Once you put it together with the previous model (Jesus as Messiah representing Israel and hence the world), you draw the sting of the main objections that have been advanced against it.

But I have become convinced, the more I have read and studied and prayed the story of Jesus, that all these constructions need to be put within a larger one again – the larger one that the gospels themselves are trying to insist on and that seems to me exactly in line with the aims and motivations of Jesus himself. Somehow, Jesus' death was seen by Jesus himself, and then by those who told and ultimately wrote his story, as the ultimate means by which God's kingdom was established. The crucifixion was the shocking answer to the prayer that God's kingdom would come on earth as in heaven. It was the ultimate Exodus event through which the tyrant was defeated, God's people were set free and given their fresh vocation, and God's presence was established in their midst in a completely new way for which the Temple itself was just an advance pointer. That is why, in John's gospel, the 'glory of God' – with all the echoes of the anticipated return of YHWH to Zion – is revealed in and through Jesus, throughout his public career, in the 'signs' he performed, but fully and finally as he is 'lifted up' on the cross.

How can this be? How can the horrible, ugly and brutal execution of a young prophet be the means of establishing God's kingdom? What does it mean to say, as we have done throughout this book, that the point of the story is that God is now in charge, if the means by which that is accomplished is the death of the one who had gone about making it happen?

There is of course much more that could be said on this subject. But, trying to boil it down and keep it simple, I think we can and must say at least this. In Jesus' own understanding of the battle he was fighting, Rome was not the real enemy. Rome provided the great gale, and the distorted ambitions of Israel the high-pressure system, but the real enemy, to be met head-on by the power and love of God, was the anti-creation power, the power of death and destruction, the force of accusation, the Accuser who lays a charge, against the whole human race and the world itself, that all are corrupt and decaying, that all humans have contributed to this by their own idolatry and sin. The terrible thing is that this charge is true. All humans have indeed worshipped what is not divine and so have failed to reflect God's image into the world. They, and creation, are therefore subject to corruption and death. At this level the Accuser is absolutely right.

But the Accuser is wrong to imagine that this is the creator's last word. What we see throughout Jesus' public career is that he himself is being accused – accused of being a blasphemer by the self-appointed thought police, accused of being out of his mind by his own family, even accused by his followers of taking his vocation in the wrong direction. All the strands of evil throughout human history, throughout the ancient biblical story, come rushing together as the gospels tell the story of Jesus, from the demons shrieking at him in the synagogue to the sneering misunderstanding of the power brokers to the frailty and folly of his own friends and followers. Finally, of course – and this is the point in the story to which the evangelists are drawing our attention – he is accused in front of the chief priests and the council and, in the end, by the high priest himself. He is accused of plotting against the Temple; he is accused of forbidding the giving of tribute to Caesar (a standard ploy of revolutionaries); he is accused of claiming to be king of the Jews, a rebel leader; he is accused of blasphemy, of claiming to be God's son. Accusations come rushing together from all sides, as the leaders accuse Jesus before Pilate; and Pilate finally does what all the accusations throughout the gospel have been demanding and has him crucified. Jesus, in other words, has taken the accusations that were outstanding against the world and against the whole human race and has borne them in himself. That is the point of the story the way the evangelists tell it.

Albert Schweitzer, one of the greatest human beings of the twentieth century, suggested that Jesus had glimpsed his own role within the long biblical story of what Schweitzer called 'the messianic woes'. Many prophets and subsequent Jewish writers spoke of the suffering that would come upon God's people – wave upon wave of suffering, reaching a climax at the time of the Messiah, a climax of horror and despair in which evil did its worst, only so that its defeat could pave the way to the redemption God had in mind. Jesus, in Schweitzer's vision, grasped this idea and believed it was his vocation to go to the point where this great 'woe', this great 'time of testing', would burst in with its full force. That is why he told his disciples to pray that they would be spared the time of testing. He had to go into it himself, but they must not. There are signs, particularly in the garden of Gethsemane, that Jesus was indeed thinking this way. Schweitzer then used the image of the great wheel of history. Jesus had hoped that it would begin to turn in the opposite direction, and when it refused, he threw himself upon it. It crushed him; but it did indeed start to move in the opposite direction.

A violent image for a violent reality. I have in this book used the analogy of the perfect storm partly as a way of picking up Schweitzer's point and developing it further. But even this, like all analogies, inevitably breaks down. What we might need, in addition, is to imagine some forces in different planes. In addition to the gale of Rome, the high-pressure system of Israel's distorted ambitions, and the cyclone of the returning purposes of God, we perhaps need a downward vortex, a giant whirlpool, that threatens to suck down into the black depths all who sail too close to it. One might even tie the themes together and suggest that the gale and the pressure system are themselves driven by the same forces that are dragging down the dark waters: Rome and rebel Israel are the unwitting tools of the satan, the Accuser, the great force of anti-creation.

And one might suggest that Jesus, precisely because he believed that in his public career 'the time was fulfilled', believed too that all these powers of evil were gathering themselves for one last battle, one last attempt to thwart the good purposes of the creator God, to pull the cosmos and the human race down into the depths. The only way, he believed, by which this great anti-creation power could be stopped and defeated would be for him, Jesus, anointed with God's spirit to fight the real battle against the real enemy, to take the full power of evil and accusation upon himself, to let it do its worst to him, so that it would thereby be exhausted, its main force spent. He would be the David for this ultimate Goliath – though with the difference that, since violence and death were themselves the ultimate enemy, this David would win the battle by losing his life, with the four nails of crucifixion and the spear thrust in his side taking the place of the five stones David took for his sling. Jesus' own mind, heart and body would be the battlefield on which the final victory would be won, as they were also the Temple in which the powerful, loving presence of Israel's returning God had made his home.

The key to it all, as the earliest Christian writers saw clearly, is the belief that, as Israel's Messiah, Jesus did indeed *represent* his people. The life of the nation is bound up in the king. As, once more, with David fighting Goliath, the one stands in for the many, so that his victory becomes theirs. The representative is thus the only fitting *substitute* (despite generations of theologians playing those two categories off against one another). And the point, then, is that Israel is the representative of the world; God called Abraham's family in the first place to be the people through whom the whole world would be blessed, would finally be released from the ancient curse. If you skip the middle stage, the Israel stage, as so many Christian theologians have done, forgetting the vital role of Abraham's descendants in the whole saving plan, you will have to force your categories to make sense of Jesus in some other way. You may even try to make his 'divinity' accomplish this, though this is not what the New Testament says. What we have, rather, is the extraordinary story of Israel's Messiah taking upon himself the Accuser's sharpest arrow and, dying under its force, robbing the Accuser of any further real power.

We must stress, in closing this account of Jesus' death, that the earliest testimony insists on its being an act, primarily, of *love*. 'He loved me,' wrote Paul within twenty years of the event, 'and gave himself for me' (Galatians 2.20). 'No one has a love greater than this,' says Jesus himself in John 15.13, 'to lay down your life for your friends.' Take the outpouring of care and concern for the sick, the weak, the vulnerable and the sinners that were characteristic of Jesus' public career. Wrap them all together in a single bundle. Then remind yourself that this whole bundle was what it looked like when the living God began to reign on earth as in heaven, began to roll back the sickly tide of the rule of sin and death. Then remind yourself once more that the announcement only made sense if it was to be backed up by the final victory, the final re-establishment of God's presence and rule. As with the brief rule of Simon the Star, Jesus' short public career, his inauguration of God's kingdom, needed to be completed with the last battle and the rebuilding of the Temple. Thus the compassion that overflowed in all directions in the first part of Jesus' work was the same compassion with which he went to his death. Having loved his own who were in the world, wrote John, he loved them to the end. To the uttermost.

I am absolutely sure that there is far, far more that could and perhaps should be said about the meaning of Jesus' death. The world would not suffice. But I am equally sure that one should not say significantly less than this. If the Christian faith is true – if, in other words, Jesus of Nazareth rose from the dead three days later to launch God's new creation and, by his Spirit, to re-energize his followers to be its active agents – then the moment of Jesus' death is, like Jerusalem on those ancient maps, the central point of the world. Even if the Christian faith were not true, we would still have to say that the death of this man, possessed of a vocation like this in which a thousand years of history and hope came rushing together in a great act of generous, compassionate love, was one of the most noble, if not the most noble, in history. Even the death of Socrates, so powerful in itself as a witness to the beliefs that had sustained his public career, cannot compete. But of course, as I shall now suggest, Jesus' death is in fact given its full meaning, and its fully central place in the history of the world, by what happened next.

14

Under new management:
Easter and beyond

If I say that there is a whole book to be written on the subject of this chapter, writer and readers may be permitted to share a wry smile. I have already published extensively on Easter and its meaning, and for much of this chapter I shall simply summarize what I have argued at length there.[1] But for the purposes of this book we need to draw out one strand in particular. At its simplest, the meaning of Easter and what quickly followed was the meaning that resulted from the events about *this* Jesus, the Jesus we have been studying so far. The difference between this Jesus and the various 'Jesuses' of popular imagination – inside the church as well as outside – will emerge as we proceed.

A new world

When Jesus rose from the dead on Easter morning, he rose as the beginning of the new world that Israel's God had always intended to make. That is the first and perhaps the most important thing to know about the meaning of Easter.

Of course, I have said 'when', not 'if'. I have argued in detail else-where that the only possible explanation for the rise of Christianity and for its taking the shape it did was that Jesus of Nazareth, three days after being very thoroughly dead (Roman executioners were professional killers and didn't let would-be rebel leaders slip out of their clutches), was found by his followers to be very thoroughly and very bodily alive again. His tomb was empty; had it not been, his followers would have believed they were seeing some kind of an apparition. Such things were well known in the ancient world, as in fact they are today. Equally, they really did see, touch and share food with Jesus as a real, bodily presence; had they not, they would have concluded that an empty tomb meant that the grave had been robbed. Such things were better known in the ancient world than they are today. The combination of empty tomb and definite, solid appearances is far and away the best explanation for everything that happened subsequently.

'Solid?' I hear someone ask. Didn't they tell stories about this risen Jesus going through locked doors, not always being recognized right away, and eventually vanishing upwards into thin air? Yes, they did, and we have to take those stories seriously too. They don't correspond to what first-century Jews, the majority of whom believed in eventual resurrection, would have thought 'the resurrection' would be like. (For another thing, they never imagined that 'resurrection' would happen to one person in the middle of time; they believed it would happen to all people at the end of time. The Easter stories are very strange, but they are not projections of what people 'always hoped would happen'.) The stories don't fit, in fact, into either of our regular categories. We tend to divide things up into solid, physical objects, on the one hand, and evanescent, insubstantial 'objects' or appearances, on the other, such as (so we imagine) ghosts. But the stories of the risen Jesus have a different quality altogether. They seem to be about *a person who is equally at home 'on earth' and 'in heaven'*. And that is, in fact, exactly what they are.

Remember – before this gets too confusing! – that 'heaven' in biblical thought is not a long way away from 'earth'. In the Bible, 'heaven' and 'earth' overlap and interlock, as the ancient Jews believed they did above all in the Temple. Remember too that 'heaven' and 'earth' are not like oil and water, resisting one another and separating themselves out. Most people in today's Western world imagine that 'heaven', by definition, could not contain what we think of as a solid, physical body. That's because we are Platonists at heart, supposing that if there is a 'heaven', it must be non-physical, beyond the reach of space, time and matter. But suppose Plato was wrong?

Suppose, in other words, that the ancient Israelite scriptures were right, and that heaven and earth were after all the twin halves of God's created reality, designed eventually to come together. Suppose that what has kept them apart all this time is that the human creatures who were put in charge of the 'earthly' part of this creation had rebelled, and that their rebellion had generated a sufficient head of steam for 'earth' to declare, as it were, independence, the desire to rule itself. And suppose that this self-rule had become extremely powerful, keeping the two spheres separate and effectively tyrannizing 'earth' with the regular weapon of the tyrant, that is, death itself.

Suppose, then, that the creator God had finally come in person to break the tyrant's weapon and inaugurate the new world in which the original purpose of creation would be fulfilled after all. That, it seems, is what the early Christians believed was going on when they met Jesus, very much alive again and appearing to be equally at home in 'heaven', where they couldn't see him, and on 'earth', where they could. Think back to what we said earlier about space, time and matter. What we are witnessing in the resurrection stories – which, obviously, are quite unlike any other stories before or since and there-fore invite the scepticism they have received as much in the ancient as in the modern world – is *the birth of new creation*. The power that has tyrannized the old creation has been broken, defeated, overthrown. *God's kingdom is now launched, and launched in power and glory, on earth as in heaven.*

This is what Jesus said would happen within the lifetime of his hearers. A new power is let loose in the world, the power to remake what was broken, to heal what was diseased, to restore what was lost. The kingdom that Jesus had inaugurated strangely, mysteriously and partially during his public career through his healings, feastings and teachings was now unveiled in a totally new dimension. If we think of Jesus during his lifetime in the way we have throughout this book and then ask about the meaning of Easter, the answer is obvious. This is the real beginning of the kingdom. Jesus' risen person – body, mind, heart and soul – is *the prototype of the new creation*. We have already seen him as the Temple in person, as the jubilee in person. Now we see him as the new creation in person.

The thing about the new creation is that it simply overflows with the power of love. Read the stories, especially the longer ones in Luke 24 and John 20—21. Jesus meets his followers. They are sorrowful, ashamed and anxious. He calls them by name. He tells them not to be afraid. He explains what's going on. He deals with them individually. The meeting with the two on the road to Emmaus (Luke 24) is one of the most gently powerful stories ever written. The brief conversation between Jesus and Peter in John 21 is one of the most moving human encounters ever recorded. There is a love, a deep, moving warmth that goes out from Jesus. But this love is strong, powerful, life-changing, life-directing. New creation has begun; and its motivating power is love.

That is why, in Luke's gospel, the risen Jesus tells his followers to go and announce to the world that a new way of life has been opened, the way of 'repentance' and 'forgiveness' (24.47). To us Westerners, that sounds a bit gloomy, as though it's a perpetual act of contrition, dredging up our 'sins' in order to hear someone declare them forgiven (until next time!). But it's far, far bigger than that. The old creation lives by pride and retribution: I stand up for myself, and if someone gets in my way I try to get even. We've been there, done that, and got the scars to prove it. Now there is a completely different way to live, a way of love and reconciliation and healing and hope. It's a way nobody's ever tried before, a way that is as unthinkable to most human beings and societies as – well, as resurrection itself. Precisely. That's the point. Welcome to Jesus' new world.

Here, then, is the message of Easter, or at least the beginning of that message. The resurrection of Jesus doesn't mean, 'It's all right. We're going to heaven now.' No, the life of heaven has been born on this earth. It doesn't mean, 'So there *is* a life after death.' Well, there is, but Easter says much, much more than that. It speaks of a life that is neither ghostly nor unreal, but solid and definite and practical. The Easter stories come at the end of the four gospels, but they are not about an 'end'. They are about a beginning. The beginning of God's new world. The beginning of the kingdom. God is now in charge, on earth as in heaven. And God's 'being-in-charge' is focused on Jesus himself being king and Lord. The title on the cross was true after all. The resurrection proves it.

Ascension and enthronement

If Easter is about Jesus as the *prototype* of the new creation, his ascension is about his *enthronement* as the one who is now in charge.

Easter tells us that Jesus is himself the first part of new creation; his ascension tells us that he is now running it.

Once more, you can only understand the ascension if you push out of your mind the idea of 'heaven' you began with and try to imagine a more biblical picture instead. For most people today, as we've said already, 'heaven' is a location of a completely different sort from the world in which we live. It is timeless, non-physical, immaterial. (People sometimes say 'spiritual' at this point, but that's a misleading description of the way the early Christians thought and spoke. For them, 'spiritual' had to do with the work of God's Spirit; and God's Spirit was at work most definitely within, not apart from, the world of space, time and matter.) So when Luke tells the story of Jesus going up to heaven in a cloud, forty days after his resurrection, and when Paul writes of Jesus being 'exalted' to heaven (e.g. Philippians 2.9–11), the one thing we should *not* think of is that, after his death, Jesus is now 'going to heaven' in the normal modern sense of that phrase.

There are four things to remember about the ascension. Each of them contributes to its meaning within the story we have been telling. First, to repeat, heaven and earth are not a long way apart. They are meant to overlap and interlock and finally to be joined fully and for ever. And the whole point of Jesus' identity, all along, is that he has been a one-man walking Temple; he has been, already, the place where heaven and earth have met, where people on earth have come into contact with the life and power of heaven. So for Jesus 'going to heaven' isn't a matter of disappearing into the far distance. Jesus is like somebody who has two homes. The homes are right next door to each other, and there is a connecting door. One day the partition wall will be knocked down and there will be one, glorious, heaven-and-earth mixture.

What that illustration doesn't quite catch is that heaven and earth are not the same *kind* of space. They are not merely contiguous, like two next-door houses. Heaven permeates earth. If Jesus is now in 'heaven', he is present to every place on earth. Had he remained on earth, he wouldn't have been present anywhere except the one place where he was. The ascension enables him to be present everywhere.

Second, and most important for our whole theme, heaven is the place from which the world is run. It is the CEO's office. You can see this in the dramatic scenes in the book of Daniel, where this or that pagan king is warned about 'the God of heaven'. That doesn't mean, 'Good, he's safely in heaven, a long way away, so we can do as we like.' It means, 'God is in the place where he can call the shots, and you'd better watch out!' This is how, in the story of Jesus, the long narrative stretching back to his baptism (and, in Luke particularly, to his birth) comes to its climax. He was born to be king of the world, the king who would upstage Caesar himself; he was baptized as Israel's Messiah, who in Psalm 2 would rule the nations; and now he is enthroned, installed officially as what he already was in theory. This, along with the resurrection, is part of what Jesus meant when he told his followers that the 'son of man' would 'come in his kingdom' and that they would see it (Matthew 16.28).

This, indeed, is part of the point of Luke's description about Jesus being 'lifted up' and taken out of sight by a 'cloud' (Acts 1.9), which brings us to the third point about ascension. If, as I have stressed, 'heaven' and 'earth' are not far apart, but are actually meeting and mingling in and through Jesus, why this vertical movement? Here we may want to remain open-minded as to how much Luke intends this description to be a literal account of a concrete reality and how much he is intending primarily to evoke that famous passage in Daniel 7.13 in which 'one like a son of man' comes on the clouds of heaven to be presented before and enthroned beside one who is called 'the Ancient One'.

What I mean is this. Luke certainly intends us to be thinking of Daniel 7 in all its political significance. This is the moment at which Israel's representative is installed as the true world ruler, with all the warring pagan nations made subject to him. How much Luke intends us also to be thinking of an actual physical event it is hard to say. There is no problem, as far as I can see, about it *being* a physical event; as some have suggested, an upward movement is perhaps the best way of indicating a departure from one sphere in order to arrive in another. But neither the ancient Jews nor the early Christians believed that 'heaven' was a location within our present continuum of space and matter, a location situated at some distance from our world and to be reached by a primitive form of space travel. We are, after all, at this point at the edge of worldview, of language, of all human thought. We should not expect to be able to put a story like this into easy contemporary categories. Better to stick with this third point about ascension, that it is the fulfilment of Daniel 7. This is the great reversal, the moment when God welcomes the one who has suffered as Israel's representative at the hands of the monsters and is now to exercise judgment over them.

This brings us to the fourth and last point about the ascension. Anyone reading Luke's account at the beginning of Acts and already being familiar with the world of the early Roman Empire would realize what was happening. After the death of Julius Caesar, people swore they had seen his soul ascending to heaven. Augustus, Caesar's adopted son, promptly declared that Julius was therefore a god; which meant that he, Augustus, was now 'son of god'. This was, to put it mildly, of considerable political advantage. When Augustus himself died, the process was repeated, as it was with many (though not all) of his successors.

Luke's story isn't an exact copy of this tradition. Luke, after all, like all the early Christians, is a monotheist. There is no sense in which he supposes he is describing the adding of another god to the collection of them already 'in heaven'. And Jesus himself is 'son of God' in a sense that would take several generations of prayerful thinkers to explore fully. Nevertheless, the parallel is sufficiently close to make any readers in the Roman world realize what is going on. Jesus is radically upstaging Caesar. Actually, if we think of the story as the opening frame of the book of Acts, we get the point, because the closing frame is Paul in Rome, under Caesar's nose, announcing God as king and Jesus as Lord 'with all boldness, and with no one stopping him'. The whole book is the story of how Jesus, exercising his power as the CEO of earth as of heaven, sends out his followers as ambassadors to make his kingdom a reality, climaxing with the strange paradox of Paul in chains announcing that the Roman world has a new emperor. It is that paradox, indeed, that sets the tone for all kingdom-work in the present time, as we shall see again presently.

But even ascension is not the last moment in the story. Something stranger still is to happen in the future. The Jesus of 'yesterday' is to become the Jesus of 'tomorrow'. The story is incomplete without its final scene.

The return of Jesus

'Look out of the window,' say the sceptics. 'If you think Jesus is already installed as king of the world, why is the world still such a mess?' Fair question. But actually the story so far – even the story of the ascension itself – is not designed to make the sort of claim to which that sort of objection would pose an ultimate problem. Even the story of Jesus' resurrection and his going into 'heaven' are only the beginning of something new, something that will be completed one day, but that none of the early Christians supposed had been fully accomplished yet.

The early Christians were, after all, a small minority, staking their daring and apparently crazy claim about Jesus from a position of great weakness and vulnerability. They were perceived, with some justification, as a threat to the established order, and so they attracted criticism, threats, punishment and even death. But their threat to the present world was not of the usual kind. They were not ordinary revolutionaries, ready to take up arms to overthrow an existing regime and establish their own instead. Celebrating Jesus as the world's rightful king – as we see them doing in our earliest documents, the letters of Paul – was indeed a way of posing a challenge to Caesar and all other earthly 'lords'. But it was a different sort of challenge. It was not only the announcement of Jesus as the true king, albeit still the king-in-waiting, but the announcement of him as the true *sort* of king. Addressing the ambitious pair James and John, he put it like this: 'Pagan rulers . . . lord it over their subjects . . . But that's not how it's to be with you' (Matthew 20.25–26). And, as he said to Pilate, the kingdoms that are characteristic of 'this world' make their way by violence, but his sort of kingdom doesn't do that (John 18.36). We all know the irony of empires that offer people peace, prosperity, freedom and justice – and kill tens of thousands of people to make the point. Jesus' kingdom isn't like that. With him, the irony works the other way round. Jesus' death and his followers' suffering are the means by which his peace, freedom and justice come to birth on earth as in heaven.

Jesus' kingdom must come, then, by the *means* that correspond to the *message*. It's no good announcing love and peace if you make

194

angry, violent war to achieve it! That, as we shall see, is the watchword for the 'today' bit of the story of Jesus. But what about the 'tomorrow' or 'for ever' bit? What is the ultimate future?

Jesus' first followers were unequivocal: Jesus will return. He will come again. He will reappear in power and glory, triumphing over all the forces of death, decay and destruction, including the structures that have used those horrible forces to enslave and devastate human lives. The present mode of the story is not the end. Pundits debate the origin of the phrase, 'It ain't over till the fat lady sings' (the best guess is that it's a metaphor from opera, though it is applied to sport and even to church services). But in the Christian story it ain't over till the Master returns.

As with the ascension, there are several things we need to say right away about this extraordinary claim. (By now we ought to be getting used to extraordinary claims, not because we are dealing with fantasy or 'supernatural' speculation, but because Jesus himself opens the window on a world that, though real and solid, is very different from the world as most people see it.) And the first thing is: don't believe everything you read about the Rapture.

In fact, don't believe most of what you read about the Rapture. Many Christians, particularly in North America, have been taught for the last century and a half that when Jesus returns he will come down from 'heaven' and that his faithful people (i.e. Christians) will then fly upwards into the sky to meet him and be taken to heaven with him for ever. Sermons, books, films, and even radio and TV shows have fostered this image, at least in certain church traditions. Indeed, for some people today the Rapture is more or less the centre of their faith.

But it's a complete misunderstanding. It's based on a misreading of what Paul says about the return of Jesus in 1 Thessalonians 4.14–17, just four verses, with 'rapture' in only one, as the basis for a complete theory of everything:

> For, you see, if we believe that Jesus died and rose, that's the way God will also, through Jesus, bring with him those who have fallen asleep.
>
> Let me explain (this is the word of the Lord I'm speaking to you!). We who are alive, who remain until the Lord is present, will not find ourselves ahead of those who fell asleep. The Lord himself will come

down from heaven with a shouted order, with the voice of an archangel and the sound of God's trumpet. The Messiah's dead will rise first; then we who are alive, who are left, will be snatched up with them among the clouds, to meet the Lord in the air. And in this way we shall always be with the Lord.

What Paul is doing, not for the first time, is mixing his metaphors. The basis of it all, offered here as comfort and hope for the grieving, is that the Lord 'will come down from heaven'. Paul describes this in language that would remind biblically minded hearers of the scene in which Moses comes down the mountain. That's the significance of the archangel's voice and the trumpet. But then God's people will be exalted, like the 'one like a son of man' in Daniel 7.13, so that after their own suffering and death they will be with their Lord for ever. And the result is that Jesus will have his 'royal appearing', like Caesar coming back to Rome after a visit to the colonies. His glad, loyal citizens will 'go out to meet him', not in order to stay with him out in the countryside, away from the city, but to escort him in triumph and splendour back into his capital.

Of course these metaphors, when pressed, don't all fit together. You're not supposed to be able to draw the scene in a sketch-pad. Think of the book of Revelation, where in 5.6 we find the lion who is also a lamb 'standing there as though it had been slaughtered' (slaughtered lambs don't normally stand up), with seven horns (we can just about imagine that) and seven eyes (that's a bit harder). The point is that this language is *not meant to be taken literally*. It's a mixture of code, metaphor and political cartoon.

But the fact that this particular picture is a rich mixture of such styles of writing doesn't mean that nothing is going to happen. Some think that once you've said something is 'metaphorical', you mean it's 'all in the mind', with no corresponding events in the real world. On the contrary. Paul is giving his readers a set of lenses through which to look, but the event itself at which they are to look is definite, clear and vital. Lose this and you lose everything. Without the 'second coming', seen in proper biblical terms, following Jesus is reduced to a 'way of being religious', a private spirituality with a vague and uncertain personal hope, but with no prospect at all of a world radically transformed by Jesus as its rightful Lord. Some, indeed, are content to make that reduction, leaving Christian faith as a 'spirituality' that one might find helpful, but without any thought of the ancient vision of the Psalms and Isaiah, of the whole world healed, judged, put right, transformed under the sovereign rule of Israel's Messiah. That fits quite nicely within the postmodern reaction against an older and arrogant Christian 'triumphalism', but it is a lot less Jewish and a lot less Christian, and it has little to do with the actual Jesus himself.

Believing in the second coming itself is anything but arrogant. The whole point of it is to insist, over against not only the wider pagan world, but against all self-delusion or pretension within the church, that Jesus remains sovereign and will return at last to put everything right. This putting right (the biblical word for it is 'justice') is the sort of sigh-of-relief event that the whole world, at its best and at many other times too, longs for most deeply. All sorts of things are out of joint, both on a large and a small scale, in the world; and God the creator will put them straight. All sorts of things are still going wrong, corrupting the lives of human beings and the larger life of the environment, the planet itself; God the creator will put them right. All sorts of things are still wrong *with us, Jesus' followers*; Jesus, when he comes, will put us right as well. That may not be comfortable, but it's what we need. Believing he will do it is part of Christian humility. Waiting for it is part of Christian patience:

> When the king is revealed (and he is your life, remember), then you too will be revealed with him in glory.   (Colossians 3.4)

> Beloved ones, we are now, already, God's children; it hasn't yet been revealed what we are going to be. We know that when he is revealed we shall be like him, because we shall see him as he is.   (1 John 3.2)

But how will it happen? Thinking of the second coming or of Jesus 'returning' often raises the same kind of problems that we saw with the ascension. People who still think that 'heaven' is a long way away, up in the sky, and that that's where Jesus has gone, imagine that the second coming will be an event somewhat like the return of a space shuttle from its far-off orbit. Not so. *Heaven is God's space, God's dimension of present reality*, so that to think of Jesus 'returning' is actually, as both Paul and John say in the passages just quoted, to think of him presently invisible, but one day *reappearing*. It won't be

197

the case that Jesus will simply reappear within the world the way it presently is. His return – his reappearing – will be the central feature of the much greater event that the New Testament writers promise, based on Jesus' resurrection itself: heaven and earth will one day come together and be present and transparent to each other. That's what they were made for, and that's what God will accomplish one day. It has, in fact, already been accomplished in the person of Jesus himself; and what God has done in Jesus, bringing heaven and earth together at immense cost and with immense joy, will be achieved in and for the whole cosmos at last. That is what Paul says at the heart of one of his great visionary prayers:

> His plan was to sum up the whole cosmos in the king – yes, everything in heaven and on earth, in him.   (Ephesians 1.10)

This means that the second coming takes on all the dimensions present in Israel's scriptures, the dimensions of the whole creation singing with delight when Israel's God comes to 'judge' the world (Psalms 96; 98). 'Judgment' in this sense is like the 'judgment' given when a poor widow finally has her case heard, the bullies who have been oppressing her are firmly rebuked, and she is vindicated. 'Judgment' is what happens when someone who has been robbed of home and dignity and livelihood is upheld, with everything restored. 'Judgment' is what happens when a forest that has been damaged through over-zealous logging, on the one hand, and acid rain, on the other, is wisely replanted and the source of pollution identified and stopped. The world is out of joint, and God's 'judgment' will perform a great act of new creation through which it will be restored to the way God always intended it to be.

To speak of the second coming is therefore to speak of God's whole new world, the new world envisaged in Revelation 21—22 or Romans 8, and of Jesus at the middle of it, administering God's just, wise and healing rule. Jesus is the truly human being who will, in the end, take the properly human role (as in Genesis) of reflecting the creator's image of wise and fruitful order into the whole creation. That is what his 'coming' and his 'judgment' will mean. God will do for the whole cosmos, in the end, what he did for Jesus at Easter; the risen Jesus, remember, is the *prototype* of the new creation. God will do this *through* Jesus himself; the ascended Jesus, remember, is the *ruler* within the new creation as it bursts in upon the old. And God will do it through the *presence* of the risen and ascended Jesus when he comes to heal, to save, and also to judge.

That is why it is not arrogant to believe in the second coming. There are arrogant ways of thinking and speaking about it, of course, as though when Jesus returns we, his people, will be able to put our noses in the air and look down smugly on everyone else. A moment's reflection will show how silly this would be. Think back over the last twenty-four hours or the last seven days. Suppose Jesus had been there, physically present beside you, throughout that time. Would you have been happy to have him see what you did? Hear what you said? Know what you thought? When he comes, as the New Testament insists, he will bring to light all the hidden things that are now in darkness and expose the thoughts and intentions of the heart. He comes, of course, as the one who died for us; there is no doubting his love. But his love is the love that wants the very best for us and from us, not the sentimental kind that doesn't want to make a fuss and so refuses to confront the thing that's actually wrong. He loves in the way a doctor or a surgeon loves, wanting the best, working for life, dealing powerfully and drastically with the cancer or the blocked artery. The only proper Christian way to think of the second coming is, as I said, with humility and patience.

But also with faith, hope and love. 'And our eyes at last shall see him, through his own redeeming love.' That is our hope, our longing, our delight. Even so, we pray with the second to last verse of the Bible, 'Come, Lord Jesus.'

Jesus today

Jesus yesterday, Jesus tomorrow. What about Jesus today?

We omitted (deliberately) one of the other vital events that, in the New Testament, complete the story of Jesus. The resurrection is all about Jesus as the *prototype* of the new creation. The ascension is all about Jesus as the *ruler* of the new creation as it breaks into the world of the old. The second coming is all about Jesus as the *coming Lord and judge* who will transform the entire creation. And, in between resurrection and ascension, on the one hand, and the second coming, on the other, Jesus is the one who sends the Holy Spirit, his own Spirit, into the lives of his followers, so that he himself is powerfully present with them and in them, guiding them, directing them, and above all enabling them to bear witness to him as the world's true Lord and work to make that sovereign rule a reality. This – the coming of the Spirit, the story of Pentecost as in Acts 2 – is a vital part of the story of Jesus. Again, I and others have written a good deal about this. All we can do here is to summarize the main points in the light of what we've said about Jesus so far.

The Acts of the Apostles is the New Testament book that is most obviously about what happens when the Spirit comes. It should be equally obvious that the Spirit enables Jesus' followers to do and say things that the authorities, both Jewish and pagan, see as dangerous nonsense – just as they did with Jesus himself. When many people today think of the Holy Spirit, they think simply of personal spiritual experience (perhaps including 'charismatic' gifts such as 'speaking in tongues') or powerfully effective spiritual gifts such as healing. These are there in Acts, to be sure. But the story line is not about the church discovering these gifts and simply enjoying them for their own sake. It is about the church living as a new community, giving allegiance to Jesus as Lord rather than to the kings and chief priests who rule the Jewish world or the emperor or magistrates who rule the non-Jewish world. 'We must obey God,' declares Peter, 'not human beings!' (Acts 5.29).

We shouldn't be surprised, then, at how it works out. Since the whole story of Jesus' ascension and the Spirit's arrival in Acts 1—2 is basically about Jesus as the new Temple (joining heaven and earth together) and the Spirit enabling the church itself to be an outpost of that new Temple (humans, creatures of earth, being indwelt by the very breath of heaven), the conflict focuses on temples: first, the Temple in Jerusalem (ch. 7), and later the temples in Athens (ch. 17) and Corinth (ch. 19), before coming back to the one in Jerusalem (chs 22—26). The underlying issues in Acts – provoked by the Spirit – are about the things that come together in the Temple, namely, God and power. Who is the true God? Where is he now living? And, above all, *who is now in charge?* For the early Christians, the answer was,

'Jesus.' 'They're saying', said their accusers in Thessalonica, 'that there is another king, Jesus!' (17.7). Well, precisely. That's what the whole story has been about.

But, again, it's a different *kind* of kingship. That too is what the whole story has been about. The story of 'how Jesus became king' in Jerusalem, Judaea, Samaria and across the world (the programme announced in Acts 1.8) is anything but the smooth, triumphant procession of a conquering worldly monarch, obliterating the opposition by the normal military methods. *The methods of kingdom-work are in accordance with the message of Jesus as king*; that is, they involve suffering, misunderstanding, violence, execution and, in the final spectacular scene (before Paul gets to Rome with the message of this new world emperor), shipwreck. Luke tells the story of how Jesus becomes king in Acts in a way that matches exactly the message of how Jesus became king in his own public career.

We see the same picture when we look at the other books of the New Testament. Whether it's Paul's letters or the ones ascribed to Peter, whether it's Hebrews or that spectacular set piece of apocalyptic imagery we call Revelation, the message is the same. Jesus is the Lord, but it's the *crucified* Jesus who is Lord – precisely because it's his crucifixion that has won the victory over all the other powers that think of themselves as in charge of the world. But that means that his followers, charged with implementing his victory in the world, will themselves have to do so by the same method. One of the most striking things about some of (what we normally see as) the later material in the New Testament is the constant theme of suffering, suffering not as something merely to be bravely borne for Jesus' sake, but as something that is mysteriously taken up into the redemptive suffering of Jesus himself. He won his victory through suffering; his followers win theirs through sharing in his.

The Spirit and suffering. Great joy and great cost. Those who follow Jesus and claim him (and proclaim him) as Lord learn both of them. It's as simple as that.

So how does all this work out today? How does the vision of Acts look – the vision of the risen and ascended Jesus sending out his followers to proclaim him as the world's true Lord – when we come forward twenty-one centuries and into our own day?

Part 3

15

Jesus: the ruler of the world

What on earth does it mean, today, to say that Jesus is king, that he is Lord of the world? How can we say such a thing in our confused world? If we do want to say it, what are we saying that Jesus is up to, in our swirling mix of modern, postmodern and other cultural movements? What is he doing, in the midst of the dangerous clash of the new secularisms and the new fundamentalisms? What does the lordship of Jesus look like in practice in the world where we bail out the big banks when they suddenly run out of cash, but don't lift a finger to help the poorest of the poor who are paying the banks interest so the banks can get rich again?

All this is, of course, the subject for another book, or perhaps several. There are a thousand issues crying out for serious engagement. But part of the problem, I think, is farther back. Most Christians in today's world have not even begun to think how calling Jesus 'Lord' might affect the real world. When I said 'what on earth' at the start of this chapter, I meant, of course, what Jesus meant in the Lord's Prayer: 'Thy kingdom come *on earth* as in heaven.' How do we even get to first base in thinking about this today?

There are, broadly, four positions people can take as they face this question. There are plenty of local variations, but these four will do for a start. To help keep track of them, I'm going to invent four conversation partners: Andy, Billy, Chris and Davie. You can decide which of them are male and which are female (though that's not the point).

For Andy, it is straightforwardly meaningless to talk of Jesus being king or Lord. He's gone; the church has messed things up; nothing has really changed. It was a nice dream, but it's over. If there is any truth in Christianity, it's about a private spiritual experience. Nothing to do with the real, public world.

Billy disagrees. Yes, it doesn't look much as though Jesus is running the world right now, but that's because he is at the moment Lord of the *upper* world, of 'heaven', not of earth. 'Now above the sky he's king,' as the hymn puts it. But one day, Billy believes, Jesus will return to sort it all out. Then, and only then, he'll be truly the king of everything. Billy prefers to believe that Jesus will do this by establishing a new heaven-and-earth reality, but knows of some other Christians who think that the final kingdom-establishing act will be blowing creation to bits in a huge Armageddon moment and establishing a completely other-worldly 'kingdom' in a different sphere altogether. This reminds Billy of the soldiers in Vietnam who explained that they had to destroy the village in order to save it. But the point remains: Jesus *will* be Lord one day, but he isn't really at the moment.

Chris and Davie are both convinced that neither Andy nor Billy is taking seriously the claims either of Jesus himself or of the New Testament. Jesus, as we have seen throughout this book, believed that God was indeed becoming king in and through his own work and that his death would be critical in bringing this about. After his resurrection, he really does seem to have taught and claimed that God's kingdom was now becoming a reality in a new way. It really had been launched. This is the claim that Andy denies and Billy postpones.

Do Chris and Davie have anything better to offer?

Chris is excited about the vision of Paul in Colossians, according to which Jesus is *already* in charge of the world. Paul declares that 'the gospel has been announced in all creation under heaven' (1.23), and he can't mean that every human being then alive had heard about Jesus. He must mean that with Jesus' death and resurrection something happened to the very structure of the cosmos itself: a kind of deep-level earthquake running through all reality. So Chris declares that the lordship of Jesus isn't a matter of church members going out and telling people about him, or working to improve the world. That, Chris thinks, is simply dualistic, as though the church is 'outside' the world and trying to 'do things to it'.

Instead, it's a matter of the church waking up to what God is doing in the world already. The signs of Jesus' kingdom are to be seen, Chris suggests enthusiastically, in the movements of thought and belief that shape the lives of millions. Chris is old enough to remember the groundswell of horror that, in the 1960s, recognized racism for what it was, in America and South Africa in particular, and worked to eliminate it. (It took longer in South Africa, but the movements were clearly related.) Such movements may or may not have been initiated or led by Christians; some were, some weren't. That's not the point: God isn't confined to the church. Chris is now inclined to see a similar God-given groundswell of opinion in the feminist movement and the green agenda. For Chris, God is at work in the world, and our task is to see what he's doing and to join in, to do it with him. That is how the kingship of Jesus is to be worked out in the world today.

Davie pours cold water on Chris's hot-headed enthusiasm. Chris is simply repeating what Hitler's tame theologians said in the 1930s: 'God has raised up the German nation to transform the world; the church must get in line and lend its support to what God is already doing.' That, Davie recalls, is partly why Karl Barth uttered his famous 'No!' There are many times when the church needs to recognize quite other 'forces' at work in the great movements of ideas and beliefs, forces that worship the idols of money, military power, blood and soil, and not least the supposed 'life force' of sex itself. All these, Davie insists, drag the church down into a form of pantheism, where God and the world are simply confused with one another, and dark, deathly forces within the world are given a cheerful would-be Christian whitewashing.

Instead of that, Davie proposes, what we need is a fresh word from God, a word from outside, a fresh summons to worship Jesus and so to be fortified in our stand against all human power systems and idolatries. The church must not collude with the world! Jesus is driving the car, not merely steering a toboggan carried downhill by its own weight. And sometimes the car has to go in the opposite direction to the rest of the traffic. This isn't dualism, Davie insists. This is how Jesus is claiming what is rightfully his own in the first place, but has been under enemy rule. This is what it looks like for Jesus to be king today.

Andy, of course, listens to this discussion and thinks it's a waste of time. Billy, naturally, thinks it's a category mistake, since, though Jesus does care about the way the world is at the moment, the only way he's going to fix it is by coming back once and for all.

Chris, meanwhile, is uncomfortably aware of leaving open the question of *which* of the movements of history we claim as the work of God. Communism or capitalism? Rationalism or Romanticism? Modernism or postmodernism? Davie, similarly, is uncomfortably aware that, among those who look for a fresh word from God to say no to the idols of our time, some of those 'fresh words' sound like Christian versions of the ideology of the Right and some like Christian versions of today's Left. Others, again, call for a plague on both houses and see the 'fresh word' as a summons to Christians to abandon the structures and to live a holy, detached, separate life. Chris and Davie are both convinced that Jesus is, in some sense, already Lord of the world. But they can't agree on how that lordship, that sovereign, saving rule, is to make its way in the world.

Sharp-eyed readers will have spotted that Chris and Davie are playing out a much older debate. The ancient Stoics thought that God and the world were more or less the same thing, so that the inner workings of the world were the inner workings of the divine itself. The ancient Epicureans believed that the gods, having set the world in motion, had left it to its own devices and that they seldom if ever stepped in to redirect traffic, to perform strange 'interventions' or 'miracles'.

The Stoics and the Epicureans were successful precisely because these are the two 'natural' positions towards which people who reflect about the nature of reality can easily be drawn. Either God and the world collapse into one another, or they are divided by a great gulf. Just as one of W. S. Gilbert's characters declares, 'Every boy and every girl / that's born into the world alive / is either a little Liberal / or else a little Conservative,' so it sometimes seems as though people naturally tend to be either Stoics or Epicureans. Either we see the world, and indeed ourselves, as full of signals of the presence of divinity, or we see the world empty of the divine, doing its own thing, with the gods now far away. We become, in other words, either pantheists or dualists.

Christians have tended to produce would-be Christian versions of these two positions, but, as I have argued elsewhere (particularly in *Simply Christian*[1]), the classic Jewish and Christian viewpoint does it all differently. In ancient Judaism and early Christianity, heaven and earth, God's world and our world, overlap and interlock in various ways that put quite a different spin on all sorts of things. How does this, then, play out in relation to the absolutely central question: what might it mean, today, to say that Jesus is Lord? What would it look like if we took seriously the claim that in his death and resurrection Jesus really did complete what he had been doing during his public career, that he really did launch God's sovereign rule on earth as in heaven? What does it mean, today, to say that Jesus is already ruling the world?

One additional note before we continue. As I stressed in *Surprised by Hope*,[2] when we think about God's kingdom in the present and the future, we must always be clear that the ultimate triumph is God's work and God's alone. Billy reacts rightly against any suggestion that we, in the present, are 'building God's kingdom'. Only God does that. We do not have God's kingdom in our pockets, to dispense at will. But what Billy doesn't realize is that we may be called, nonetheless, to build *for* God's kingdom. What we do in the present, as Paul insists, is not wasted (1 Corinthians 15.58). It will all be part of the eventual structure, even though at the moment we have no idea how.

So what is Jesus up to in the present time? What does it mean to think of him as king, already, now? What will it look like, particularly, not only to think of him in this way, but actually to work for his kingdom?

God's rule – through us

As usual, when a discussion reaches deadlock, it's probably because one or more key factors have been left out of consideration. And in this case we don't have to look far to see what's missing. The crucial factor in Jesus' kingdom-project picks up the crucial factor in God's creation project. God intended to rule the world *through human beings*. Jesus picks up this principle, rescues it and transforms it.

Rescues it? Yes, because humans, of course, have messed the world up. Whatever you think of the much misunderstood doctrine of original sin (that's a topic for another time), it would be extremely foolish to suppose that humans, left to themselves, have not done amazingly horrible things as well as amazingly wonderful ones. Humans make bombs as well as music. They build torture chambers as well as hospitals and schools. They create deserts as well as gardens.

And yet the vocation sketched in Genesis 1 remains: humans are to be God's image-bearers, that is, they are to reflect his sovereign rule into the world. Humans are the vital ingredient in God's kingdom-project. When we ask about the way in which God wants to run the world and then focus on the sharper question of how Jesus now runs the world, we should expect, from the whole of scripture, that the answer will have something to do with the delegation of God's authority, of Jesus' authority, to human beings.

This is why several of the New Testament writers make a direct connection between Jesus' rescue project, climaxing in his crucifixion, and the renewal of the human project. *Jesus rescues human beings in order that through them he may rule his world in the new way he always intended.* Thus the heavenly chorus sings the new song:

> 'You are worthy to take the scroll;
> you are worthy to open its seals;
> for you were slaughtered and with your own blood
> you purchased a people for God,
> from every tribe and tongue,
> from every people and nation,
> and made them a kingdom and priests to our God
> and they will reign on the earth.'
> (Revelation 5.9–10)

This, then, is how Jesus puts his kingdom-achievement into operation: through the humans he has rescued. That is why, right at the start of his public career, he called associates to share his work and then to carry it on after he had laid the foundations, particularly in his saving death. It has been all too easy for us to suppose that, if Jesus really was king of the world, he would, as it were, do the whole thing all by himself. But that was never his way – because it was never God's way. It wasn't how creation itself was supposed to work. And Jesus' kingdom-project is nothing if not the rescue and renewal of God's creation-project.

Nor was this simply pragmatic, as though God (or Jesus) wanted a bit of help, needed someone to whom certain tasks could be delegated. It has to do with something deep within the very being of God, the same thing that led him to create a world that was other than himself. One name for this something is Love. Another is Trinity.

Either way, deeply mysterious though it remains, we should recognize that when Jesus announced his intention to launch God's kingdom at last, he did it in a way that involved and included other human beings. God works through Jesus; Jesus works through his followers. This is not accidental.

Some things (like the crucifixion itself) had to be done by Jesus himself, alone. Other things (like the itinerant ministry around Galilee) could and should be shared. God and Jesus don't do what they do by blasting a way through all opposition. They do what they do by working with the grain of the cosmos, by planting seeds that grow secretly, by calling humans to be co-creators. God's kingdom comes like a farmer sowing a fresh crop or like a vineyard owner looking for workers to pick the grapes, bringing people on board to help. When God goes to work – when Jesus becomes king – human beings are not downgraded, reduced to being pawns or ciphers. In God's kingdom, humans get to reflect God at last into the world, in the way they were meant to. They become more fully what humans were meant to be. That is how God becomes king. That is how Jesus goes to work in the present time. Exactly as he always did.

That is why Jesus answers his followers the way he does at the start of the book of Acts (where we left them at the end of the previous chapter). The disciples ask Jesus if this is now the moment for God's kingdom to be 'restored to Israel'. Jesus, answering obliquely, as he does so often when correcting the assumptions of questioners, tells them that they are to be his 'witnesses':

> So when the apostles came together, they put this question to Jesus.
> 'Master,' they said, 'is this the time when you are going to restore the kingdom to Israel?'
> 'It's not your business to know about times and dates,' he replied. 'The father has placed all that under his own direct authority. What will happen, though, is that you will receive power when the holy spirit comes upon you. Then you will be my witnesses in Jerusalem, in all Judaea and Samaria, and to the very ends of the earth.' (Acts 1.6–8)

We have to imagine the disciples here in a strange mixture of joy and bewilderment. Jesus' resurrection had caught them gloriously by surprise. It didn't fit at all into the game plan they thought they had been working with. It didn't fit the plan they had assumed that *Jesus himself* had had. They were expecting him to become king of Israel, in some reasonable if revolutionary way. With that, he would become (according to the ancient scriptural promises about Israel's king) Lord of the world. So what does Jesus' answer mean?

Here once again we have to avoid the usual downgrading and domesticating of the apostolic mission. We have to train ourselves to see it with first-century Jewish and Christian eyes. It isn't a matter of Jesus saying, in effect, 'No, you've got it wrong. Forget the idea of me being some sort of a king. You just have to go and tell people to believe in me, and then you and they will all come and join me in heaven.' That is certainly not how Luke, telling the story, sees it, and it wouldn't fit with all that we have seen of how Jesus himself saw his mission during his public career. Instead, Jesus' answer here is designed to say that, yes, the kingdom is indeed now being launched. He is indeed Israel's king; he is therefore, indeed, the Lord of the world. But the way his kingdom is being implemented is, once more, *through these human beings*. Modern Christians use the word 'witness' to mean 'tell someone else about your faith'. The way Luke seems to be using it is, 'tell someone else that Jesus is the world's true Lord'. The story of what happened next is written in such a way as to say, 'This is how the kingdom is to come. This is how Jesus is starting to rule the world. This is what it will look like when God becomes king on earth as in heaven.'

We therefore have to reread the book of Acts with a relentless determination not to be drawn down into the usual categories, into stories of spiritual experiences, remarkable healings, strange divine promptings and leadings, conversions, and so on. All of these matter. They matter very much indeed. But they are the modus operandi of the thing that *really* matters, the fact that through Jesus' followers God is establishing his kingdom and the rule of Jesus himself on earth as in heaven. Underneath the exciting 'spiritual' experiences there is a constant theme that emerges, for instance, when Jesus' followers speak of having to obey God rather than human beings. The powers of the world do their utmost to stamp out the new vision, the new Way. But, despite the best efforts of chief priests and governors, of kings and mobs and courts and councils, Jesus is celebrated as Lord, even over the wild waves that shipwreck Paul and threaten to stop his getting to Rome to announce God as king and Jesus as Lord at the heart of the greatest superpower the world had ever known.

An additional theme in Acts ties this kingdom-work of the disciples with the theme we saw again and again in Jesus' public career. Jesus, we remember, redefined 'space' around himself, so that the 'holy place' of the Temple in Jerusalem was upstaged by his own work, by his own person. (This was not an unnatural thing for a Jewish reform movement to do, as we know from Qumran, where the Essene community saw its own common life as the replacement for the Jerusalem Temple.) But now, with Jesus joining heaven and earth together in his own person, the Holy Spirit, which anointed and equipped Jesus himself for his kingdom-work, comes pouring out onto his followers, so that they become as it were an extension of that new Temple. Where they are, heaven and earth are joined together. Jesus is with them, his life is at work in and through them, and, whether in Jerusalem or out in the wider world, they are the place where the living God, the God who is reclaiming the world for his own, is alive and active and establishing his sovereign rule.

That is why, as we saw earlier, the great scenes of confrontation and conflict in Acts all focus on the question of temples, both Jewish and pagan, and on the role and claim of the Christian community in relation to them (chs 7, 14, 17, 19, 22—26). The Temple was the place, like the tabernacle in the wilderness, from which God ruled Israel. Now the new Temple – Jesus and his Spirit-filled followers – is the place from which and through which God is beginning to implement the world-transforming kingdom that was achieved in and through Jesus and his death and resurrection.

Let's pause there and see how this short study of the role of humans in God's plan and the opening of Acts have contributed to the discussion we listened to earlier.

Andy, grudgingly, can see that Acts really does claim that Jesus is now the Lord of the world, but he still insists that it's really all wishful thinking. Nothing has really changed; it's still just a few fanatics rushing around the world thinking they're doing God's will.

Billy is still looking for the final second coming when all will be fulfilled. That's there in Acts 1 as well. But Billy too has to admit that

Luke really does seem to have thought that Jesus' resurrection and the sending of the Spirit meant the arrival – albeit not yet the full completion – of the kingdom of which Jesus had spoken during his public ministry. Perhaps it isn't all postponed to the last day after all. But what sense can we make of this?

Chris is unsure, not wanting to say that God was simply at work in the Roman Empire, yet pointing out that without Roman roads and magistrates Paul would not have been able to do half of what he did. God does seem to have provided, as it were, the infrastructure through the work of people totally outside Israel and the church, even if then the good news had to be taken by the apostles themselves.

Davie is inclined to stress the 'miraculous' – the sudden rush of wind at Pentecost, the dramatic divine 'interventions'. Yet even here Luke's story seems to be one not merely of something new, but of the deep-seated renewal of the old order, the old world. The disciples are rescued from further persecution by a leading, and still unbelieving, Jewish rabbi, Gamaliel. Paul is rescued from certain death by a Roman centurion. God seems to be at work not only through the church, but also in the world outside. How, once more, can we make sense of all of this? What is Jesus up to?

All four, Chris and Davie especially, would do well to study Acts 17, where Luke gives a summary account of Paul's speech to the philosophically minded high court in Athens. Paul's speech is both a defence against serious charges ('proclaiming foreign divinities', which is close to what got Socrates condemned) and an explanation of the Christian worldview in which the fresh news of Jesus' resurrection and of God's upcoming judgment of the world completes, and does not destroy, the ancient Jewish wisdom of the creator God, who has remained as close as breath to his creation and to human beings. Somehow, if we are to speak wisely of God as king and Jesus as Lord, we have to speak of something radically new *and* the refreshment of something radically ancient, something fundamental in the way the world is. And if we are not just to speak of it, but to be *part* of it – to be among the humans who are enlisted in God's project – then we need to understand the framework within which it all makes sense.

The centrality of worship

All kingdom-work is rooted in *worship*. Or, to put it the other way round, worshipping the God we see at work in Jesus is the most politically charged act we can ever perform. Christian worship declares that *Jesus* is Lord and that therefore, by strong implication, nobody else is. What's more, it doesn't just declare it as something to be believed, like the fact that the sun is hot or the sea wet. It commits the worshipper to allegiance, to following this Jesus, to being shaped and directed by him. Worshipping the God we see in Jesus orients our whole being, our imagination, our will, our hopes and our fears away from the world where Mars, Mammon and Aphrodite (violence, money and sex) make absolute demands and punish anyone who resists. It orients us instead to a world in which love is stronger than death, the poor are promised the kingdom, and chastity (whether married or single) reflects the holiness and faithfulness of God himself. Acclaiming Jesus as Lord plants a flag that supersedes the flags of the nations, however 'free' or 'democratic' they may be. It challenges *both* the tyrants who think they are, in effect, divine *and* the 'secular democracies' that have effectively become, if not divine, at least ecclesial, that is, communities that are trying to do and be what the church was supposed to do and be, but without recourse to the one who sustains the church's life. Worship creates – or should create, if it is allowed to be truly itself – a community that marches to a different beat, that keeps in step with a different Lord.

Ideally, then – I shall come to the problems with this in a moment – the church, the community that hails Jesus as Lord and king, and feasts at his table celebrating his victorious death and resurrection, is constituted as the 'body of the Messiah'. This famous Pauline image is not a random 'illustration'. It expresses Paul's conviction that *this is the way in which Jesus now exercises his rule in the world – through the church, which is his Body*. Paul, rooted as he was in the ancient scriptures, knew well that the creator's plan was to look after his creation through obedient humankind. For Paul, Jesus himself is the Obedient Man who is now therefore in charge of the world; and the church is 'his body, the fullness of the one who fills all in all' (Ephesians 1.23). It is this vocation that gives the church courage to stand up in the face of the bullying self-appointed masters of the world, to resist them when they are forcing their communities to go in the wrong way, while at the same time demonstrating, in its own life, that there is a different way of being human, a way pioneered and now made possible by Jesus himself. 'God's wisdom, in all its rich variety', is to be 'made known to the rulers and authorities in the heavenly places – through the church!' (Ephesians 3.10).

This is the point at which a great deal of Jesus' own kingdom-agenda comes into its own. His great Sermon on the Mount opens with the Beatitudes, which are normally read either as a special form of 'Christian ethic' ('This is how you are to behave, if you want to be really special people') or as the rules you must keep in order to 'go to heaven when you die'. This latter view has been reinforced by the standard misreading of the first Beatitude. 'Blessings on the poor in spirit! The kingdom of heaven is yours' (Matthew 5.3) doesn't mean, 'You will go to heaven when you die.' It means *you will be one of those through whom God's kingdom, heaven's rule, begins to appear on earth as in heaven.* The Beatitudes are the agenda for kingdom-people. They are not simply about how to behave, so that God will do something nice *to* you. They are about the way in which Jesus wants to rule the world. He wants to do it *through* this sort of people – people, actually, just like himself (read the Beatitudes again and see). The Sermon on the Mount is a call to Jesus' followers to take up their vocation as light to the world, as salt to the earth – in other words, as people through whom Jesus' kingdom-vision is to become a reality. This is how to be the people through whom the victory of Jesus over the powers of sin and death is to be implemented in the wider world.

The work of the kingdom, in fact, is summed up pretty well in those Beatitudes. When God wants to change the world, he doesn't send in the tanks. He sends in the meek, the mourners, those who are hungry and thirsty for God's justice, the peacemakers, and so on. Just as God's whole *style*, his chosen way of operating, reflects his generous love, sharing his rule with his human creatures, so the way in which those humans then have to behave if they are to be agents of Jesus' lordship reflects in its turn the same sense of vulnerable, gentle, but powerful self-giving love. It is because of this that the world has been changed by people like William Wilberforce, campaigning tirelessly to abolish slavery; by Desmond Tutu, working and praying not just to end apartheid, but to end it in such a way as to produce a reconciled, forgiving South Africa; by Cicely Saunders, starting a hospice for terminally ill patients ignored by the medical profession and launching a movement that has, within a generation, spread right around the globe.

These are paradigm cases. Jesus rules the world today not just through his people 'behaving themselves', keeping a code of ethics, and engaging in certain spiritual practices, important though those are. The Beatitudes are much more than a 'new rule of life', as though one could practise them in private, away from the world. Jesus rules the world through those who launch new initiatives that radically challenge the accepted ways of doing things: jubilee projects to remit ridiculous and unpayable debt, housing trusts that provide accommodation for low-income families or homeless people, local and sustainable agricultural projects that care for creation instead of destroying it in the hope of quick profit, and so on. We have domesticated the Christian idea of 'good works', so that it has simply become 'the keeping of ethical commands'. In the New Testament, 'good works' are what Christians are supposed to be doing in and for the wider community. *That is how the sovereignty of Jesus is put into effect.*

What, then, does it look like when Jesus is enthroned? It looks like new projects that do what Jesus' mother's great song announced: put down the mighty from their seat, exalt the humble and meek, fulfil ancient promises, but send the rich away empty. The church made its way in the world for many centuries by doing all this kind of thing. Now that in many countries the 'state' has assumed responsibility for many of them (that's part of what I mean by saying that the state, not least in Western democracies, has become 'ecclesial', a kind of secular shadow church), the church has been in danger of forgetting that these are its primary tasks. Jesus went about feeding the hungry, curing the sick and rescuing lost sheep; his Body is supposed to be doing the same. That is how his kingdom is at work. That is how *he* is at work. Acts begins by saying that in the first book (i.e. the gospel of Luke) the writer described 'everything Jesus *began* to do and teach' (Acts 1.1). The implication is clear. The story of Acts, even after Jesus' ascension, is about what Jesus *continued* to do and teach. And the way he did it and taught it was – through his followers.

But of course it doesn't stop there. When the church does and teaches what Jesus is doing and teaching, it will produce the same reaction that Jesus produced during his public career. A good deal of what the church has to do and say will fly in the face of the 'spirit of the age', what passes for 'received wisdom' in this or that generation. So be it. The day the church can no longer say, 'We must obey God rather than human beings' (Acts 5.29), it ceases to be the church. This may well mean suffering or persecution. That has been a reality since the very beginning, and for many Christians it is still the case today. Some of the most profound passages in the New Testament are those in which the church's own sufferings are related directly to those of Jesus, its Messiah and Lord. Kingdom and cross went together in his own work; they will go together in the kingdom-work of his followers.

The role of the church

This vision of the church's calling – to be the means through which Jesus continues to work and to teach, to establish his sovereign rule on earth as in heaven – is an ideal so high that it might seem not only unattainable, but hopelessly out of touch, triumphalistic and self-congratulatory. One of today's most-repeated clichés is that there are lots of people who find God believable, but the church unbearable, Jesus appealing, but the church appalling. We are never short of ecclesial follies and failings, as the sorrowing faithful and the salivating journalists know well. What does it mean to say that Jesus is king when the people who are supposed to be putting his kingship into practice are letting the side down so badly?

There are three things to say here, and each of them matters quite a lot. To begin with, for every foolish or wicked Christian leader who ends up in court, in the newspapers, or both, there are dozens, hundreds, thousands who are doing a great job, often unnoticed except within their own communities. The effect of perspective (we only notice the things that get into the papers, but the papers only report the odd and the scandalous) means that almost all of what is done by the churches goes unreported, allowing sneering outsiders to assume that the church is collapsing into a little heap of squabbling factions. Mostly it isn't. The newspaper perspective is like that of someone who walks down a certain street on the one day a week when people put out their rubbish for collection and who then reports that the street is always full of rubbish. Christians ought not to collude with the sneerers. 'Walk down the street some other time,' we ought to say. 'Come and see us on a normal day.'

Second, though, we must never forget that the way Jesus worked then and works now is through forgiveness and restoration. His spectacular conversation with Peter (John 21.15–19), who would certainly have had his name in the papers after his appalling behaviour on the night Jesus was arrested, shows a depth of love and trust. The church is not supposed to be a society of perfect people doing great work. It's a society of forgiven sinners repaying their unpayable debt of love by working for Jesus' kingdom in every way they can, knowing themselves to be unworthy of the task. The moment any Christian, particularly any Christian leader, forgets that – the moment any of us imagine that we are automatically special or above the dangers and temptations that afflict ordinary mortals – that is the moment when we are in gravest danger. Peter's disastrous, humiliating crash came an hour or two after he had declared that he would follow Jesus to prison and even to death.

I suspect that part at least of the cause of the scandals that have afflicted some parts of the church is creeping triumphalism, which allows some people to think that because of their baptism, vocation, ordination or whatever, they are immune to serious sin – or that, if it happens, it must be a 'blip' rather than a telltale sign of a serious problem. Nor will it do to refer to Jesus' love and forgiveness as an excuse for sweeping things under the carpet. That's just cheap grace; real forgiveness involves real confrontation with what has gone wrong. Nobody reading John 21 could doubt that Peter's problem had been addressed and dealt with. The kingdom-message of forgiveness, healing and reconciliation applies as much to those who are now implementing it as to those to whom they minister. This is a vital part of the way in which Jesus operates right now, today, as part of his kingdom-project.

But the third point is perhaps the most important, and it opens up a whole new area at which we hinted earlier on and to which we now return. The way in which Jesus exercises his sovereign lordship in the present time includes his strange, often secret, sovereignty over the nations and their rulers. What does this mean? How does the kingship of Jesus, at work in the wider world, relate to the specific vocation of the church to be Jesus' agents in implementing his sovereign rule?

Some, indeed, have been so overwhelmed by the failure, short-sightedness and sin of the church that they have trumpeted God's work in the wider world as though to put the church in its place. To listen to some theologians, you might think that God was wonderfully at work everywhere in the world *except* in the church. This position is always in danger of the trap towards which, in our earlier discussion, Chris seemed to be marching: hailing movements of thought and opinion, the rise and fall of empires, as places where 'God was at work', so that one simply had to 'do it with him' to get on board with the forward movement of the divine purpose.

This point of view has had a huge boost, over the last two centuries, by the latent Whig view of history, according to which things are moving inexorably towards a more 'open', freedom-loving, Western, democratic kind of society. People even talk of being 'on the wrong side of history', as though they knew not only what the last twenty years had produced, but what the next twenty years were going to produce as well. The idolization of 'progress', of 'moving with the times', is part of the same movement. 'Now that we live in the twenty-first century . . .' people begin, as though it were obvious that one's ethics or theology ought to change with the calendar. All this is a form of creeping pantheism, of looking at certain trends in the wider world and deducing that they are what 'God' is doing. (It's also very selective; it cheerfully screens out all the inventions of modernism, such as guillotines and gas chambers, which do not exactly fit the picture of an upward journey into light.) Just as we must not be triumphalistic or complacent about what Jesus is doing in and through the church, so we ought not to be complacent about how 'wonder-fully' God is at work in the world outside the church.

But we must give full weight to the difficult but important biblical vision of God's sovereignty over the nations and his determination to shape their fortunes to serve his larger purposes. This belief is so important for any vision of what it means to speak of Jesus' kingship in the present time that we must spell it out slightly more fully before drawing the threads together.

Once again, three things need to be said very clearly. The first is that God's principle of operation (his intention to run his world through human beings) applies just as much here as elsewhere. God wants the world to be ordered, not chaotic. He intends to bring that order to the world through the work, the thought, the planning and the wisdom of human beings. Human rulers were God's idea in the first place. The Bible insists that this was a good and wise plan.

This is so whether or not the human beings in question have any thought of God or any desire to serve him. If they have, so much the better, though that will by no means guarantee that all their decisions are either wise, good or correct. To be a Christian and to be a ruler does not mean that one can claim an infallibility that Christians believe belongs only to God (and that Roman Catholics believe that God shares, on certain occasions, with the pope). Likewise, if the rulers are not God-fearing, that does not mean they are not performing a task God wants to have performed. Precisely because God cares passionately for the weak, the vulnerable and the poor, God desires that in each society there should be rulers who will see to it that such people are looked after and given their rights rather than, as is bound to happen in a state of anarchy, left to the mercy of the unscrupulous and the bullies. Strictly speaking, in fact, there is actually no such thing as anarchy, or not for very long. Pretty soon those with money and muscle take over, and woe betide the helpless when that happens. No: God desires order, not chaos, and calls human rulers, whether they know it or not, to bring that order about. Just as you don't have to tell people (unless there is something very unusual about them) that they are made for human relationships, on the one hand, and made to look after the natural world, on the other (friendship and gardening just happen; you don't have to compel people to do them), so you don't have to tell people that they are made to organize their world, whether it's their personal space or a city council.

Second, even when the rulers are wild or wicked, God can bend their imaginings to serve his purpose. The Bible tells many stories in which God seems to take charge and overrule the intentions of pagan monarchs. He uses the Assyrians as a stick with which to beat his own people (Isaiah 10), even though he then punishes the Assyrians in turn, because they did what they did with a haughty arrogance. He raises up the Chaldeans, 'that fierce and impetuous nation' (Habakkuk 1.6), to bring his wrath upon his own wayward people. But it isn't all bad: God also raises up a pagan king, Cyrus the Persian, to bring his people back from exile in Babylon (Isaiah 45.1–7, 12–13). Even when looking back at a fairly godless and arrogant set of regimes, the book of Daniel affirms again and again the sovereignty of God over the nations of the world, the kingdom of God over the kingdoms of the world. They are not necessarily doing what God would have wanted, but nor are they entirely outside his will and power. God will, sooner or later, bring about the final judgment of the powers that range themselves arrogantly against him. But, in the meantime, his 'sovereignty' works not by cutting them off the moment they do anything wrong, but by turning and bending them to his will. 'The Most High has sovereignty over the kingdom of mortals and gives it to whom he will' (Daniel 4.32).

Third, then, God will in the end call the nations to account. This is the further manifestation of his sovereignty over them. Daniel 7, with its great judgment scene, belongs with such seminal passages as Psalm 2 in declaring that, though the nations may rage and bluster, God will eventually have them judged and put in their place. He will do so, what's more, in the same way that he has chosen to act throughout his creation: through a human being. In Psalm 2 it is the king. In Daniel 7 it is 'one like a son of man', representing God's people. Not surprisingly, people in the first century, both Jewish and Christian, saw the two pictures as one.

The judgment scene in Daniel 7 serves as the backdrop for Jesus' own sense of vocation. As we saw earlier, this is a key entry point for understanding what God's kingdom as inaugurated in Jesus' life, death, resurrection and ascension might actually mean. There can be no doubt that Jesus' first followers believed that Jesus had fulfilled this vision of Psalm 2 and Daniel 7. Jesus himself had constantly hinted at something like this, though until the great events of Calvary and Easter nobody had worked out either what it might mean or how it would be put into effect. But these events, seen in this light, mean that we have to take very seriously the early Christian belief that Jesus was indeed now exalted; he was now in charge; he was already, now, calling the nations to account.

And he was going to do so through his followers, those to whom he had given his Spirit. This, whether we like it or not, is where we come in.

Yes, God can and does work in all sorts of ways outside the church. There are many movements of thought and energy totally beyond the life of the church in which wise Christians can discern and celebrate God's sovereign and gracious presence. Paul, in a moment of visionary affirmation, looks out on a world full of things to celebrate: 'whatever is true, whatever is holy, whatever is upright, whatever is pure, whatever is attractive, whatever has a good reputation; anything virtuous, anything praiseworthy' (Philippians 4.8). We thank God for his wonderful work well beyond the borders of Christendom. God is the sovereign creator; he can and does do all sorts of things without our knowing, without our involvement.

But we do not, because of that, lose sight of one of the church's primary roles: *to bear witness to the sovereign rule of Jesus, holding the world to account.* And when I say 'bear witness', I mean it in the strong sense I spoke of earlier. Like a witness in a lawcourt, we are not just telling about our private experiences. We are declaring things that, by their declaration, will change the way things are going.

This means that the church has a task that, in our modern Western democracies, we have attempted to replicate in other ways. We have tried to have some semblance of 'accountability'. If the voters don't like someone, they don't have to vote for that candidate next time. We all know that this is a very blunt instrument. Here in Britain, the majority of Parliamentary seats are 'safe'. In any case, even if you vote for 'the other lot', you are still voting for politicians, and many people now believe that politicians are, as a class, part of the problem rather than part of the solution. In the United States, whoever you vote for, you still get a millionaire. And so on. Accountability isn't all it's cracked up to be.

So those who follow Jesus have, front and centre within their vocation, the task of being the real 'opposition'. This doesn't mean, of course, that they must actually oppose everything that the official government tries to do. They must weigh it, sift it, hold it to account, affirm what can be affirmed, point out things that are lacking or not quite in focus, critique what needs critiquing, and denounce, on occasion, what needs denouncing. It is very telling that, in the early centuries of church history, the Christian bishops gained a reputation in the wider world of being the champions of the poor. They spoke up for their rights; they spoke out against those who would abuse and ill-treat them. Of course! The bishops were followers of Jesus – what else would you expect? That role continues to this day. And it goes much wider. The church has a wealth of experience and centuries of careful reflection in the fields of education, health care, the treatment of the elderly, the needs and vulnerabilities of refugees and migrants, and so on. We should use these to full effect.

This facet of the church's 'witness', this central vocation through which Jesus continues his work to this day, has been marginalized. Modern Western democracies haven't wanted to be held to account in this way and so have either officially or unofficially driven a fat wedge between 'church' and 'state'. But, as we have hinted already, this has actually changed the meanings of both words. 'State' has expanded to do some of what 'church' should be doing; and the churches themselves have colluded with the privatization of 'religion', leaving all the things that the church used to be best at to the 'state' or other agencies. 'Religion', as one recent writer says, then 'dwindles to a kind of personal pastime, like breeding gerbils or collecting porcelain'.[3] No wonder, when people within the church speak up or speak out on key issues of the day, those who don't like what they say tell them to go back to their private 'religious' world.

But speak up and speak out we must, because we have not only the clear instruction of Jesus himself, but the clear promise that *this is how he will exercise his sovereignty; this is how he will make his kingdom a reality.* In John's gospel Jesus tells his followers that the Spirit will call the world to account:

'When he comes, he will prove the world to be in the wrong on three counts: sin, justice and judgment. In relation to sin – because they don't believe in me. In relation to justice – because I'm going to the father, and you won't see me any more. In relation to judgment – because the ruler of this world is judged.' (16.8–11)

And the point of this dense little promise is worryingly clear: the Spirit will do all this *through the church*. That is the mandate. That is how Jesus intends to operate. That is how the victory he won at Calvary is to be implemented in the world.

In particular, we must take seriously the early Christian belief that with the death and resurrection of Jesus something decisive happened to the 'principalities and powers'. Paul, writing to the Colossians from a Roman prison, is under no illusions about the continuing actual bodily power of the pagan empire whose captive he is. But he can still speak of the great victory that Jesus has already won over the rulers. The crucifixion looked as though they were celebrating a triumph over him, but in fact the boot was on the other foot:

He stripped the rulers and authorities of their armour, and displayed them contemptuously to public view, celebrating his triumph over them in him. (2.15)

As a result, Paul can even talk about all the principalities, powers, rulers and authorities not only being created in, through and for Jesus, but about them now being *reconciled*. He has made 'peace by the blood of his cross' (1.20).

This cannot mean – it obviously cannot mean! – that all rulers and authorities are now kindly disposed towards the message of Jesus and its messengers. Paul, as we said, is writing this letter from prison. The early church knew all about authorities that got it wrong, that imprisoned, beat or killed Jesus' followers. The early Christians were not living in a cloud-cuckoo-land, imagining that the rulers and authorities were really 'on their side'. But, at the same time, they addressed the authorities, explained to them what they were doing, and appealed to them (you can see Paul doing it in Acts) to do their job properly. We can see the same thing going on in the second century, when bishops like Polycarp and apologists like Justin showed proper respect for the authorities, even though those authorities were obviously bent on killing them. Just as the early church refused to collapse its faith into a dualism in which the created order itself, the world of space, time and matter, was evil and to be shunned, so it refused to collapse its witness to Jesus' kingdom into a *political* dualism in which the rulers and authorities were straightforwardly wicked and to be condemned (or, as in gnosticism and much modern Western spirituality, irrelevant and to be ignored). The only exception – which is obviously important – comes where the rulers actually divinize themselves; then they become demonic and shift into a different category altogether, as we see happening in Revelation 13.

Of course, the church will sometimes get it wrong. The church must exercise a prophetic gift towards the world, but this will require further prophetic ministries within the church itself, to challenge and correct as well as to endorse what has been said. And all would-be prophetic ministries are subject to further scrutiny; not for nothing does John warn his readers to 'test the spirits', since many false prophets have gone out into the world (1 John 4.1–6). The rule of thumb, interestingly enough, is to look back to Jesus himself. Do the voices that are being raised confess him as Messiah, as having 'come in the flesh'? Do these would-be prophecies, in other words, reflect the truth of Jesus' kingdom really arriving 'on earth as in heaven', or do they lead the church away from that reality and into the seductively safe space of detached 'religion'? There was, after all, plenty of 'religion' around in the ancient world, and much of it was of a sort that was deeply out of tune with the dangerous message of Jesus. The Roman Empire could tolerate any number of spiritualities, mysticisms and other-worldly hopes. They threatened nobody. John, in line with the other New Testament writings, was holding onto the confession of faith according to which the one true God had acted uniquely and decisively *in the world, the material world*, in and as Jesus, Israel's Messiah. That was, and is, fighting talk.

This, then, is a central and often ignored part of the meaning of Jesus' kingdom for today. Each generation and each local church needs to pray for its civic leaders. Granted the wide variety of forms of government, types of constitutions and so forth that obtain across the world, each generation and each local church needs to figure out wise and appropriate ways of speaking the truth to power. *That is a central part of the present-day meaning of Jesus' universal kingship.*

Summing up

We can sum it all up like this. We live in the period of Jesus' sovereign rule over the world – a reign that has not yet been completed, since, as Paul says in 1 Corinthians 15.20–28, he must reign until 'he has put all his enemies under his feet', including death itself. But Paul is clear that we do not have to wait until the second coming to say that Jesus is already reigning. In fact, Paul in that passage says something we might not otherwise have guessed: the reign of Jesus, in its present mode, is strictly temporary. God the father has installed Jesus in power, to act on his behalf; but when his task is complete, 'the son himself will be placed in proper order' under God the father, 'so that God may be all in all'. I do not think that Paul would have quarrelled with the Nicene Creed when it says, of Jesus, that his kingdom 'will have no end'. That, after all, is what the book of Revelation states on page after page. But I stress this point in 1 Corinthians because it makes it very clear that the present age is indeed the age of the reign of Jesus the Messiah. We cannot, in other words, agree with Billy that this reign is postponed to the second coming. That, on the contrary, is when it will be complete.

In trying to understand that present reign of Jesus, though, we have seen two apparently quite different strands. On the one hand, we have seen that all the powers and authorities in the universe are now, in some sense or other, subject to Jesus. This doesn't mean that they all do what he wants all the time, only that Jesus intends that there should be social and political structures of governance. Jesus himself pointed out to Pilate that the authority that the Roman governor had over him had been given to him 'from above' (John 19.11). Once that has been said, we should not be shy about recognizing – however paradoxical it seems to our black-and-white minds! – the God-givenness of structures of authority, even when they are tyrannical and violent. Part of what we say when we say that a structure is God-given is also that God will hold it to account. We have trained ourselves to think of political legitimacy simply in terms of the method or mode of appointment (e.g. if you've won an election). The ancient Jews and early Christians were far more interested in holding rulers to account with regard to what they were actually doing. God wants rulers, but God will call them to account.

Where does Jesus come into all this? From his own perspective, he was himself both upstaging the power structures of his day and also calling them to account, then and there. That's what his action in the Temple was all about. But his death, resurrection and ascension were the demonstration that he was Lord and they were not. The calling to account has, in other words, already begun – and will be completed at the second coming. *And the church's work of speaking the truth to power means what it means because it is based on the first of these and anticipates the second.* What the church does, in the power of the Spirit, is rooted in the achievement of Jesus and looks ahead to the final completion of his work. This is how Jesus is running the world in the present.

But, happily, it doesn't stop there, with the constant critique, both positive and negative, of what the world's rulers are up to. There are millions of things that the church should be getting into that the rulers of the world either don't bother about or don't have the resources to support. Jesus has all kinds of projects up his sleeve and is simply waiting for faithful people to say their prayers, to read the signs of the times and to get busy. Nobody would have dreamed of a Truth and Reconciliation Commission if Desmond Tutu hadn't prayed, and pushed, and made it happen. Nobody would have worked out the Jubilee movement, to campaign for international debt relief, if people in the churches had not become serious about the ridiculous plight of the poor. Closer to home, nobody else is likely to organize a car shuttle to get old people to and from the shops. Nobody else is likely to volunteer to play the piano for the service at the local prison. Few other people will start a play group for the children of single mothers who are still at work when school finishes. Nobody else, in my experience, will listen very hard to the plight of isolated rural communities or equally isolated inner-city enclaves. Nobody else thought of organizing the 'Street Pastors' scheme, which has had remarkable success in reducing crime. And so on. And so on.

And if the response is that these things are all very small and in themselves insignificant, I reply in two ways. First, didn't Jesus explain his own actions by talking about the smallest of the seeds that then grows into the largest kind of shrub? And second, it is remarkable how one small action can start a trend. One theologian has called it 'cascading grace'. Word gets around that a church in the next town has begun a particular project, and the good news story invites people to try something similar for themselves. That's how the Hospice movement spread, transforming within a generation the care of terminally ill patients. *Jesus is at work, taking forward his kingdom-project.*

He is, no doubt, doing this in a million ways of which we see little. He is, for sure, at work far outside the confines of the church. The cosmic vision of Colossians is true and should give us hope, not least when we have to stand before local government officials and explain what we were doing praying for people on the street, or why we need to rent a public hall for a series of meetings, or why we remain implacably opposed to a new business that is seeking shamelessly to exploit young people or low-income families, for instance by encouraging them to gamble with their limited resources. When we explain ourselves, we do so before people who, whether or not they know it, have been appointed to their jobs by God himself. Jesus has defeated on the cross the power that would make them malevolent. And, as we pray and celebrate his death in the sacraments, we claim that victory and go to our work calmly and without fear.

But Jesus is also at work in all sorts of ways in and through the church itself. We are to be, as Paul says, 'renewed in the image of the creator' (Colossians 3.10) – renewed, that is, by worship of God and the Lamb, so that we are able to serve as 'kings and priests', putting Jesus' rule into effect in the world and summing up creation's praise before him. This is what it looks like, today, when Jesus is running the world. This is, after all, what he told us to expect. The poor in spirit will be making the kingdom of heaven happen. The meek will be taking over the earth, so gently that the powerful won't notice until it's too late. The peacemakers will be putting the arms manufacturers out of business. Those who are hungry and thirsty for God's justice will be analysing government policy and legal rulings and speaking up on behalf of those at the bottom of the pile. The merciful will be surprising everybody by showing that there is a different way to do human relations other than being judgmental, eager to put everyone else down. 'You are the light of the world,' said Jesus. 'You are the salt of the earth.' He was announcing a programme yet to be completed. He was inviting his hearers, then and now, to join him in making it happen. This is, quite simply, what it looks like when Jesus is enthroned.

Notes

Preface

1 *Jesus and the Victory of God* (London: SPCK; Minneapolis: Fortress, 1996); *The Challenge of Jesus* (London: SPCK; Downers Grove, IL: InterVarsity, 2000).

2 *The New Testament and the People of God* (London: SPCK; Minneapolis: Fortress, 1992).

3 The perfect storm

1 *National Oceanographic and Atmospheric Administration News*, 16 June 2000.

4 The making of a first-century storm

1 *Eclogues* 4.

5 The hurricane

1 For others, see Psalms 22.27–28; 44.4–5; 74.12–13, 22; 93.1–2; 99.1–5.

2 See also Isaiah 33.22; Obadiah 17, 21; Zechariah 14.9.

3 Yes, today many people are shocked at the idea of animal sacrifice. It was part of most ancient religions, Judaism included. That's a subject for another time.

11 Space, Time and Matter

1 From V. Sander, *St Seraphim of Sarov*, trans. Sr Gabriel Anne (London: SPCK, 1975), pp. 15–16, as quoted in Roger Pooley and Philip Seddon, *The Lord of the Journey* (London: Collins, 1986), p. 51.

13 Why did the Messiah have to die?

1 G. B. Caird, *Jesus and the Jewish Nation* (London: Athlone, 1965), p. 22.

14 Under new management: Easter and beyond

1 *The Resurrection of the Son of God* (London: SPCK; Minneapolis: Augsburg Fortress, 2003); *Surprised by Hope* (London: SPCK, 2007; San Francisco: HarperOne, 2008).

15 Jesus: the ruler of the world

1 *Simply Christian* (London: SPCK; San Francisco: HarperSanFrancisco, 2006).

2 *Surprised by Hope* (London: SPCK, 2007; San Francisco: HarperOne, 2008).

3 Terry Eagleton, 'Who Needs Darwin?', *New Statesman*, 13 June 2011, p. 58.

Further reading

It would be possible to compile a bibliography for the present book that would be almost as long as a chapter. An annotated bibliography could easily be as long as the book itself. Instead, I content myself here with noting some recent books that I regard as supplementing (and quite often challenging) the work I set out in *Jesus and the Victory of God* (London: SPCK; Minneapolis: Fortress, 1996) and *The Challenge of Jesus* (London: SPCK; Downers Grove, IL: InterVarsity, 2000). They remain basic for my own account of Jesus, standing firmly on the foundations laid (not least in regard to Second Temple Judaism) in *The New Testament and the People of God* (London: SPCK; Minneapolis: Fortress, 1992). For the resurrection, one may cite *The Resurrection of the son of God* (London: SPCK; Minneapolis: Fortress, 2003). A team of scholars has engaged with my work in the recent symposium *Jesus, Paul and the People of God: A Theological Dialogue with N. T. Wright*, edited by Nicholas Perrin and Richard B. Hays (London: SPCK; Downers Grove, IL: InterVarsity, 2011), to which I contributed a substantial essay (pp. 115–58) that indicates some of the background and sketches some of the questions I have attempted to take further in this book.

A splendid recent reference work for the whole area of first-century Judaism is *The Eerdmans Dictionary of Early Judaism*, edited by John J. Collins and Daniel C. Harlow (Grand Rapids, MI: Eerdmans, 2010). Those who want to track more recent scholarship in the many areas relevant to the present book might begin by consulting one of the recent excellent Bible dictionaries, such as the one-volume *Eerdmans Dictionary of the Bible*, edited by David Noel Freedman (Grand Rapids, MI: Eerdmans, 2000) or the five-volume *New Interpreters Dictionary of the Bible*, edited by Katharine Doob Sakenfeld (Nashville: Abingdon, 2006). Each verse and phrase in the four canonical gospels has been studied relentlessly in commentaries large and small, and this is not the place to attempt even to list them.

Books on Jesus come in all sorts, shapes and sizes: scholarly, popular, critical, devotional, political, historical or – quite frequently, as with the present book – several of these at once. What follows is a not quite random selection of writing from the last few years, in alphabetical order. I have included books that fall into quite different categories. Several of these authors would want to raise sharp questions about my work, as I would about theirs.

Further reading

Allison, Dale C. *The Historical Christ and the Theological Jesus.* Grand Rapids, MI and Cambridge: Eerdmans, 2009.

——. *Constructing Jesus: Memory, Imagination, and History.* Grand Rapids, MI: Baker Academic; London: SPCK, 2010.

Bailey, Kenneth E. *Jesus Through Middle Eastern Eyes: Cultural Studies in the Gospels.* Grand Rapids, MI: Eerdmans; London: SPCK, 2008.

Bauckham, Richard J. *Jesus and the Eyewitnesses: The Gospels as Eyewitness Testimony.* Grand Rapids, MI: Eerdmans, 2006.

——. *Jesus and the God of Israel: God Crucified and Other Studies on the New Testament's Christology of Divine Identity.* Milton Keynes: Paternoster; Grand Rapids, MI: Eerdmans, 2008.

Borg, Marcus J. *Jesus: Uncovering the Life, Teachings, and Relevance of a Religious Revolutionary.* San Francisco: HarperSanFrancisco, 2006.

Dunn, James D. G. *Jesus Remembered.* Christianity in the Making, vol. 1. Grand Rapids, MI: Eerdmans, 2003.

Fisk, Bruce N. *A Hitchhiker's Guide to Jesus: Reading the Gospels on the Ground.* Grand Rapids, MI: Baker Academic, 2011.

Gaventa, Beverly Roberts, and Richard B. Hays, eds. *Seeking the Identity of Jesus: A Pilgrimage.* Grand Rapids, MI: Eerdmans, 2008.

Hurtado, Larry W. *Lord Jesus Christ: Devotion to Jesus in Earliest Christianity.* Grand Rapids, MI and Cambridge: Eerdmans, 2003.

Keener, Craig S. *The Historical Jesus of the Gospels.* Grand Rapids, MI: Eerdmans, 2009.

McKnight, Scot. *Jesus and His Death: Historiography, the Historical Jesus, and Atonement Theory.* Waco, TX: Baylor University Press, 2005.

Perrin, Nicholas. *Jesus the Temple.* London: SPCK; Grand Rapids, MI: Baker Academic, 2010.

Pitre, Brant. *Jesus, the Tribulation, and the End of Exile: Restoration Eschatology and the Origin of the Atonement.* Tübingen: Mohr Siebeck; Grand Rapids, MI: Baker Academic, 2005.

Ratzinger, Joseph. *Jesus of Nazareth*, 2 vols. London: Bloomsbury, 2007, 2011.

Vermes, Geza. *Jesus in the Jewish World.* London: SCM, 2010.

Index of biblical references

Index of subjects